lonely planet

SRI LANKA

Travel Phrasebook & Dictionary

Credits

Production Editor Sofie Andersen

Language Writers Swarna Pragnaratne and Zinara Rathnayake (Sinhala); PAEN Language Services and Rakshi Thambaiah (Tamil)

Thanks

Marc Backwell, Gwen Cotter, Fergal Condon, Kellie Langdon, Darren O'Connell, Akanksha Singh, Saralinda Turner, Clifton Wilkinson

Published by Lonely Planet Global Limited
CRN 554153

Digital Depot, Roe Lane off Thomas Street, Dublin
D08 TCV4, Ireland (EU authorised representative)

6th Edition – Oct 2026
ISBN 978 1 80653 148 6

Printed in Malaysia 10 9 8 7 6 5 4 3 2 1

Contact lonelyplanet.com/contact

Make the most of this phrasebook...

Anyone can speak another language. It's all about confidence. Don't worry if you can't remember your school language lessons or if you've never learnt a language before. Even if you learn the very basics, your travel experience will be the better for it. You have nothing to lose and everything to gain when the locals hear you making an effort.

FINDING THINGS IN THIS BOOK

For easy navigation, this book is in sections. The Sinhala part of the book includes **Basics**, such as pronunciation, grammar and numbers; a **Practical** section that covers travel situations; a **Social** section that gives you handy conversational phrases to get to know people; and **Safe Travel** that equips you with health and police phrases, just in case. **Food** has a section all of its own. The Tamil part of the book includes a guide to the **Alphabet** and **Pronunciation**, followed by a section with a variety of useful **Travel Phrases**, covering basics, practical and social situations, food and eating out, emergencies and health. You can also use the comprehensive **Index**, with terms clearly marked 'Sinhala' or 'Tamil', or check the relevant **Dictionary** for the word you need.

BEING UNDERSTOOD

Throughout this book you'll see coloured phrases on each page. They're phonetic guides to help you pronounce the language. You don't even need to look at the language itself, but you'll get used to the way we've represented particular sounds. The pronunciation sections will explain more, but you can feel confident that if you read the coloured phrase slowly, you'll be understood.

COMMUNICATION TIPS

Body language, ways of doing things, sense of humour – all have a role to play in every culture. 'Local talk' boxes show you common ways of saying things, or everyday language to drop into conversation. 'Listen for' boxes supply the phrases you may hear, and 'Look for' the signs you may see. They start with the language (so local people can point out what they want to say to you) and then lead in to the pronunciation guide and the English translation.

CONTENTS

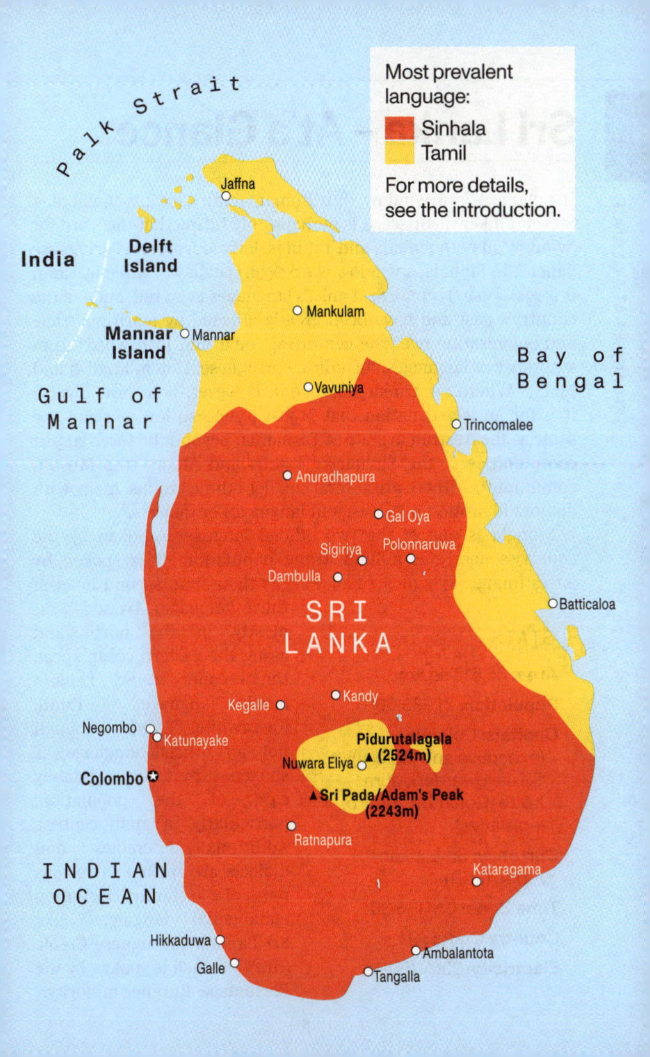
Most prevalent language:
Sinhala
Tamil
For more details, see the introduction.
Palk Strait
Jaffna
India
Delft Island
Mankulam
Mannar Island
Mannar
Bay of Bengal
Vavuniya
Gulf of Mannar
Trincomalee
Anuradhapura
Gal Oya
Sigiriya
Polonnaruwa
Dambulla
Batticaloa
SRI LANKA
Kandy
Kegalle
Negombo
Katunayake
Pidurutalagala (2524m)
Nuwara Eliya
Colombo
Sri Pada/Adam's Peak (2243m)
Ratnapura
INDIAN OCEAN
Kataragama
Hikkaduwa
Ambalantota
Galle
Tangalla

Sri Lanka – At a Glance

If language is a window into human nature, as psycholinguist Steven Pinker theorises, it is perhaps only fitting that the word for 'window' in both Sinhala and Tamil is derived from the Portuguese 'janela'. In Sinhala, a window is ජනේලය (janelaya), while in Tamil it is ஜன்னல் (jannal). Sri Lanka's languages are a reflection of the country's past and have been greatly affected by maritime trade and colonisation over the centuries; you'll find loan words from a number of languages, including Portuguese, Dutch, English and Malay. Where Sri Lanka stands out, however, is in how diverse it is for an island nation that is just 65,000 sq km – about the same as the Australian state of Tasmania. Beyond the three largest communities – the Sinhalese, Tamils and Moors (the Muslim community) – there are several smaller ethnic groups, many with distinct identities, histories, and languages or dialects.

Sinhala is one of the two official languages spoken by the country's nearly 22-million-strong population. It is spoken by an estimated 87% of Sri Lankans, as their first, second or even third language. Around 30%, mostly in the north and along the eastern coast, speak the second of Sri Lanka's official languages – Tamil. Meanwhile, English, though not an official language, is spoken by approximately 24% of the population, particularly in main centres. Additionally, creoles and dialects are spoken in various parts of the country, including endangered languages like Sri Lankan Portuguese Creole (SLPC), which is spoken by the Portuguese Burgher minority.

STATS

Area: 65,610 sq km

Population: 21,938,000

Capitals: Colombo (executive and judicial); Sri Jayewardenepura Kotte (Colombo suburb; legislative)

Currency: Sri Lankan rupee (LKR)

Time Zone: GMT+5.30

Country Code: +94

Electricity: 230V/50Hz

Beyond being a marker of identity, language in the Sri Lankan context is also a political tool. Sri Lanka's 26-year civil war between the government and the Liberation Tigers of Tamil Eelam (LTTE) was fuelled in part by language-related issues. Notably, Sri Lankan language fluency also falls along religious lines. Muslim Sri Lankans, for example, primarily speak Tamil as their first language, with most of them either bilingual (Tamil, Sinhala) or trilingual (Tamil, Sinhala and English). Hindu-Tamils as an ethno-religious group are also closely associated with the Tamil language, while a similarly strong connection exists for the Buddhist-Sinhala group and Sinhala.

Given Sri Lanka's ethnic, linguistic and religious diversity, and its complex political history, it is perhaps understandable that inter-group tensions are somewhat prevalent, even in today's post-civil-war Sri Lanka. To soothe these tensions, the country has increasingly prioritised bilingual and even trilingual education as a means of fostering social cohesion, albeit to varying degrees of success. From 2002 onwards, secondary school students learn both Sinhala and Tamil. While there's still a long road ahead, linguistic boundaries are slowly crumbling, creating new ways of reflecting a multicultural society.

ABBREVIATIONS USED IN THIS BOOK

adj	adjective	n	noun
f	feminine	neut	neuter
inf	informal	pl	plural
lit	literal	sg	singular
m	masculine	v	verb

Signs

SINHALA	
CLOSED	වසා ඇත
DANGER!	අන්තරාදායකයි!
ENTRANCE	ඇතුල්වීම
EXIT	පිටවීම
INFORMATION	තොරතුරු
NO ENTRY	ඇතුල්වීම තහනම්
NO EXIT	පිටවීම තහනම්
NO SMOKING	දුම් බීම තහනම්
OPEN	විවෘතව ඇත
POLICE	පොලීසිය
STOP	නතර වෙන්න
TOILETS	වැසිකිලි

TAMIL	
CLOSED	மூடப்பட்டுள்ளது
DANGER!	அபாயம்
ENTRANCE	நுழைவாயில்
EXIT	வெளியெறல்
INFORMATION	தகவல்
NO ENTRY	உள்நுழையக் கூடாது
NO EXIT	வெளியெறக் கூடாது
NO SMOKING	புகைபிடிக்கக் கூடாது
OPEN	திறந்துள்ளது
POLICE	பொலிஸ்
STOP	நில்
TOILETS	மலசலகூடம்

SINHALA

VOWELS

There are 12 vowels in Sinhala, which can be divided into two groups: short and long, with six in each.

Script	Transliteration	Pronunciation
Short vowels		
අ	ah	like the 'u' in 'cup'
ඇ	a	like the 'a' in 'pat'
එ	e	like the 'e' in 'pet'
ඉ	i	like the 'i' in 'pit'
ඔ	o	like the 'o' in 'pot'
උ	u	like the 'u' in 'put'
Long vowels		
ආ	aah	like the 'a' in 'part'
ඈ	aa	like the 'a' in 'ant'
ඒ	eh	like the 'a' in 'bathe'
ඊ	ee	like the 'ee' in 'see'
ඕ	oh	like the 'o' in 'port'
ඌ	oo	like the 'oo' in 'pool'

In script, vowels only appear as separate characters at the beginning of a word; for example, in ee-lahn-gah (ඊළඟ), 'next', the ඊ (ee) is clearly visible. When vowels appear elsewhere in a word, they're indicated by a symbol added to the consonant they follow. Within a word, ee is represented by ◌ී; for example, in aah-di-kaah-lee-nah (ආදිකාලීන), 'ancient', it appears in combination with ල (lah) to form ලී (lee); see Applying Vowels to Consonants on p14.

Vowel Combinations (Diphthongs)		
Script	**Transliteration**	**Pronunciation**
ආයි	ai	like the 'ai' in 'aisle'
ඖ	au	like the 'ou' in 'ounce'
ඒයි	ei	like the 'ei' in 'weight'
ඔයි	oi	like the 'oi' in 'oil'

SINHALA

Introduction

According to Sinhalese tradition, the 6th-century introduction of the Sinhala language to Sri Lanka is attributed to a sequence of events commencing with a journey by Prince Vijaya from the kingdom of Sinhapura (Bengal). Banished to the sea by the king, Vijaya and his followers landed on an island, defeated its evil 'demon inhabitants', then settled down to create a dynasty. Thus, the Sinhalese civilisation in the island began.

There is some fact behind this traditional explanation, and the date given in the story accounts neatly for the development of unique characteristics that distinguish Sinhala from other Indo-Aryan languages. The reference to demons might be more fanciful, though. Recent archaeological findings suggest that the 'demons' had, in fact, established agricultural practices, including irrigation, used iron and made pottery – not normally the work of demons.

Two forms of Sinhala are in use today, a literary written form and a spoken form. The written language retains a number of features that link it back to the ancient Indian languages Pali and Sanskrit, and is most commonly associated with Buddhism and education. Spoken Sinhala, however, is the focus of this book for obvious reasons, and it is the spoken form that everyone understands – some scholars even suggest that differences between the two forms are so great that they might almost be considered distinct languages.

Although the grammar of Sinhala may at first seem daunting to English speakers, its relative flexibility allows users to have a go at making sentences and still be understood. The sounds are quite similar to those found in English and, as is the case with every country you visit, your efforts to speak the language will be rewarded, sometimes with laughter (of the appreciative kind) and certainly with approval.

BASICS

Pronunciation

Pronunciation of Sinhala is not difficult – many of the sounds are similar to English and, unlike other languages in the region, there are no tones.

You'll find, however, that many of the transliterations contain consonant clusters that may be unfamiliar. Don't be put off by their appearance – the sounds themselves aren't too complicated. One example is sth, as in sthoo-thiy (ස්තූතියි), 'thank you'. To pronounce this correctly, try saying the 'ss' in 'hiss' followed by 'toothy'. Another example is dhy, as in vi-dhyaah-vah (විද්‍යා), 'science'. The dhyaah, here, is pronounced similarly to 'd', followed by the 'yar' in 'yarn' – but remember it's only one syllable.

Throughout the book, we've split the transliterations into syllables to aid pronunciation. This is particularly important where a consonant is doubled in a word, as you need to pronounce them both for the correct meaning to be understood. For example, to avoid confusion between mah-lah මල ('flower') and mal-lah මල්ල ('bag'), each 'l' needs to be pronounced clearly in the latter.

PRONUNCIATION TIPS

aspirated consonants	pronounced with a puff of air after the sound; this is the way the letters 'p', 't' and 'k' are pronounced in English at the beginning of a word
unaspirated consonants	pronounced without a puff of air – compare 'pot' (aspirated) with 'spot'
(unaspirated) diphthongs	the sound produced by the combination of two vowels, for example, the 'ai' in 'aisle'

VOWELS

There are 12 vowels in Sinhala, which can be divided into two groups: short and long, with six in each.

Script	Transliteration	Pronunciation
Short vowels		
අ	ah	like the 'u' in 'cup'
ඇ	a	like the 'a' in 'pat'
එ	e	like the 'e' in 'pet'
ඉ	i	like the 'i' in 'pit'
ඔ	o	like the 'o' in 'pot'
උ	u	like the 'u' in 'put'
Long vowels		
ආ	aah	like the 'a' in 'part'
ඈ	aa	like the 'a' in 'ant'
ඒ	eh	like the 'a' in 'bathe'
ඊ	ee	like the 'ee' in 'see'
ඕ	oh	like the 'o' in 'port'
ඌ	oo	like the 'oo' in 'pool'

In script, vowels only appear as separate characters at the beginning of a word; for example, in ee-lahn-gah (ඊළඟ), 'next', the ඊ (ee) is clearly visible. When vowels appear elsewhere in a word, they're indicated by a symbol added to the consonant they follow. Within a word, ee is represented by ී; for example, in aah-di-kaah-lee-nah (ආදිකාලීන), 'ancient', it appears in combination with ල (lah) to form ලී (lee); see Applying Vowels to Consonants on p14.

Vowel Combinations (Diphthongs)		
Script	**Transliteration**	**Pronunciation**
ආයි	ai	like the 'ai' in 'aisle'
ඖ	au	like the 'ou' in 'ounce'
ඒයි	ei	like the 'ei' in 'weight'
ඔයි	oi	like the 'oi' in 'oil'

CONSONANTS

Consonants in Sinhala are represented as syllabic units – they all have an inherent ah sound in their basic form. These syllabic units form the foundation for writing all of the possible sounds in Sinhala. To represent sounds other than ah sounds, the basic form is used in conjunction with additional characters or symbols (see p15).

Unaspirated Consonants		
Script	**Transliteration**	**Pronunciation**
ක	kah	like the 'cu' in 'cup'
ග	gah	like the 'gu' in 'gun'
ජ	jah	like the 'ju' in 'jump'
ට	tah	like the 'tu' in 'tug'
ඩ	dah	like the 'du' in 'duck'
ණ[1]	nah	like the 'nu' in 'nun'
ත	thah	like the 'thu' in 'thump'
ද	dhah	like the 'the' in 'mother'
න[1]	nah	like the 'nu' in 'nun'
ප	pah	like the 'pu' in 'punt'
බ	bah	like the 'bu' in 'bun'
ම	mah	like the 'mu' in 'mum'
ය	yah	like the 'yu' in 'yuck'
ර	rah	like the 'ru' in 'rum'
ල[2]	lah	like the 'lu' in 'luck'
ව	wah	like the 'wo' in 'won'
	vah*	like the 'va' in 'vantage'
හ	hah	like the 'hu' in 'hut'
ස	sah	like the 'su' in 'sun'
ළ[2]	lah	like the 'lu' in 'luck'
ශ[3]	shah	like the 'shu' in 'shut'
ෂ[3]	shah	like the 'shu' in 'shut'

ච	chah	as the 'chu' in 'chuck'
ඥ	gnah	as the 'ny' in 'Kenya', plus the 'u' in 'cup'
* generally, vah is used in verbs and wah in all other words		

Letters marked with numbers (nah, ණ; nah, න; lah, ල; lah, ළ; shah, ශ; shah, ෂ) are pronounced very similarly but are used in words totally different from each other in meaning. In spoken language, this is not a problem – your meaning would be clear through context – but in written language you'd need to be cautious to avoid confusing your message:

[1]ණ	nah	තණ	thah-nah	grass
න	nah	තන	thah-nah	breast
[2]ල	lah	මල	mah-lah	flower
ළ	lah	මළ	mah-lah	dead

With shah (ශ) and shah (ෂ), you wouldn't create the wrong word by using the wrong letter, as they're not used in the same combination of letters – you would just create a word that doesn't exist. For example, if you used ශ instead of ෂ in the word යුෂ; yu-shah ('juice'), the word would have no meaning. Likewise, if you used ෂ instead of ශ in the word මාංශ maahn-shah ('flesh'), it would have no meaning.

APPLYING VOWELS TO CONSONANTS

As mentioned earlier in this chapter, vowel sounds within a word are indicated by attaching a number of different characters or symbols to a consonant; these symbols can appear above, below, before or after the consonant. A symbol is also added to a consonant when it's pronounced on its own, without any vowel. In the following table, we've used kah (ක) as an example.

☑ SYLLABIC SINHALA

Unlike English, vowels and consonants in Sinhala aren't written separately, but together as syllabic units. That is to say, each character represents a syllable, not just a single letter.

Script	Symbol(s) added	Transliteration	Pronunciation
ක්	x්	k	like the 'k' in 'skin'
කා	xා	kaah	like 'k' plus the 'a' in 'part'
කි	xි	ki	like 'k' plus the 'i' in 'pit'
කී	xී	kee	like 'k' plus the 'ee' in 'see'
කු	xු	ku	like 'k' plus the 'u' in 'put'
කූ	xූ	koo	like 'k' plus the 'oo' in 'pool'
කෙ	ෙx	ke	like 'k' plus the 'e' in 'pet'
කේ	ෙx්	keh	like 'k' plus the 'ai' in 'bait'
කො	ෙxා	ko	like 'k' plus the 'o' in 'pot'
කෝ	ෙxෟ	koh	like 'k' plus the 'o' in 'port'

ASPIRATED CONSONANTS

There are seven aspirated consonants in Sinhala. All have unaspirated counterparts and are pronounced the same but with a puff of air (see p13).

Aspirated		Unaspirated	
ඛ	khah	ක	kah
ඝ	ghah	ග	gah
ඨ	tah*	ට	tah
ථ	thah*	ත	thah
ධ	dhah*	ද	dhah
ඵ	phah	ප	pah
භ	bhah	බ	bah

* underlining has been used in the transliterations to distinguish between the unaspirated and aspirated sounds

THE SINHALA ALPHABET

Vowels					
අ	ආ	ඇ	ඈ	එ	ඒ
ah	aah	a	aa	e	eh
ඔ	ඕ	ඉ	ඊ	උ	ඌ
o	oh	i	ee	u	oo

Consonants					
ක	ග	ජ	ට	ඩ	ඛ
kah	gah	jah	tah	dah	khah
ඝ	ඨ	ඪ	ත	ද	න
ghah	tah	dah	thah	dhah	nah
ප	බ	ම	ථ	ධ	ණ
pah	bah	mah	thah	dhah	nah
ඵ	භ	ය	ර	ල	ව
phah	bhah	yah	rah	lah	vah/wah
ස	හ	ෆ	ළ	ශ	ෂ
sah	hah	fah	lah	shah	shah
ච	ඡ	ඞ	ඹ	ඥ	
chah	chah	ngah	mbah	gnah	

Grammar

Spoken Sinhala and written Sinhala vary quite considerably. In many respects, the spoken language is far simpler – for example, you don't need to worry about gender agreement between nouns and verbs.

You'll also come across a number of words that have been borrowed from English (eg, bahs, 'bus'), which will make things easier for you.

This chapter gives the basics of Sinhala grammar, which will enable you to construct your own sentences and communicate with ease.

WORD ORDER

Unlike English, where the word order is subject-verb-object, the word order in Sinhala is generally subject-object-verb:

I bought a book.
mah-mah po-thahk gahth-thaah (lit: I book bought) — මම පොතක් ගත්තා.

ARTICLES

Sinhala doesn't use the definite article ('the'), so po-thah (පොත) can mean 'book' or 'the book' – context will usually make it clear which is meant.

Nouns borrowed from English, however, are always followed by e-kah (එක), meaning 'one':

(the) bus	bahs e-kah	බස් එක
(the) piano	pi-yaah-noh e-kah	පියානෝ එක
(the) station	steh-shahn e-kah	ස්ටේෂන් එක

There's no corresponding word for the indefinite article ('a/an'). To make a noun indefinite, just add k (ක්) to the end of the final syllable:

book	po-thah	පොත
a book	po-thahk	පොතක්
egg	bith-thah-rah-yah	බිත්තරය
an egg	bith-thah-rah-yahk	බිත්තරයක්

However, this rule only applies to nouns ending in the short vowel sounds (ah, a, e, i, o and u) - these are always inanimate (non-living) nouns.

For nouns ending in the long vowel sounds aah and ee - always animate (living) nouns - the final vowel sound changes to ek. Note that singular nouns never end in the other long vowel sounds (aa, oo, eh and oh) or in consonants unless they're loan words.

child	lah-mah-yaah	ළමයා
a child	lah-mah-yek	ළමයෙක්
passenger	mah-gi-yaah	මගියා
a passenger	mah-gi-yek	මගියෙක්

For English loan words, the final e-kah (එක) becomes e-kahk (එකක්) to indicate the indefinite article:

a bus	bahs e-kahk	බස් එකක්
a piano	pi-yaah-noh e-kahk	යානෝ එකක්
a station	steh-shahn e-kahk	ස්ටේෂන් එකක්

☑ GRAMMATICAL TERMS

A number of basic grammatical terms are used in this chapter. Here's a general summary of them:

adjective	adds information about a noun red wine
adverb	adds information about a verb or adjective He runs quickly. very big
conjunction	joins together sentences or parts of a sentence Wash the car and walk the dog.
noun	a person (John), thing (book), place (beach) or concept (happiness)
object	refers to the noun or pronoun that is affected by the verb Paul washes the dog.
preposition	introduces information about location, place or direction at the market towards the city
pronoun	usually takes the place of a noun he sings instead of Paul sings
subject	refers to the noun or pronoun that is performing an action The man washes the dog.
verb	an action or doing word He runs fast.

NOUNS

GENDER

Nouns are masculine, feminine or neuter in gender. It's important to know the gender of a noun as the verb endings must agree in written language (see Verbs, p26). In spoken language, however, there's no agreement.

Gender is easy to remember in Sinhala. Generally, it reflects human gender: boy, man, husband etc are masculine; girl, woman, wife etc are feminine; and all inanimate nouns are neuter:

man	mi-ni-haah (m)	මිනිහා
woman	ga-ha-ni-yah (f)	ගැහැණිය
knife	pi-hi-yah (neut)	පිහිය

Nouns that could refer to a male or a female (child, bus driver etc) are neuter. You can specify the gender of such nouns by placing ga-ha-nu, 'female', or pi-ri-mi, 'male', before the noun:

child	lah-mah-yaah	ළමයා
boy	pi-ri-mi lah-mah-yaah	පිරිමි ළමයා
girl	ga-ha-nu lah-mah-yaah	ගැහැණු ළමයා
driver	ri-yah-du-raah	රියදුරා
male driver	pi-ri-mi ri-yah-du-raah	පිරිමි රියදුරා
female driver	ga-ha-nu ri-yah-du-raah	ගැහැණු රියදුරා

PLURALS

Plurals of nouns vary but always involve changing the final syllable of the singular – usually it's shortened, sometimes even dropped:

tree	gah-sah	ගස
trees	gahs	ගස්

pillar	kah-nu-wah	කණුව
pillars	kah-nu	කණු

To pluralise English loan words, e-kah is always dropped:

car	kaahr e-kah	කාර් එක
cars	kaahr	කාර්

There's no single rule for pluralising nouns, however, and even words with the same or similar endings don't necessarily follow the same pattern. Don't be put off though – you'll still be understood if you use the singular form (which is given in the dictionary) and no one will mind the odd mistake.

CASE

In English, we're able to recognise the 'role' a noun plays in a sentence – who is performing an action, to whom, with what and so on – by its position in the sentence and/or by the use of prepositions.

Many other languages, however, for example, German, Russian and Sinhala, use what are know as 'cases' to make these distinctions. Different endings act as labels to indicate the role of a noun and its relationship to other words in a sentence.

In Sinhala, there are nine cases, known as vi-bahk-thi (විභක්ති):

Nominative	prah-thah-maah	ප්‍රථමා
Accusative	kahr-mah	කර්ම
Genitive	sahm-bahn-dhah	සම්බන්ධ
Dative	sahm-prah-dhaah-nah	සම්ප්‍රදාන
Instrumental	kath-roo	කතෘ
Ablative	ah-vah-dhi	අවධි
Agentive	kah-rah-nah	කරණ
Locative	aah-dhaah-rah	ආධාර
Vocative	aah-lah-pah-nah	ආලපන

While endings vary, you can use the following ones or even use no endings and still be understood. Where case endings have no English equivalent, they are given in the literal translations in their transliterated form. This has been applied throughout the book.

NOMINATIVE

The nominative case refers to the subject of the sentence, and is also the form you'll find in a dictionary. It indicates 'who' or 'what' is performing the action.

The child went home.
lah-mah-yaah ge-dhe-rah gi-yeh-yah — ළමයා ගෙදර ගියා.
(lit: child home went)

ACCUSATIVE

The accusative case refers to the direct object of a sentence. It indicates 'what' or 'whom' the verb affects.

The dog is chasing the child.
bahl-laah lah-mah-yaah-vah pahn-nah-nah-vaah — බල්ලා ළමයාව පන්නනවා.
(lit: dog child chasing)

GENITIVE

The genitive case refers to possession. It indicates 'whose', 'of what' or 'of whom'.

The child's hand is injured.
lah-mah-yaah-geh ah-thah thu-vaah-lai — ළමයාගේ අත තුවාලයි.
(lit: child's hand injured)

DATIVE

The dative case refers to the indirect object. It indicates the person or object 'to whom' or 'to which' something is given, done, lent and so on.

I gave the child some food.

mah-mah lah-mah-yaah-tah kaa-mah dun-naah — මම ළමයාට කෑම දුන්නා.

(lit: I child-to food gave)

INSTRUMENTAL

The instrumental case has several functions. It's used to answer a number of questions, including 'with what' and 'by what means'.

The child hit the dog with the stick.

lah-mah-yaah bahl-laah-tah koh-tu-ven ga-hu-vaah — ළමයා බල්ලාට කෝටුවෙන් ගැහුවා.

(lit: child to-dog with-stick hit)

ABLATIVE

The ablative case is used to denote 'from where' or 'from whom'.

The thief stole money from the child.

so-raah lah-mah-yaah-gen mu-dal so-rah-kahm kah-lah — සොරා ළමයගෙන් මුදල් සොරකම් කරා.

(lit: thief from-child money stole)

AGENTIVE

The agentive case is used to denote 'by whom'.

The vase was broken by the child.

lah-mah-yaah vi-sin mahl bah-du-nah kah-dah-nah lah-dee — ළමයා විසින් මල් බඳුන කඩන ලදී.

(lit: child by flower vase broken)

LOCATIVE

The locative case indicates where an action takes place. It's always used with prepositions indicating location, such as 'in', 'on', 'by', 'at' and 'about'.

The child's in the house.

lah-mah-yaah ge-yah a-thu-leh — ළමයා ගෙය ඇතුළේ.

(lit: child house in)

VOCATIVE

The vocative case is used when addressing people directly.

Child, come here!
lah-mah-yaah me-he en-nah! ළමයා මෙහෙ එන්න!
(lit: child here come!)

ADJECTIVES

The adjective always precedes the noun it describes:

tall man (lit: tall man)	u-sah mi-ni-haah	උස මිනිහා
big house (lit: big house)	lo-ku ge-yah	ලොකු ගෙය

COMPARATIVES

To create comparatives, simply place either i-thaah (ඉතා) or vah-daah (වඩා) before the adjective. The two alternatives are interchangeable:

tall	u-sah	උස
taller	i-thaah u-sah	ඉතා උස
big	lo-ku	ලොකු
bigger	vah-daah lo-ku	වඩා ලොකු

SUPERLATIVES

To create superlatives in Sinhala, add i-thaah-mahth (ඉතාමත්) or vah-daah-mahth (වඩාමත්) before the adjective. Another way of looking at this is to add mahth to the end of the comparative indicator (i-thaah or vah-daah):

tallest	i-thaah-mahth u-sah	ඉතාමත් උස
biggest	vah-daah-mahth lo-ku	වඩාමත් ලොකු

PRONOUNS

All subject and object pronouns are the same, except for he/him:

Subject Pronouns	Object Pronouns	Transliteration	Script
Singular			
I	me	mah-mah	මම
you	you	o-bah (written) o-yaah (spoken)	ඔබ ඔයා
he	–	o-hu	ඔහු
–	him	a-yaah	එයා
she	her	a-yah	ඇය
it	it	eh-kah / e-yah	ඒක / එය
Plural			
we	us	ah-pi	අපි
you	you	o-bah(-laa)	ඔබ(ලා)
they	them	o-vun	ඔවුන්

Note that eh-kah, 'it', is more common in spoken language than e-yah which tends to be reserved for written language.

The subject pronoun always precedes the verb. If the sentence contains an object pronoun as well, it is placed between the subject pronoun and the verb:

I gave it to my mother.

mah-mah e-yah mah-geh
ahm-maah-tah dhun-naah
(lit: I it my mother-to gave)

මම එය මගේ
අම්මට දුන්නා.

VERBS

In both spoken and written Sinhala, the present tense is the same as the future tense – context differentiates between the two. In the past tense, both the stem and the endings change.

SPOKEN LANGUAGE

In spoken language, the present/future tense is the form of the verb that usually appears in the dictionary. The verb doesn't change according to gender or number (singular or plural) and always ends in -nah-vaah (නවා).

To form the past tense, nah is dropped and the vowel in the first syllable of the verb changes. Again the verb remains the same, irrespective of gender or number. There are various patterns which affect the vowel change and it's something that must be learned, however, you'll find you'll still be understood even if you don't get it quite right.

As an example, 'eat', kah-nah-vaah (කනවා) has the following forms in the present/future and past tenses, which are added to the pronouns:

Spoken Language: Present/Future & Past tenses			
I	mah-mah	මම	Present/future: kah-nah-vaah කනවා
you (sg)	o-bah	ඔබ	
he/she	o-hu / a-yah	ඔහු / ඇය	
it	eh-kah / e-yah	ඒක / එය	
we	a-pi	අපි	Past: kaa-vaah කෑවා
you (pl)	o-bah-laah	ඔබලා	
they	o-vun	ඔවුන්	

WRITTEN LANGUAGE

In written language, the verb changes in the third person singular (he, she, it) according to the gender of the subject. Neuter takes the same verb endings as masculine:

fall va-te-nah-vaah වැටෙනවා

The boy falls. (m)
pi-ri-mi lah-mah-yaah va-tu-<u>neh-yah</u>
(lit: male child falls)
පිරිමි ළමයා වැටුණේය.

The tree falls. (neut)
gah-sah va-tu-<u>neh-yah</u>
(lit: tree falls)
ගස වැටුණේය.

The girl falls. (f)
ga-ha-nu lah-mah-yaah va-tu-<u>naah-yah</u>
(lit: female child falls)
ගැහැණු ළමයා වැටුණාය.

PRESENT/FUTURE TENSE

The verb endings for the present and future tenses in written language are as follows:

Written Language: Present/future tense		
I	mah-mah ...-n-ne-mi	මම ... න්නෙමි
you (sg)	o-bah ...-n-neh-yah	ඔබ ... න්නේය
he	o-hu ...-n-neh-yah	ඔහු ... න්නේය
she	a-yah ...-n-naah-yah	ඇය ... න්නාය
it	eh-kah/e-yah ...-n-neh-yah	ඒක/එය ... න්නේය
we	a-pi ...-n-ne-mu	අපි ... න්නෙමු
you (pl)	o-bah-laah ...-n-noh-yah	ඔබ ... න්නෝය
they	o-vun ...-n-noh-yah	ඔබලා ... න්නෝය

So, in written language, the verb kah-nah-vaah (කනවා), 'eat', would be conjugated as follows in the present/future tense:

I eat; will eat	mah-mah kahn-ne-mi	මම කන්නෙමි
you eat; will eat	o-bah kahn-neh-yah	ඔබ කන්නේය
he eats; will eat	o-hu kahn-neh-yah	ඔහු කන්නේය
she eats; will eat	a-yah kahn-naah-yah	ඇය කන්නීය
we eat; will eat	a-pi kahn-ne-mu	අපි කන්නෙමු
you eat; will eat	o-bah-laah kahn-noh-yah	ඔබලා කන්නෝය
they eat; will eat	o-vun kahn-noh-yah	ඔව්හු කන්නෝය

PAST TENSE

In the past tense, the stem is the same as in spoken language and the verb ending either starts with v or with n, depending on the last syllable of the verb stem. There's no hard-and-fast rule and whichever you choose, you'll find you'll still be understood.

Written Language: Past tense		
I	mah-mah ...-ve-mi / ne-mi	මම ...වෙමි/නෙමි
you (sg)	o-bah ...-veh-yah / neh-yah	ඔබ ...වේය/නේය
he/she	o-hu / a-yah / eh-kah / e-yah ...-veh-yah / neh-yah	ඔහු/ඇය/ඒක/එය ...වේය/නේය
it	eh-kah / e-yah	ඒක/එය
we	a-pi ...-ve-mu / ne-mu	අපි ...වෙමු/නෙමු
you (pl)	o-bah-laah ...-voh-yah / noh-yah	ඔබලා ...වෝය/නෝය
they	o-vun ...-voh-yah / noh-yah	ඔව්හු ...වෝය/නෝය

In written language, the verb kah-nah-vaah (කනවා) would be conjugated as follows in the past tense:

I ate	mah-mah kaa-ve-mi	මම කෑවෙමි
you ate	o-bah kaa-veh-yah	ඔබ කෑවේය
he ate	o-hu kaa-veh-yah	ඔහු කෑවේය
she ate	a-yah kaa-vaah-yah	ඇය කෑවාය
we ate	a-pi kaa-ve-mu	අපි කෑවෙමු
you ate	o-bah-laah kaa-voh-yah	ඔබලා කෑවෝය
they ate	o-vun kaa-voh-yah	ඔවුන් කෑවෝය

TO HAVE

The verb 'to have' doesn't change according to person; however, the forms of the pronouns are different, and, unlike other verbs, the present and future forms are not the same.

I	mah-tah	මට	Present: thi-ye-nah-vaah තියෙනවා
you	o-bah-tah	ඔබට	
he	o-hu-tah	ඔහුට	Past: thi-bu-naah තිබුණා
she	a-yah-tah	ඇයට	
it	eh-yah-tah	එයට	Future: thi-yeh vi තියේවි
we	ah-pah-tah	අපට	
you	o-bah-laah-tah	ඔබලාට	
they	o-vun-tah	ඔවුන්ට	

TO BE

There's no equivalent of the verb 'to be' in Sinhala – you just use the noun or the subject pronoun followed by the adjective or noun:

The car is blue.
kaahr e-kah nil paah-tai — කාර් එක නිල්
(lit: car one blue colour) — පාටයි

I'm frightened.
mah-mah bhah-yai — මම බයයි
(lit: I frightened)

I'm a student.
mah-mah shish-yah-yek — මම ශිෂ්‍යයෙක්
(lit: I student)

MODALS

Modals are auxiliary verbs used in conjunction with other verbs to express certainty, probability or possibility. In Sinhala, modals come immediately after the verb.

You'll notice that the syllable immediately before -nah (න) in the verb takes a final n (න්) – providing there isn't one already.

MUST/HAVE TO

To create a sense of obligation (must, have to, should, need to etc), mah (ම) replaces the final syllable (vaah, ා) of the present/future form of the verb and oh-neh (ඕනෙ) is placed after the verb:

leave	yah-nah-vaah	යනවා

I must leave now.
mah-mah dhan yahn-nah-mah oh-neh — මම දැන් යන්නම ඕනේ.
(lit: I now go must)

CAN/TO BE ABLE TO

With the modal 'can/to be able', the final syllable (vaah, වා) of the present/future form of the verb is dropped and pu-lu-vah-ni (පුළුවනි) is placed after the verb:

do	kah-rah-nah-vaah	කරනවා

I can do this.
meh-kah mah-tah kah-rahn-nah pu-lu-vah-ni — මේක මට කරන්න පුළුවනි.
(lit: this I do can)

Note, to express 'can't', you don't need pu-lu-vah-ni – just the negative form ba-ha (බැහැ), which is placed immediately after the verb:

I can't do this.
meh-kah mah-tah kah-rahn-nah ba-ha — මෙක මට කරන්න බැහැ.
(lit: this I do no)

TO LIKE

To form 'to like', the final syllable (vaah, වා) of the present/future form of the verb is dropped and ka-mah-thiy (කැමතියි) must be placed after the verb:

read	ki-yah-vah-nah-vaah	කියවනවා

I like reading.
mah-mah ki-yah-vahn-nah ka-mah-thiy — මම කියවන්න කැමතියි.
(lit: I read like)

ESSENTIAL VERBS

The verbs listed here are given in the present/future tense (spoken language), since this is the form they'll be in in the dictionary.

be able	ha-ki ve-nah-vaah	හැකි වෙනවා
become	ve-nah-vaah	වෙනවා
bring	ge-ne-nah-vaah	ගෙනෙනවා
buy	gahn nah vaah	ගන්නවා
come	e-nah-vaah	එනවා
cost	va-yah ve-nah-vaah	වැය වෙනවා
depart/leave	yah-nah-vaah	යනවා
drink	bo-nah-vaah	බොනවා
eat	kah-nah-vaah	කනවා
give	dhe-nah-vaah	දෙනවා
go	yah-nah-vaah	යනවා
have	thi-yah-nah-vaah	තියනවා
know	dhan-nah-vaah	දන්නවා
like	ka-mah-thi ve-nah-vaah	කැමති වෙනවා

live	jee-vahth ve-nah-vaah	ජීවත් වෙනවා
love	aah-dhah-rah-yah kah-rah-nah-vaah	ආදරය කරනවා
make	hah-dhah-nah-vaah	හදනවා
meet	hah-mu ve-nah-vaah	හමුවෙනවා
need	ah-vahsh-yah ve-nah-vaah	අවශ්‍ය වෙනවා
return	aah-pah-su dhe-nah-vaah say ki-yah-nah-vaah	ආපසු දෙනවා කියනවා
stay	in-nah-vaah	ඉන්නවා
take	gahn-nah-vaah	ගන්නවා
understand	theh-rum gahn-nah-vaah	තේරුම් ගන්නවා
want	oh-nah kah-rah-nah-vaah	ඕන කරනවා

ADVERBS

Adverbs are words that usually derive from adjectives and add information about verbs. They're normally formed by adding an extra syllable to the adjective. Below is a list of some of the common ones:

cheap	laah-bah	ලාභ
cheaply	laah-be-tah	ලාබෙට
close	lahn-gah	ළඟ
closely	lahn-gah-mah	ළඟම
clear	pa-ha-di-li	පැහැදිලි
clearly	pa-ha-di-li-vah	පැහැදිලිව
direct	ke-lin	කෙළින්
directly	ke-lin-mah	කෙළින්ම
free	ni-dhah-hahs	නිදහස්
freely	ni-dhah-hahs-vah	නිදහස්ව
slow	he-min	හෙමින්
slowly	he-min	හෙමින්ම

quick	ik-mah-n	ඉක්මන්
quickly	ik-mah-nin	ඉක්මනින්ම

In Sinhala, adverbs always precede the verb:

He bought it very cheaply.
o-hu eh-kah hah-ri laah-be-tah gahth-theh — ඔහු ඒක හරි ලාබෙට ගත්තේ.
(lit: he it very cheaply bought)

The dog ran quickly.
bahl-laah ik-mah-nin dhiv-veh-yah — බල්ලා ඉක්මණින් දිව්වේය.
(lit: dog quickly ran)

POSSESSIVES

Possessive adjectives and pronouns have the same form in Sinhala so mah-geh (මගේ), for example, is used to express both 'my' and 'mine':

Possessive Adjective / Pronoun		
my/mine	mah-geh	මගේ
your/ yours	o-beh, o-bah-geh (sg & pl)	ඔබේ, ඔබගේ
his	o-hu-geh	ඔහුගේ
her/hers	a-(yah)-geh	ඇයගේ
its	u-geh, eh-kah	උගේ, ඒකේ
our/ours	ah-peh, ah-pah-geh	අපේ, අපගේ
their/ theirs	o-vun-geh	ඔවුන්ගේ

Occasionally, o-beh, 'your/yours', and ah-peh, 'our/ours', are used rather than o-bah-geh and ah-pah-geh, and that a-yah-geh, 'her/hers', is abbreviated to a-geh. In addition, be aware that u-geh, 'its', is used only to refer to animals. Instead of o-bah (you) / o-beh, o-bah-geh (your/yours), o-yaah (you) / o-yaah-tah (your) / o-yaah-geh (yours) are commonly used in Spoken Sinhala.

Possessive adjectives come before the noun they possess and possessive pronouns are placed after:

This is my car.
meh mah-geh kaahr e-kah — මේ මගේ කාර් එක.
(lit: this my car one)

This car is mine.
meh kaahr e-kah mah-geh — මේ කාර් එක මගේ.
(lit: this car one mine)

QUESTIONS

Question words usually appear at the end of the sentence, but there's no hard-and-fast rule, so you can place them anywhere and still be understood. You'll notice that -dhah (ද), which denotes an inquiry, appears at the end of all question words.

Common question words are listed below. Where two alternatives appear, the first is used in spoken language and the second in written language.

Where? ko-heh-dhah? කොහේද?

Where's the bank?
ban-ku-wah ko-heh-dhah? — බැංකුව කොහේද?
(lit: bank where?)

Why? a-yi/a-yi-dhah? ඇයි/ඇයිද?

Why is the office closed?
kahn-thoh-ru-wah vah-hah-laah a-yi? — කන්තෝරුව වහල ඇයි?
(lit: office closed why?)

When? kah-vah-dhaah-dhah? කවදාද?

When are you coming?
o-bah en-neh kah-vah-dhaah-dhah? — ඔබ එන්නේ කවදාද?
(lit: you coming when?)

What? ku-mahk-dah?/ mo-kahk-dah? කුමක්ද?ශ්‍රී මොකක්ද?

What happened?
mo-kahk-dhah vu-neh? මොකක්ද වුණේ?
(lit: what happened?)

How? ko-ho-mah-dhah? කොහොමද?

How did you come? (get here)
aah-veh ko-ho-mah-dhah? ආවේ කොහොමද?
(lit: came how?)

Who? kahv-dhah? කව්ද?

Who came today?
ah-dhah kahv-dhah aah-veh? අද කව්ද ආවේ?
(lit: today who came?)

Which? koi e-kah-dhah?; ku-mahk-dhah? කොයි එකද?; කුමක්ද?

Which one is mine?
koi e-kah-dhah mah-geh? කොයි එකද මගේ?
(lit: which one mine?)

As already mentioned, word order in Sinhala questions is very flexible, so the same question can be phrased in a number of different ways. Two common variations are as follows:

What's the time?
veh-laah-vah kee-yah-dhah? වේලාව කීයද?
(lit: time how-much?)

What's the time?
kee-yah-dhah veh-laah-vah? කීයද වේලාව?
(lit: how-much time?)

'YES/NO' QUESTIONS

To form a yes/no question, ie a question that elicits a 'yes/no' answer, simply add -dhah (ද) to the end of any sentence – there's no need to change the word order at all.

You're going.
o-bah yah-nah-vaah — ඔබ යනවා.
(lit: you going)

Are you going?
o-bah yah-nah-vaah-dhah? — ඔබ යනවාද?
(lit: you going?)

NEGATIVES

Negative sentences are formed by changing the verb ending from nah-vaah (නවා) to neh (නේ) and adding an extra n (න්) to the preceding syllable. The negative particle na-ha (නැහැ) is placed immediately after the verb.

I'm going today.
mah-mah ah-dhah yah-nah-vaah — මම අද යනවා.
(lit: I today am-going)

I'm not going today.
mah-mah ah-dhah yahn-neh na-ha — මම අද යන්නේ නැහැ.
(lit: I today go no)

For emphasis, you may hear na-ha placed twice in a sentence – at the beginning, as well as after the verb:

No, I'm not going today.
na-ha, mah-mah ah-dhah yahn-neh na-ha — නැහැ, මම අද යන්නේ නැහැ.
(lit: no I today go no)

PREPOSITIONS

Sinhala prepositions are placed after the noun or pronoun they refer to. The prepositions most commonly used are:

above	u-din	උඩින්
below	pah-hah-lin	පහලින්
beside	ah-yi-neh	අයිනේ
by	lahn-gah	ළඟ
from	si-tah	සිට
in	a-thu-leh	ඇතුලේ
on	mah-thah / u-dah	මත/උඩ
over	u-din	උඩින්
to	tah	ට
under	yah-tah	යට

The dog is in the house.
bahl-laah ge-yah a-thu-leh — බල්ලා ගෙය ඇතුලේ.
(lit: dog house in)

Sit under the tree.
gah-hah yah-tah — ගහ යට
in-dhah gahn-nah — ඉඳ ගන්න.
(lit: tree under sit)

Look over your shoulder.
o-beh u-rah-hi-sah-tah — ඔබේ උරහිසට
u-din bah-lahn-nah — උඩින් බලන්න.
(lit: your shoulder over look)

CONJUNCTIONS

Conjunctions join together sentences or parts of a sentence. The following is a list of the most common conjunctions:

and	sah-hah	සහ
as	ni-saah	නිසා
because	he-yin; ni-saah (spoken)	හෙයින්; නිසා
but	eh u-naah-tah	ඒ උනාට
although	u-naah-tah	උනාට
however	e-she-dhah/	එසේද/
	ke-seh ve-thahth	කෙසේ වෙතත්
since	ni-saah	නිසා

I can't go because I'm sick.
ah-sah-nee-pah ni-saah mah-tah yahn-nah ba-ha
(lit: sick because to-me go not)
අසනීප නිසා මට යන්න බැහැ

I like it, but it's too expensive for me.
mah-mah eh-kah-tah kah-mah-thiy, eh-u-naah-tah gaah-nah va-diy
(lit: I it like but expensive too)
මම ඒකට කැමතියි, ඒ උනාට ගාණ වැඩියි

Time & Dates

වේලාව සහ දිනයන්

TELLING THE TIME

වේලාව කියවීම

You'll notice that telling the time in Sinhala is just as simple as saying it in English - you follow the same pattern. Numerically speaking, you'll need to know the Sinhala version of your figures up to sixty (see p43 and p44).

What time is it?
veh-laah-vah kee-yah-dhah? වේලාව කීයද?

It's (one) o'clock.
dhan veh-laah-vah (e-kai) දැන් වේලාව (එකයි).
(lit: now time one)

Half past one.
e-kah-hah-maah-rai එකහමාරයි.
(lit: one-half)

Quarter past one.
e-kai kah-lai එකයි කාලයි.
(lit: one quarter)

Quarter to one.
e-kah-tah kaah-lai එකට කාලයි.
(lit: to-one quarter)

Twenty to one.
e-kah-tah vis-sai එකට විස්සයි.
(lit: to-one twenty)

DAYS OF THE WEEK

සතියේ දින

Monday	sahn-dhu-dhaah	සඳුදා
Tuesday	ahn-gah-hah-ru-vaah-dhaah	අඟහරුවාදා
Wednesday	bah-dhaah-dhaah	බදාදා

Thursday	brah-has-pah-thin-dhaah	බ්‍රහස්පතින්දා
Friday	si-ku-raah-dhaah	සිකුරාදා
Saturday	se-nah-su-raah-dhaah	සෙනසුරාදා
Sunday	i-ri-dhaah	ඉරිදා

MONTHS

මාසයන්

January	jah-nah-vaah-ri	ජනවාරි
February	pe-bah-rah-vaah-ri	පෙබරවාරි
March	maahr-thu	මාර්තු
April	ahp-rehl	අප්‍රේල්
May	ma-yi	මැයි
June	joo-ni	ජූනි
July	joo-li	ජූලි
August	ah-gohs-thu	අගෝස්තු
September	sep-tham-bahr	සෙප්තැම්බර්
October	ok-thoh-bahr	ඔක්තෝබර්
November	no-vam-bahr	නොවැම්බර්
December	dhe-sahm-bahr	දෙසැම්බර්

SEASONS

සෘතු කාල

summer	greesh-mah kaah-lah-yah	ග්‍රීෂ්ම කාලය
autumn	sah-rahth kaah-lah-yah	සරත් කාලය
winter	shee-thah kaah-lah-yah	ශීත කාලය
spring	wah-sahn-thah kaah-lah-yah	වසන්ත කාලය

For more on weather, see p146.

DATES

දින

What date is it today?
ah-dhah dhi-nah-yah mo-kahk-dhah? අද දිනය මොකක්ද?

It's 18 October.
ah-dhah ok-thoh-bahr 18 ve-ni-dhaah — අද ඔක්තෝබර්18 වෙනිදා.

PRESENT වර්තමානය

today	ah-dhah	අද
this morning	ah-dhah u-dheh	අද උදේ
this afternoon	ah-dhah dhah-vahl	අද දවල්
tonight	ah-dhah raa	අද රෑ
this week	meh sah-thi-yeh	මේ සතියේ
this month	meh maah-sah-yeh	මේ මාසයේ
this year	meh ah-vu-rud-dheh	මේ අවුරුද්දේ
now	dhan	දැන්
right now	dhan-mah	දැන්ම

PAST අතීතය

yesterday	ee-yeh	ඊයේ
day before yesterday	pe-reh-dhaah	පෙරේදා
yesterday ...	ee-yeh ...	ඊයේ
morning	u-dheh	උදේ
afternoon	dhah-vahl	දවල්
evening	han-daa-veh	හැන්දෑවේ
last night	ee-yeh raa	ඊයේ රෑ
last week	gi-yah sah-thi-yeh	ගිය සතියේ
last month	gi-yah maah-seh	ගිය මාසේ
last year	gi-yah ah-vu-rudh-dheh	ගිය අවුරුද්දේ
(half an hour) ago	(pa-yah bhaah-gah-yah) kah-tah is-sah-rah	(පැය භාගය) කට ඉස්සර
(three) days ago	dhah-vahs (thu-nah)-kah-tah kah-lin	දවස් (තුනා)කට කලින්
(five) years ago	ah-vu-rudh-dhu (pah-hah)-kah-tah is-sah-rah	අවුරුදු (පහ) කට ඉස්සර
a while ago	kah-lah-kah-tah pe-rah	කලකට පෙර
since (May)	(ma-yi) maah-seh si-tah	(මැයි) මාසේ සිට

FUTURE අනාගතය

tomorrow	he-tah	හෙට
day after tomorrow	ah-nidh-dhaah	අනිද්දා
tomorrow ...	he-tah ...	හෙට ...
morning	u-dheh	උදේ
afternoon	dhah-vahl	දවල්
evening	han-dhaa-weh	හැන්දෑවේ
next week	ee-lahn-gah sah-thi-yeh	ඊළඟ සතියේ
next month	ee-lahn-gah maah-seh	ඊළඟ මාසේ
next year	ee-lahn-gah ah-vu-rudh-dheh	ඊළඟ අවුරුද්දේ
in (five) minutes	vi-naah-di (pah-hah)-kin	විනාඩි (පහ)කින්
in (six) days	dhi-nah (hah-yah)-kin	දින (හය)කින්
until (June)	(joo-ni) maah-sah-yah thek	(ජූනි) මාසය තෙක්

DURING THE DAY

දවස තුළ

It's early.	veh-laah-sah-nai	වේලාසනයි.
It's late.	pah-rahk-kuy	පරක්කුයි.
early	veh-laah-sah-nah	වේලාසන
afternoon	dhah-vahl	දවල්
dawn	paahn-dhah-ra	පාන්දර
day	dhah-vah-sah	දවස
evening	han-dhaa-wah	හැන්දෑව
lunchtime	dah-vahl kaa-mah veh-laah-vah	දවල් කෑම වේලාව
midday	dhah-hah-vah-lah	දහවල
midnight	ma-dhi-yahm ra-yah	මැදියම් රැය
morning	u-dheh	උදේ
night	raa	රෑ
noon	dhah-vahl	දවල්
sunrise	hi-ru u-dhaah-vah	හිරු උදාව
sunset	hi-ru ba-see-mah	හිරු බැසීම

Numbers & Amounts

අංක සහ ප්‍රමාණයන්

If you follow the pattern of Sinhala numbers, you'll notice that one to 12 differ from one another, but from 20 onwards there is a set pattern, with only a change in each series of tens up to one hundred.

CARDINAL NUMBERS

අනු අංක

1	e-kah	එක
2	dhe-kah	දෙක
3	thu-nah	තුන
4	hah-thah-rah	හතර
5	pah-hah	පහ
6	hah-yah	හය
7	hah-thah	හත
8	ah-tah	අට
9	nah-vah-yah	නවය
10	dhah-hah-yah	දහය
11	e-ko-lah-hah	එකොළහ
12	dho-lah-hah	දොළහ
13	dhah-hah-thu-nah	දහතුන
14	dhah-hah-hah-thah-rah	දහහතර
15	pah-hah-lah-vah	පහළොව
16	dhah-hah-sah-yah	දහසය
17	dhah-hah-hah-thah	දහහත
18	dhah-hah-ah-tah	දහඅට
19	dhah-hah-nah-vah-yah	දහනවය
20	vis-sah	විස්ස

☑ FIGURING IT OUT

In Sinhala, figures are only written in script when they're spelled out – the figures themselves are written as in English.

Numbers 21-29 start with vis-si-:		විස්
21	vis-si-e-kah	විස්එක
22	vi-si-dhe-kah	විස්දෙක
30	thi-hah	තිහ
Numbers 31-39 start with this-:		තිස්
33	this-thu-nah	තිස්තුන
37	this-hah-thah	තිස්හත
40	hah-thah-li-hah	හතලිහ
Numbers 41-49 start with ha-thah-lis:		හතලිස්
43	hah-thah-lis thu-nah	හතලිස් තුන
46	hah-thah-lis hah-yah	හතලිස් හය
50	pah-nah-hah	පනහ
Numbers 51-59 start with pah-nahs:		පනස්
52	pah-nahs dhe-kah	පනස් දෙක
55	pah-nahs pah-hah	පනස් පහ
60	ha-tah	හැට
Numbers 61-69 start with ha-tah:		හැට
61	ha-tah e-kah	හැට එක
66	ha-tah hah-yah	හැට හය
70	hath-thaa-wah	හැත්තෑව
Numbers 71-79 start with hath-thaah:		හැත්තා
73	hath-thaah thu-nah	හැත්තා තුන
75	hath-thaah pah-hah	හැත්තා පහ
80	ah-soo-wah	අසූව
Numbers 81-89 start with ah-soo:		අසූ
84	ah-soo hah-thah-rah	අසූ හතර
88	ah-soo ah-tah	අසූ අට
90	ah-noo-wah	අනූව
Numbers 81-89 start with ah-noo:		අනූ
96	ah-noo hah-yah	අනූ හය
99	ah-noo nah-vah-yah	අනූ නවය

All numbers in the hundreds end with see-yah:

100	e-kah see-yah	එකසීය
200	dhe-see-yah	දෙසීය
300	thun-see-yah	තුන්සීය
400	haah-rah-see-yah	හාරසීය
500	pahn-see-yah	පන්සීය
600	hah-yah-see-yah	හයසීය
700	hath-see-yah	හත්සීය
800	ah-tah-see-yah	අටසීය
900	nah-vah-see-yah	නවසීය
1000	daah-hah	දාහ
one lakh (100,000)	ek lahk-shah-yah	එක් ලක්ශය
one million	mi-li-yah-nah-yah	මිලියනය

ORDINAL NUMBERS

ක්‍රමාංක

1st	pah-lah-mu-ve-ni	පළමුවෙනි
2nd	dhe-vah-ni	දෙවනි
3rd	thun-ve-ni	තුන්වෙනි
4th	hah-thah-rah-ve-ni	හතරවෙනි
5th	pahs-ve-ni	පස්වෙනි

FRACTIONS

භාග

a quarter	kaah-lah	කාල
a half	bhaah-gah-yah	භාගය
a third	thu-nen pahn-gu-wah	තුනෙන් පංගුව
three-quarters	hah-thah-ren thu-nah	හතරෙන් තුන

USEFUL AMOUNTS

ප්‍රයෝජනවත් ප්‍රමාණ

How much?	koch-chah-rah-dhah?	කොච්චරද?
How many?	kee-yah-dhah?	කීයද?
Could you please give me ...? (f.)	kah-ru-naah-kah-rah mah-tah ... dhen-nah?	කරුණාකර මට ... දෙන්න?
Please (inf.)	plees	ප්ලීස්
I need ...	mah-tah ... oh-neh	මට ... ඕනේ
all (written)	sahm-poor-nah	සම්පූර්ණ
all (spoken)	ok-ko-mah	ඔක්කොම
double	dhe-kah dhe-kah	දෙක දෙක
a dozen	dhu-si-mahk	දුසිමක්
half a dozen	dhu-sim baah-gah-yahk	දුසිම් භාගයක්
(a) few	ti-kahk	ටිකක්
less	ah-du	අඩු
a little	bo-hoh-mah ti-kahk	බොහෝම ටිකක්
a lot	hun-gahk	හුඟාක්
(too) many	bo-hoh (va-di)	බොහෝ (වැඩි)
more	thah-vah	තව
(too) much	go-daahk (va-di)	ගොඩක් (වැඩි)
none	ki-si-wahk na-thi	කිසිවක් නැති
a pair	joh-du-wahk/dhe-kahk	ජෝවක්/දෙකක්
some	sah-mah-hah-rehk	සමහරෙක්
a bottle/jar	boh-thah-lah-yahk	බෝතලයක්
a packet	pa-kaht-tu-wahk	පැකට්ටුවක්
a slice	peth-thahk	පෙත්තක්
a tin	tin e-kahk	ටින් එකක්
once	ek vah-rahk	එක් වරක්
twice	dhe-sa-rah-yahk	දෙසැරයක්

PRACTICAL

Getting Around

ගමනේ බිමනේ යෙදීම්

Sri Lanka has a good network of roads connecting the principal towns and places of interest, as well as a train service linking the island's key tourist destinations.

Cars can be hired with or without drivers, and taxis are available in all the main towns. Taxis usually have meters, but if not, the fare must be negotiated – ideally, before the journey begins. For an open-air experience, try a three-wheeled 'autorickshaw'.

Bus travel is cheap and there's an island-wide service. Express buses run to all main towns and seats can be booked in advance.

FINDING YOUR WAY

ගමන් බිමන් යෑමේදී

Where's the ...?	... ko-heh-dhah thi-yen-neh?	... කොහේද තියෙන්නේ?
bus stop	bahs staand e-kah	බස් ස්ටෑන්ඩ් එක
road to ...	...-tah yah-nah paah-rah	...ට යන පාර
train station	dhum-ri-yah sthaah-nah-yah	දුම්රිය ස්ථානය
What time does the ... leave/arrive?	... pi-tahth ven-neh/ en-neh kee-yah-tah-dhah?	... පිටත් වෙන්නේ/ එන්නේ කීයටද?
boat	boht-tu-wah	බෝට්ටුව
bus	bahs e-kah	බස් එක
plane	ah-hahs-yaah thraah-vah	අහස් යාත්‍රාව
train	dhum-ri-yah	දුම්රිය

How do we get to ...?
...-tah yahn-neh ko-ho-mah-dhah? — ...ට යන්නේ කොහොමද?

Is it close by?
dhan lahn-gah-dhah? — දැන් ළඟද?

Can we walk there?
ah-pi-tah eh-haah-tah a-vi-dhan yah-nnah pu-lu-vahn-dhah? — අපිට එහාට ඇවිදන් යන්න පුළුවන්ද?

Although the translation of 'walk' is a-vi-dhin-nah, in the above context, it's more common to say pah-yin meaning 'on foot'.

Can you show me (on the map)?
mah-tah (si-thi-yah-meh) pen-vahn-nah pu-lu-vahn-dhah? — මට (සිතියමේ) පෙන්වන්න පුළුවන්ද?

Are there other means of getting there?
e-haah-tah ve-nah vi-dhi-yah-kin yahn-nah ba-ri-dhah? — එහාට වෙන විදියකින් යන්න බැරිද?

What ... is this?	meh mo-nah ...-dhah?	මේ මොන ...ද?
city	nah-gah-rah-yah	නගරය
street	paah-rah	පාර
village	gah-mah	ගම

DIRECTIONS මග සලකුණු

Turn at the ...	... ha-ren-nah	... හැරෙන්න.
next corner	ee-lahn-gah ko-neh-dhee	ඊළඟ කොණේදී
traffic lights	tra-fic lait vah-lah-dhee	ට්‍රැෆික් ලයිට් වලදී
next crossroads	ee-lahn-gah hahn-dhi-yeh-dhee	ඊළඟ හන්දියේදී

Go straight ahead.	ke-lin is-sah-rah-hah-tah yahn-nah	කෙලින් ඉස්සරහට යන්න.
Turn left/right.	vah-mah-tah/ dhah-ku-nah-tah ha-ren-nah	වමට/දකුණට හැරෙන්න.

behind	pahs-sah-tah/ pahs-sen	පස්සට/ පස්සෙන්
in front of	is-sah-rah-hin	ඉස්සරහින්
far	aa-thah	ඈත
near	lan-gah	ළඟ
here	me-thah-nah	මෙතන
there	ah-tha-nah	අතන
opposite	i-di-ri-pah-sah	ඉදිරිපස
north	u-thu-rah	උතුර
south	dhah-ku-nah	දකුණ
east	na-ge-nah-hi-rah	නැගෙනහිර
west	bah-tah-hi-rah	බටහිර

Thank you for showing us the way.
ah-pah-tah paah-rah pen-nu-waah-tah sthoo-thiy — අපට පාර පෙන්නුවාට ස්තූතියි.

ADDRESSES

ලිපිනයන්

Addresses are often written in English, but occasionally they're in Sinhala – particularly in suburban and rural areas. A written address in Sinhala would give the person's name, the number and street, the suburb and the city. For Colombo addresses usually only the suburb is given, unless the address is in one of the city zones. For example:

සීතා හේරත්	see-thaah heh rah-th	**Seetha Herath**
45 නාවල පාර	45 naah-wah-lah paah-rah	**45 Nawala Road**
නුගේගොඩ	nu-geh-go-dah	**Nugegoda**

TAXI

කුලී රථ

Is this taxi free?
yahn-nah pu-lu-vahn-dhah? — යන්න පුළුවන්ද?

Please take me to ...
kah-ru-naah-kah-rah-lah maah-wah ...-tah ge-ni-yahn-nah — කරුණාකරල මාව ...ට ගෙනියන්න.

How much is it to go to ...?
...-tah yahn-nah kee-yahk gahn-nah-vaah-dhah? — ...ට යන්න කීයක් ගන්නවද?

Do we pay extra for luggage?
bah-du ge-ni-yah-nah-vaah-tah va-di-pu-rah ge-vahn-nah oh-ne-dhah? — බඩු ගෙනියනවාට වැඩිපුර ගෙවන්න ඕනෙද?

INSTRUCTIONS නියෝග

Continue!
no-na-vah-thee yahn-nah! — නොනැවතී යන්න!

Take the next street to the left/right.
vah-mah-tah/dhah-ku-nah-tah a-thi ee-lahn-gah paah-reh yahn-nah — වමට/දකුණට ඇති ඊළඟ පාරේ යන්න.

Please slow down.
kah-ru-naah-kah-rah-lah he-min yahn-nah — කරුණාකරල හෙමින් යන්න.

Please wait here.
kah-ru-naah-kah-rah-lah me-thah-nah in-nah — කරුණාකරල මෙතන ඉන්න.

Stop here.
me-thah-nah nah-vah-thin-nah — මෙතන නවතින්න.

Stop at the corner.
ko-ne nah-vah-thin-nah — කොණේ නවතින්න.

BUYING TICKETS

ටිකට් මිලදී ගැනීම

Where can I buy a ticket?
mah-tah ti-kaht e-kahk gahn-neh ko-hen-dhah? — මට ටිකට් එකක් ගන්නේ කොහෙන්ද?

We want to go to ...
ah-pah-tah ...-tah yahn-nah oh-neh — අපට ...ට යන්න ඕනේ.

Do I need to book?
mah-mah seet ven-kah-rah gahn-nah oh-neh-dhah? — මම සීට් වෙන්කර ගන්න ඕනේද?

I'd like to book a seat to ...
mah-tah ...-tah seet e-kahk buk kah-rahn-nah oh-neh — මට ...ට සීට් එකක් බුක් කරන්න ඕනේ.

How long does the trip take?
gah-mah-nah-tah koch-chah-rah ve-laah gah-thah ve-nah-vaah-dhah? — ගමනට කොච්චර වෙලා ගත වෙනවාද?

I'd like a luggage locker.
bah-du dhah-mahn-nah yah-thu-rahk ek-kah sehp-pu-wak oh-neh — බඩු දමන්න යතුරක් එක්ක සේප්පුවක් ඕනේ.

I'd like (a) ...	mah-tah oh-neh ...	මට ඕනේ ...
one-way ticket	yahn-nah vi-thah-rahk ti-kaht e-kahk	යන්න විතරක් ටිකට් එකක්
return ticket	yahn-nah en-nah dhe-kah-tah-mah ti-kaht e-kahk	යන්න එන්න දෙකටම ටිකට් එකක්
two tickets	ti-kaht dhe-kahk	ටිකට් දෙකක්
1st-class ticket	pah-lah-mu-vah-nah pahn-thi-yeh ti-kaht e-kahk	පළමුවන පංතියේ ටිකට් එකක්
2nd-class ticket	dhe-vah-nah pahn-thi-yeh ti-kaht e-kahk	දෙවන පංතියේ ටිකට් එකක්

AIR

ගුවනින්

When's the the next flight to ...?

...-tah ee-lan-gah flait e-kah kee-yah-tah-dhah?
...ට ඊළඟ ෆ්ලයිට් එක කීයටද?

What time do I have to check in at the airport?

mah-mah e-yaah-poht e-kah-tah en-nah oh-neh kee-yah-tah-dhah?
මම එයාපෝට් එකට එන්න ඕනේ කීයටද?

I'd like vegetarian meals.

mah-mah ka-mah-thi mahs maah-lu na-thi kaa-mah
මම කැමති මස් මාළු නැති කෑම.

I'd like to cancel my reservation.

mah-geh seet e-kah can-sahl kah-rahn-nah ka-mah-thiy
මගේ සීට් එක කැන්සල් කරන්න කැමතියි.

I'd like to make change my reservation.

mah-mah buk kah-lah seet e-kah ve-nahs kah-rahn-nah ka-mah-thiy
මම බුක් කළ සීට් එක වෙනස් කරන්න කැමතියි.

My luggage hasn't arrived.

mah-geh baag thah-vah-mah a-vith na-ha
මගේ බෑග් තවම ඇවිත් නැහැ

LOOK FOR

බඩු ලබා ගැනීම්	**baggage claim**
රේගුව	**customs**
අභ්‍යන්තර	**domestic**
ජාත්‍යන්තර	**international**
ගමන් බලපත්‍ර කටයුතු	**passport control**

AT CUSTOMS රේගුවේදී

I have nothing to declare.
mah-tah pen-vahn-nah ki-si-vahk na-ha — මට පෙන්වන්න කිසිවක් නැහැ.

I have something to declare.
mah-tah pen-vahn-nah yah-mahk thi-yah-nah-vaah — මට පෙන්වන්න යමක් තියනවා.

Although the translation of 'to declare' is prah-kaah-shah, in the above context you would say pen-vahn-nah, meaning 'to show'.

This is all my luggage.
meh ok-kah-mah bah-du mah-geh — මේ ඔක්කම බඩු මගේ.

It's also very common to use the English word 'bag' (බෑග්) for luggage in this instance instead of using the translation for luggage, which is bah-du.

That's not mine.
eh-kah mah-geh no-veh — ඒක මගෙ නොවේ.

I didn't know I had to declare it.
eh ga-nah ki-yahn-nah oh-neh ki-yah-lah mah-mah dha-nah-ge-nah hi-ti-yeh na-ha — ඒ ගැන කියන්න ඕනේ කියලා මම දැනගෙන හිටියේ නැහැ.

In this last example, although 'to declare' is prah-kaah-shah, ki-yahn-nah, 'to tell', is more suitable in this context.

LISTEN FOR

seet na-ha	**It's full.**

BOAT

බෝට්ටු

Where does the boat leave from?

boht-tu-wah ko-hen-dhah pi-tahth ven-neh? — බෝට්ටුව කොහෙන්ද පිටත් වෙන්නේ?

What time does the boat arrive?

boht-tu-wah en-neh kee-yah-tah-dhah? — බෝට්ටුව එන්නේ කීයටද?

BUS

බස් රථ

Where's the bus stop?

bahs e-kah nah-vaht-vahn-neh ko-thah-nah-dhah? — බස් එක නවත්වන්නේ කොතනද?

Does this bus go to ...?

meh bahs e-kah ...-tah yah-nah-vaah-dhah? — මේ බස් එක ...ට යනවාද?

How often do buses come?

koch-chah-rah veh-laah-vah-kah-tah va-thaah-vahk-dhah bahs en-neh? — කොච්චර වෙලාවකට වතාවක්ද බස් එන්නේ?

What time's the ... bus?	... bahs eh-kah kee-yah-tah-dhah?	... බස් එක කීයටද?
first	pah-lah-mu	පළමු
last	ahn-thi-mah	අන්තිම
next	ee-lahn-gah	ඊළඟ

Could you let me know when we get to ...?

...-tah gi-yaah-mah mah-tah ki-yah-nah-vaah-dhah? — ...ට ගියාම මට කියනවාද?

Where do I get the bus for ...?

...-tah bahs e-kah gahn-neh ko-thah-nin-dhah? — ...ට බස් එක ගන්නේ කොතනින්ද?

TRAIN

දුම්රිය/කෝච්චිය

Which station is this?

meh mo-nah steh-shah-mah-dhah?

මේ මොන ස්ටේෂමද?

What's the next station?

ee-lahn-gah steh-shah-mah mo-kahk-dhah?

ඊළඟ ස්ටේෂම මොකක්ද?

Does this train stop at ...?

meh koch-chi-yah ... nah-thah-rah kah-rah-nah-vaah-dhah?

මේ කෝච්චිය ... නතර කරනවාද?

The train is delayed/cancelled.

koch-chi-yah [prah-maah-dhai; dhu-vahn-neh na-ha]

කෝච්චිය ප්‍රමාදයි; දුවන්නේ නැහැ.

Do I have to change?

ah-tha-rah mah-gah maah-ru ven-nah oh-ne-dhah?

අතර මඟ මාරු වෙන්න ඕනෙද?

Is that seat taken?

meh seet e-keh kau-ru hah-ri in-nah-vaah-dhah?

මේ සීට් එකේ කවුරු හරි ඉන්නවාද?

I want to get off in (Kandy).

mah-tah (nu-wah-rin) bah-hin-nah oh-neh

මට (නුවරින්) බහින්න ඕනේ.

CAR

කාර් එක

When hiring a car in Sri Lanka, you can either drive yourself or hire a vehicle with a driver. The latter is a popular option, as most drivers are happy to provide you with local knowledge and act as a tour guide.

Where can I hire a car (and driver)?

kaahr e-kahk (sah-hah drai-vah ke-nek) hah-yahr kah-rahn-neh ko-hen-dhah?

කාර් එකක් (සහ ඩ්‍රයිවර් කෙනෙක්) හයර් කරන්නේ කොහෙන්ද?

How much is it daily/weekly?
dhah-vah-sah-kah-tah/ sah-thi-yah-kah-tah kee-yah-dhah? — දවසකට/ සතියකට කීයද?

Does that include insurance/mileage?
meh rakh-sha-nah/sa-thah-pum gah-nah-nah ek-kah-dhah? — මේ රක්ෂණ/සැතපුම් ගණන එක්කද?

Where's the next petrol station?
ee-lahn-gah pet-rohl sta-shah-mah ko-heh-dhah? — ඊළඟ පෙට්‍රල් ස්ටේෂම කොහේද?

Please fill the tank.
kah-ru-naah-kah-rah-lah tan-ki-yah pu-rah-vahn-nah — කරුණාකරල ටැංකිය පුරවන්න.

Does this road lead to ...?
meh paah-rah ... yah-nah-vaah-dhah? — මේ පාර ... යනවාද?

Please check the ...	kah-ru-naah-kah-rah-lah ... bah-lahn-nah	කරුණාකරල ... බලන්න.
oil	thel	තෙල්
tyre pressure	hu-lahng	හුළං
water	wah-thu-rah	වතුර

LOOK FOR

අන්තරාදායකයි	**danger**
ඉඩ දෙන්න	**give way**
නතර කිරීම තහනම්	**no parking**
ඒකීය ධාවනය	**one way**
පාර අළුත්වැඩියා කෙරේ	**roadworks**
සෙමින් පදවන්න	**slow down**
නතර වෙන්න	**stop**

air	hu-lahng	හුළං
battery	ba-tri-yah	බැට්‍රිය
brakes	brehk	බ්‍රේක්
clutch	klahch e-kah	ක්ලච් එක
driver's licence	lai-sahn e-kah	ලයිසන් එක
lights	lait	ලයිට්
... petrol (gas)	... pet-rohl	... පෙට්‍රෝල්
leaded	led ek-kah	ලෙඩ් එක්ක
regular	saah-maan-yah	සාමාන්‍ය
unleaded	led na-thi	ලෙඩ් නැති
puncture	tah-yahr e-keh hu-lahng gi-hil-laah	ටයර් එකේ හුළං ගිහිල්ලා
radiator	reh-di-yeh-tah-rah-yah	රේඩියේටරය
seatbelt	seet belt e-kah	සීට් බෙල්ට් එක
tyres	tah-yahr	ටයර්
windscreen	vin skreen e-kah	වින් ස්ක්‍රීන් එක

BICYCLE

බයිසිකලය

Is it within cycling distance?
bai-si-kah-lah-yen yah-nah dhu-rah-dhah? — බයිසිකලයෙන් යන දුරද?

Where can I hire a bicycle?
bai-si-kah-lah-yahk ku-li-yah-tah gahn-neh ko-hen-dhah? — බයිසිකලයක් කුලියට ගන්නේ කොහෙන්ද?

How much is it for ...?	... gaah-nah kee-yah-dhah?	... ගාන කීයද?
an hour	pa-yah-kah-tah	පැයකට
the morning	u-dheh-tah	උදේට
the afternoon	hah-vah-sah-tah	හවසට
the day	dhah-vah-sah-tah	දවසට

I have a flat tyre.

mah-geh tah-yahr e-keh hu-lahng ba-ha-laah	මගේ ටයර් එකේ හුළං බැහැලා.

bike	bai-si-kah-la-yah	බයිසිකලය
handlebars	han-dhahl baahr e-kah	හැන්ඩල් බාර් එක
helmet	hel-maht e-kah	හෙල්මට් එක
inner tube	a-thu-leh ti-yub e-kah	ඇතුලෙ ටියුබ් එක
lights	lait	ලයිට්
padlock	ib-baah	ඉබ්බා
pump	pom-pah-yah	පොම්පය
puncture	tah-yahr e-keh hu-lahng gi-hil-laah	ටයර් එකේ හුළං ගිහිල්ලා
saddle	sa-dah-lah-yah	සැඩලය
wheel	roh-dhah	රෝද

Accommodation

නවාතැන්

Sri Lanka has a wide variety of accommodation options, ranging from family homes, guesthouses and rest houses to hotels, motels, lodges and tourist resorts.

FINDING ACCOMMODATION

නවාතැන් සොයා ගැනීම

I'm looking for a ...	mah-mah so-yahn-neh ...	මම සොයන්නේ ...
backpack hostel	bak-pak hos-tahl e-kahk	බැක්පැක් හොස්ටල් එකක්
guesthouse	gest hah-vus e-kahk	ගෙස්ට් හවුස් එකක්
hotel	hoh-tah-lah-yahk	හෝටලයක්
motel	mo-tehl e-kahk	මොටේල් එකක්

Where can I find a ... hotel?	mah-mah ... hoh-tah-lah-yahk so-yaah gahn-neh ko-hen-dhah?	මම ... හෝටලයක් සොයා ගන්නේ කොහෙන්ද?
clean	pi-ri-si-du	පිරිසිදු
good	hon-dhah	හොඳ

Where's the ... hotel?	... hoh-tah-lah-yah thi-yen-neh ko-heh-dhah?	... හෝටලය තියෙන්නේ කොහේද?
best	hon-dhah-mah	හොඳම
cheapest	laah-bah-mah	ලාභම
nearest	lahn-gah-mah	ළඟම

LOOK FOR

නවාතැන් නැත	**no vacancies**
නවාතැන් ඇත	**rooms available**

What's the address?
e-keh li-pi-nah-yah mo-kahk-dhah? — ඒකේ ලිපිනය මොකක්ද?

Could you write the address, please?
kah-ru-naah-kah-rah-lah lipi-nah-yah li-yah-laah dhen-nah? — කරුණාකරල ලිපිනය ලියලා දෙන්න?

BOOKING AHEAD

කලින් වෙන්කරවා ගැනීම

I'd like to book a (single/double) room, please.
kah-ru-naah-kah-rah-lah mah-tah (thah-ni/dhen-ne-ku-tah) kaah-mah-rah-yahk gahn-nah ha-ki-dhah? — කරුණාකරල මට (තනි/දෙන්නෙකුට) කාමරයක් ගන්න හැකිද?

For (three) nights.
raa (thu-nah-)kah-tah — රෑ (තුන)කට.

How much for ...?	... kee-yah-dhah?	... කීයද?
one night	e-kah ra-yah-kahk	එක රැයක්
a week	e-kah sah-thi-yah-kah-tah	එක සතියකට
two people	dhen-ne-ku-tah	දෙන්නෙකුට

Is there a discount for children/students?
lah-mun-tah/shish-yah-yahn-tah mi-lah ah-du-dhah? — ළමුන්ට/ශිෂ්‍යයන්ට මිළ අඩුද?

I'll/We'll be arriving at ...
mah-mah/ah-pi ... e-nah-vaah — මම/අපි ... එනවා.

My name's ...
mah-geh nah-mah ... — මගේ නම ...

Can I pay by credit card?
kaahd e-ken ge-vahn-nah ha-ki-dhah? — කාඩ් එකෙන් ගෙවන්න හැකිද?

CHECKING IN

පැමිණීමේදී

Do you have any rooms/beds available?
kaah-mah-rah/a-dahn thi-yeh-dhah? — කාමර/ඇඳන් තියේද?

Do you have a room with two beds?
a-dhahn dhe-keh kaah-mah-rah thi-yeh-dhah? — ඇඳන් දෙකේ කාමර තියේද?

Do you have a room with a double bed?
dah-bahl an-dahk ek-kah kaah-mah-rah-yak thi-yeh-dhah? — ඩබල් ඇඳක් එක්ක කාමරයක් තියේද?

I'd like ...	mah-mah ka-mah-thiy ...	මම කැමතියි ...
to share a dorm	dohm-room-e-kahk-she-yaah-kah-rahn-nah	ඩෝම් රූම් එකක් ශෙයා කරන්න
a single room	thah-ni kaah-mah-rah-yahk	තනි කාමරයක්

I/We want a room with a ...	mah-tah/ah-pi-tah oh-neh ... ek-kah kaah-mah-rah-yahk	මට/අපට ඕනේ ... එක්ක කාමරයක්.
bathroom	naah-nah kaah-mah-rah-yahk	නාන කාමරයක්
shower	shah-vahr e-kahk	ෂවර් එකක්
TV	tee-vee e-kahk	ටී.වී. එකක්
window	jah-neh-lah-yahk	ජනේලයක්

LISTEN FOR

kah-nah-gaah-tuy kaah-mah-rah na-ha — **Sorry, we're full.**

Can I see it?
mah-tah bah-lahn-nah ha-ki-dhah? — මට බලන්න හැකිද?

Are there any others?
ve-nah kaah-mah-rah thi-yeh-dhah? — වෙන කාමර තියේද?

It's fine. I'll take it.
eh-kah hon-dhai. mah-mah eh-kah gahn-nam — ඒක හොඳයි. මම ඒක ගන්නම්.

REQUESTS & QUERIES

ඉල්ලීම් හා විමසීම්

Where's the bathroom?
naah-nah kaah-mah-rah-yah ko-heh-dhah? — නාන කාමරය කොහේද?

Where's breakfast served?
u-dheh kaa-mah gahn-neh ko-heh-dhah? — උදේ කෑම ගන්නේ කොහේද?

Is there somewhere to wash clothes?
an-dum soh-dhaah gahn-nah tha-nahk thi-yeh-dhah? — ඇඳුම් සෝදා ගන්න තැනක් තියේද?

Is there hot water all day?
dhah-vah-sah pu-raah u-nu wah-thu-rah thi-yeh-dhah? — දවස පුරා උණු වතුර තියේද?

Can we use the kitchen?
a-pah-tah kus-si-yah paah-vich-chi kah-rahn-nah ha-ki-dhah? — අපට කුස්සිය පාවිච්චි කරන්න හැකිද?

Can we use the telephone?
a-pah-tah te-li-fohn e-kah paah-vich-chi kah-rahn-nah ha-ki-dhah? — අපට ටෙලිෆෝන් ඒක පාවිච්චි කරන්න හැකිද?

Do you have a safe where I can leave my valuables?

mah-geh vah-ti-naah bah-du
thi-yahn-nah ha-ki
sehp-pu-wahk thi-yeh-dhah?

මගේ වටිනා බ
තියන්න හැකි
සේප්පුවක් තියේද?

Could I have a receipt for them?

eh-vah-tah ri-seet e-kahk
gahn-nah ha-ki-dhah?

ඒවාට රිසීට් එකක්
ගන්න හැකිද?

Do you change money here?

o-bah sahl-li maah-ru
kah-rah-nah-vaah-dhah?

ඔබ සල්ලි මාරු
කරනවාද?

Do you arrange tours?

o-bah sahn-chaah-rah gah-mahn
laas-thi kah-rah-nah-vaah-dhah?

ඔබ සංචාර ගමන්
ලෑස්ති කරනවාද?

Can I leave a message?

mah-tah pah-ni-vu-dah-yak
thi-yahn-nah ha-ki-dhah?

මට පණිවුඩයක්
තියන්න හැකිද?

Is there a message for me?

mah-tah pah-ni-vu-dah-yak
thi-yeh-dhah?

මට පණිවුඩයක්
තියේද?

Please wake us at (seven).

kah-ru-naah-kah-rah-lah
ah-pah-vah (hah-thah-tah)
ah-rah-vahn-nah

කරුණාකරල අපව
(හතට) ඇහැරවන්න

Please change the sheets.

kah-ru-naah-kah-rah-lah
sheet maah-ru kah-rahn-nah

කරුණාකරල ශීට්
මාරු කරන්න.

The room needs to be cleaned.

kaah-mah-rah-yah pi-ri-si-du
kah-rahn-nah oh-neh

කාමරය පිරිසිදු
කරන්න ඕනේ.

I need a/another ...

mah-tah thah-vahth ... oh-neh

මට තවත් ... ඕනේ.

Could we have ...?	ah-pah-tah ... gahn-nah pu-lu-vahn-dhah?	අපට ... ගන්න පුළුවන්ද?
an extra blanket	va-di-pu-rah blan-kaht e-kahk	වැඩිපුර බ්ලැන්කට් එකක්
a mosquito net	mah-dhu-ru dha-lahk	මදුරු දැලක්
our key	ah-peh yah-thu-rah	අපේ යතුර

I've locked myself out of my room.
yah-thu-rah kaah-mah-rah-yah a-thu-leh dhah-mah-laah mah-mah dho-rah vah-hah-lah
යතුර කාමරය ඇතුලේ දමලා මම දොර වහලා.

We left the key at reception.
ah-pi yah-thu-rah is-sah-rah-hah kaun-tah-reh thib-baah
අපි යතුර ඉස්සරහ කවුන්ටරයේ තිබ්බා.

COMPLAINTS

පැමිණිලි

I can't open/close the window.
mah-tah jah-neh-lah-yah ah-rin-nah/vah-hahn-nah ba-ha
මට ජනේලය අරින්න/වහන්න බැහැ.

I don't like this room.
mah-mah meh kaah-mah-rah-yah-tah ka-mah-thi na-ha
මම මේ කාමරයට කැමති නැහැ.

The toilet won't flush.
toi-laht e-kah va-dah kah-rahn-neh na-ha
ටොයිලට් එක වැඩ කරන්නේ නැහැ.

Can I change to another room?
mah-tah ve-nah kaah-mah-rah-yah-kah-tah yahn-nah ha-ki-dhah?
මට වෙන කාමරයකට යන්න හැකිද?

It's too ...	meh-kah hu-gaahk ...	මේක හුගාක් ...
cold	see-thah-lai	සීතලයි
dark	kah-lu-vah-rai	කළුවරයි
expensive	gah-nahn va-diy	ගණන් වැඩියි
light/bright	e-li-yah va-diy	එලිය වැඩියි
noisy	shahb-dhah va-diy	ශබ්ද වැඩියි
small	po-di va-diy	පොඩි වැඩියි

This ... is not clean.	meh ... pi-ri-si-du na-ha	මේ ... පිරිසිදු නැහැ.
blanket	blan-kaht e-kah	බ්ලැන්කට් එක
pillow	kot-tah-yah	කොට්ටය
pillowcase	kot-tah u-rah-yah	කොට්ට උරය
sheet	sheet e-kah	ශීට් එක

CHECKING OUT

බැහැරව යෑම

What time do we have to check out?
ah-pah i-vahth-vah yahn-nah oh-neh kee-yah-tah-dhah?
අප ඉවත්ව යන්න ඕනේ කීයටද?

I'm/We're leaving now.
mah-mah/ah-pi dhan yah-nah-vaah
මම/අපි දැන් යනවා.

We had a great stay, thank you.
ah-pi-go-dahk-ka-mah-thiy-o-yaah-lah-ge-ho-tehl-e-kah-tah
අපි ගොඩක් කැමතියි ඔයාලගේ හොටෙල් එකට

Thank you for all your help.
kah-lah u-dhahv vah-lah-lah sthoo-thiy
කළ උදව් වලට ස්තුතියි.

The room was perfect.
kaah-mah-rah-yah ni-yah-mah-yi
කාමරය නියමයි.

We hope we can return some day.
na-vah-thah kah-vah-dhaah hoh en-nah ah-pi bah-laah-po-roth-thu ve-nah-vaah
නැවත කවදා හෝ එන්න අපි බලාපොරොත්තු වෙනවා.

I'd like to pay the bill.
mah-tah bi-lah ge-vahn-nah oh-neh — මට බිල ගෙවන්න ඕනේ.

There's a mistake in the bill.
bi-leh vah-rah-dhahk thi-ye-nah-vaah — බිලේ වරදක් තියෙනවා.

Can I leave my backpack here until tonight?
ah-dhah raa vah-nah thu-ru mah-geh bak-pak e-kah me-heh thi-yahn-nah ha-ki-dhah? — අද රෑ වන තුරු මගේ බැක්පැක් එක මෙහේ තියන්න හැකිද?

We'll be back in (three) days.
ah-pi dhah-vas (thu-nah) kin aah-pah-su e-nah-vaah — අපි දවස් (තුන) කින් ආපසු එනවා.

Can you call a taxi for me?
mah-tah tak-si e-kahk kah-thaah kah-rah-lah dhe-nah-vaah-dhah? — මට ටැක්සි එකක් කතා කරල දෙනවාද?

RENTING

කුලියට ගැනීම

Renting in Sri Lanka is another accommodation option, with many people renting out individual rooms or even part of their house on a short- or long-term basis.

I'm here about your advertisement for a room to rent.
kaah-mah-rah-yahk ku-li-yah-tah dhee-mah-tah a-thi dhan-vee-mah ga-nai mah-mah aah-veh
කාමරයක් කුලියට දීමට ඇති දැන්වීම ගැනයි මම ආවේ.

I'm looking for a flat to rent for (two) months.
maah-sah (dhe-kah)-kah-tah ku-li-yah-tah gahn nah po-di ge-yak mah-mah so-yah-nah-vaah
මාස (දෙකකට) කුලියට ගන්න පොඩි ගෙයක් මම සොයනවා.

I'm looking for something close to the ...	mah-mah so-yahn-neh ...-tah kit-tu-ven	මම සොයන්නේ ...ට කිට්ටුවෙන්.
beach	mu-hu-du ve-rah-lah	මුහුදු වෙරළ
city centre	nah-gah-rah mah-dhyah-yah	නගර මධ්‍යය
train station	dhum-ri-yah sthaah-nah-yah	දුම්රිය ස්ථානය

Could I see it?
mah-tah bah-lahn-nah ha-ki-dhah?
මට බලන්න හැකිද?

How much is it per ...? ... kee-yah-dhah? ... කීයද?

- **week** sah-thi-yah-kah-tah සතියකට
- **month** maah-sah-yah-kah-tah මාසයකට

Is there anything cheaper?
mi-lah ah-du ve-nah ki-si-vahk thi-yeh-dhah? මිළ අ වෙන කිසිවක් තියේද?

Do you need a deposit?
ad-vaahns-e-kahk oh-ne-dhah? ඇඩ්වාන්ස් එකක් ඕනෙද?

I'd like to rent it for (a month).
(maah-sah-yah-kah-tah) ku-li-yah-tah gahn-nah mah-mah ka-mah-thiy (මාසයකට) කුලියට ගන්න මම කැමතියි.

Around Town

නගරබද ගමන්

In many of the major cities, you'll find that English is widely understood. However, in the suburbs or country you may have to rely on Sinhala, so it's best to familiarise yourself with commonly used terms and phrases before venturing out onto the streets. Besides, your efforts to communicate in Sinhala will be much appreciated.

LOOKING FOR ...

... සොයා බැලීම

Where's a/an/the ...?	... ko-heh-dhah thi-yen-neh?	... කොහේද තියෙන්නේ?
art gallery	aaht-gal- lahri-e-kah	ආට් ගැලරි එක
bank	ban-ku-wah	බැංකුව
cinema	si-nah-maah shaah-laah-wah	සිනමා ශාලාව
city centre	nah-gah-rah-yah	නගරය
... consulate	... kon-sahl kaahr-yaah-lah-yah	... කොන්සල් කායක්‍රාලය
... embassy	... thaah-naah-pah-thi kaahr-yaah-lah-yah	... තානාපති කාර්යාලය
... hotel	... hoh-tah-lah-yah	... හෝටලය
market	ve-lahn-dhah po-lah	වෙළඳ පොළ
museum	mu-se-um e-kah; kau-thu-kaah-gaah-rah-yah	ම්‍යුසියම් එක කෞතුකාගාරය
police station	po-lee-si-yah	පොලීසිය
post office	tha-pal kahn-thoh-ru-wah	තැපැල් කන්තෝරුව
public toilet	po-dhu va-si-ki-li-yah	පොදු වැසිකිලිය
temple	pahn-sah-lah	පන්සල

AT THE BANK

බැංකුවේදී

No doubt, at some stage during your visit to Sri Lanka, you'll need to visit a bank. Again, any attempts you make at Sinhala will be appreciated and, as you tour the more remote parts of the country, you'll find it a necessity.

I want to change (a) ... mah-tah ... maah-ru-kah-rahn-nah oh-neh මට ... මාරු-කරන්න ඕනේ.

cash/money mu-dahl/sahl-li මුදල්/සල්ලි

What time does the bank open?
ban-ku-wah ah-rin-neh kee-yah-tah-dhah? බැංකුව අරින්නේ කීයටද?

Can I use my credit card to withdraw money?
sahl-li gahn-nah mah-geh kaahd e-kah paah-vich-chi kah-rahn-nah pu-lu-vahn-dhah? සල්ලි ගන්න මගේ කාඩ් එක පාවිච්චි කරන්න පුළුවන්ද?

The automatic teller machine (ATM) swallowed my card.
eh-tee-am me-shin-e-kah mah-geh kaahd e-kah gahth-thaah ඒටීඇම් මැෂින් එක මගේ කාඩ් එක ගත්තා.

Can I exchange money here?
mah-tah me-thah-nah sahl-li maah-ru kah-rahn-nah pu-lu-vahn-dhah? මට මෙතන සල්ලි මාරු කරන්න පුළුවන්ද?

How many rupees per dollar?
dor-lah e-kah-kah-tah ru-pi-yahl kee-yahk la-be-nah-vaah-dhah? ඩොලර් එකකට රුපියල් කීයක් ලැබෙනවාද?

What's your commission?
sahl-li maah-ru kah-rahn-nah ko-mis kee-yah-dhah? සල්ලි මාරු කරන්න කොමිස් කීයද?

Please write it down.
kah-ru-naah-kah-rah-lah mah-tah eh-kah li-yaah dhen-nah කරුණාකරල මට එක ලියා දෙන්න.

Can I have smaller notes?
mah-tah po-di sahl-li dhe-nah-vaah-dhah?
මට පොඩි සල්ලි දෙනවද?

Can I have change?
mah-tah maah-ru sah-li dhe-nah-vah-dhah?
මට මාරු සල්ලි දෙනවද?

Can I transfer money here from my bank?
mah-geh ban-ku-wen me-haah-tah sahl-li maah-ru kah-rahn-nah pu-lu-vahn-dhah?
මගේ බැංකුවෙන් මෙහාට සල්ලි මාරු කරන්න පුළුවන්ද?

How long will it take to arrive?
me-haah-tah la-ben-nah koch-chah-rah kah-lahk yaah-vi-dhah?
මෙහාට ලැබෙන්න කොච්චර කලක් යාවිද?

Has my money arrived yet?
mah-geh sahl-li dhan a-vith ath-dhah?
මගේ සල්ලි දැන් ඇවිත් ඇත්ද?

Can I transfer money overseas?
sahl-li pi-tah-rah-tah yah-vahn-nah mah-tah pu-lu-vahn-dha?
සල්ලි පිටරට යවන්න මට පුළුවන්ද?

Where do I sign?
ko-heh-dhah mah-mah ahth-sahn kah-rahn-neh?
කොහේද මම අත්සන් කරන්නේ?

LOOK FOR

වසා ඇත	**closed**
ඇතුල්වීම	**entrance**
පිටවීම	**exit**
තොරතුරු	**information**
විමසීම	**inquiries**
ඇතුල්වීම තහනම්	**no entry**
දුම් බීම තහනම්	**no smoking**
විවෘතව ඇත	**open**

AT THE POST OFFICE

තැපැල් කන්තෝරුවේදී

I want to buy ...	mah-tah ... gahn-nah oh-neh	මට ... ගන්න ඕනේ.
postcards	pohst kaahd; tha-pal pahth	පෝස්ට් කාඩ් තැපැල් පත්
stamps	mudh-dhah-rah	මුද්දර
I want to send a ...	mah-tah ... yah-vahn-nah oh-neh	මට ... යවන්න ඕනේ.
letter	li-yu-mahk	ලියුමක්
parcel	paahr-sah-lah-yahk	පාර්සලයක්
postcard	pohst kaahd e-kahk; tha-pal pah-thahk	පෝස්ට් කාඩ් එකකෂ තැපැල් පතක්

How much is it to send this to ...?
meh-kah ...-tah yah-vahn-nah kee-yahk ve-nah-vaah-dhah? මේක ...ට යවන්න කීයක් වෙනවාද?

Is there any mail for me?
mah-tah li-yum thi-yah-nah-vaah-dhah? මට ලියුම් තියෙනවාද?

air mail	e-yaah mehl	එයා මේල්
envelope	li-yum kah-vah-rah-yah	ලියුම් කවරය
express mail	see-grah-gaah-mi tha-pal	සීඝ්‍රගාමී තැපැල්
mail box	tha-pal pet-ti-yah	තැපැල් පෙට්ටිය
parcel	paahr-sah-lah-yah	පාර්සලය
pen	paa-nah	පෑන
postcode	tha-pal sahn-keh-thah	තැපැල් සංකේත
registered mail	li-yaah-pah-dhin-chi tha-pal	ලියාපදිංචි තැපැල්

TELECOMMUNICATIONS

විදුලි සංදේශ

Could I please use the telephone?
mah-tah te-li-fohn korl e-kahk gahn-nah pu-lu-vahn-dhah?
මට ටෙලිෆෝන් කෝල් එකක් ගන්න පුළුවන්ද?

The number is ...
ahn-kah-yah ...
අංකය ...

What's the area code for ...?
...(-veh) tha-pal sahn-keh-thah-yah mo-kahk-dhah?
...(වේ) තැපැල් සංකේතය මොකක්ද?

It's engaged.
eh-kah kaahr-yah-bah-hu-lah-yi
ඒක කාර්යබහුලයි

I've been cut off.
maah-wah ka-pu-nah
මාව කැප්‍රුණා.

mobile phone; cell phone	moh-bail e-kahk; sel-tel e-kahk	මෝබයිල් එකක්; සෙල්ටෙල් එකක්
telephone	te-li-fohn e-kah	ටෙලිෆෝන් එක
urgent	hah-dhi-siy	හදිසියි

MAKING A CALL දුරකථන ඇමතුම් ගැනීම

Hello, is ... there?
he-loh ... in-nah-vaah-dhah? — හෙලෝ ... ඉන්නවාද?

Hello. (answering a call)
he-loh — හෙලෝ.

Can I speak to ...?
mah-tah ...-tah kah-thaah kah-rahn-nah pu-lu-vahn-dhah? — මට ...ට කතා කරන්න පුළුවන්ද?

Who's calling?
kau-dhah kah-thaah kah-rahn-neh? — කව්ද කතා කරන්නේ?

It's ...
meh ... — මේ ...

One moment (please).
pod-dahk in-nah (ka-ru-naah-kah-rah-lah) — පොඩ්ඩක් ඉන්න (කරුණාකරල).

I'm sorry, he's/she's not here.
kah-nah-gaah-tuy, e-yaah na-ha — කණගාටුයි, එයා නැහැ.

What time will he/she be back?
e-yaah koi ve-laah-veh-dhah aah-pah-su en-neh? — එයා කොයි වෙලාවේද ආපසු එන්නේ?

Can I leave a message?
mah-tah pah-ni-vu-dah-yahk thi-yahn-nah pu-lu-vahn-dhah? — මට පණිවුඩයක් තියන්න පුළුවන්ද?

Please tell ... I called.
ka-ru-naah-kah-rah-lah ...-tah ki-yahn-nah mah-mah kah-thaah kah-laah ki-yah-lah — කරුණාකරල ...ට කියන්න මම කතා කළා කියල.

My number is ...
mah-geh nom-mah-rah-yah ... — මගේ නොම්මරය ...

I don't have a contact number.
aah-pah-su kah-thaah kah-rahn-nah ha-ki nom-mah-rah-yahk mah-tah na-ha — ආපසු කතා කරන්න හැකි නොම්මරයක් මට නැහැ.

I'll call back later.

mah-mah pahs-seh kah-thaah kah-rahn-nahm — මම පස්සේ කතා කරන්නම්.

SIGHTSEEING

සංචාර ගමන්

Where's the tourist office?

tu-wah-rist kahn-thoh-ru-wah ko-heh-dhah thi-yen-neh? — ටුවරිස්ට් කන්තෝරුව කොහේද තියෙන්නේ?

Do you have a local map?

o-bah lahn-gah meh pah-laah-theh si-thi-yah-mahk thi-ye-nah-vaah-dhah? — ඔබ ළඟ මේ පළාතේ සිතියමක් තියනවාද?

Do you have a guidebook in English?

o-bah lahn-gah in-gree-si gaid buk e-kahk thi-ye-nah-vaah-dhah? — ඔබ ළඟ ඉංග්‍රීසි ගෛඩ් බුක් එකක් තියෙනවාද?

What are the main attractions?
vah-daahth sith gahn-naah dheh-vahl mo-nah-vaah-dhah thi-yen-neh?
වඩාත් සිත් ගන්නා දේවල් මොනවාද තියෙන්නේ?

We only have (one day; two days).
ah-pah-tah thah-vah thi-yen-neh (e-kah dhah-vah-sai; dhah-vahs dhe-kai)
අපට තව තියෙන්නේ ධඑක දවසයි; දවස් දෙකයි.

I'd like to see ...
mah-tah ... bah-lahn-nah aah-sai
මට ... බලන්න ආසයි.

Can we take photographs?
ah-pah-tah pin-thoo-ru gahn-nah pu-lu-vahn-dha?
අපට පිංතූර ගන්න පුළුවන්ද?

Could you take a photograph of me?
o-yaah-tah pu-lu-vahn-dhah mah-geh fo-toh e-kahk gahn-nah?
ඔයාට ප්‍රළුවන්ද මගේ ෆොටෝ එකක් ගන්න?

LOOK FOR

අල්ලන්න එපා	**do not touch**
නො මිළයේ ඇතුල්වීම	**free admission**
තණකොළ මග හරින්න	**keep off the grass**
වෙන් කර ඇත	**reserved**
වැසිකිළි	**toilets**

What time does it open/close?
eh-kah ah-rin-neh/wah-han-neh kee-yah-tah-dhah? — ඒක අරින්නේ/ වහන්නේ කීයටද?

Is there an admission charge?
a-thul-vee-meh gaahs-thu-vahk thi-yah-nah-vaah-dhah? — ඇතුල්වීමේ ගාස්තුවක් තියනවාද?

THE SIGHTS දර්ශනයන්

What's that building?
ah-rah go-dah-na-gil-lah mo-kahk-dhah? — අර ගොඩනැගිල්ල මොකක්ද?

What's this monument?
meh smaah-rah-kah-yah mo-kahk-dhah? — මේ ස්මාරකය මොකක්ද?

What's that?
ah-rah mo-kahk-dhah? — අර මොකක්ද?

How old is it?
eh-kah koch-chah-rah pah-rah-nah-dhah? — ඒක කොච්චර පරණද?

church	pahl-li-yah/ dhev-ma-dhu-rah	පල්ලිය/දෙව්මැදුර
cinema	si-nah-maah shaah-laah-wah	සිනමා ශාලාව
museum	kah-tu-ge-yah/ kau-thu-kaah-gaah-rah-yah	කටුගෙය/ කෞතුකාගාරය
park	u-dhyaah-nah-yah	උද්‍යානය
ruins	nah-tah-bun	නටබුන්
statue	pi-li-mah-yah	පිළිමය
temple	pahn-sah-lah	පන්සල
university	vish-vah vi-dhyaah-lah-yah	විශ්ව විද්‍යාලය

COLOMBO SIGHTS

Changing Guard (at President's Residence)	jah-naah-di-pah-thi mahn-dee-rah-yeh mu-rah-kaah-vahl maah-ru-wah	ජනාදිපති මන්දීරයේ මුරකාවල් මාරුව
Clock Tower	o-rah-loh-su kah-nu-wah	ඔරලෝසු කණුව
Fort Train Station	ko-tu-wah dhum-ri-yah sthaah-nah-yah	කොටුව දුම්රිය ස්තානය
Galle Buck	gaah-lu mu-vah-dho-rah	ගාලු මුවදොර
Lighthouse	prah-dee-paah-gaah-rah-yah	ප්‍රදීපාගාරය
New Parliament House	nah-vah paahr-li-mehn-thu-wah	නව පාර්ලිමේන්තුව
Old Parliament House	pa-rah-ni paahr-li-mehn-thu-wah	පැරණි පාර්ලිමේන්තුව
Port (of Colombo)	ko-lom-bah vah-raah-yah	කොළඹ වරාය
President's Residence	jah-naah-dhi-pah-thi mahn-dhee-rah-yah	ජනාදිපති මන්දීරය
'Temple-Trees' (Prime Minister's residence)	ah-rah-li-yah gah-hah mahn-dhee-rah-yah (ah-gah-ma-thi ni-lah ni-vah-sah)	අරලිය ගහ මන්දීරය (අගමැති නිල නිවස)

TOURS චාරිකා

Are there regular tours we can join?
ah-pah-tah yaah ha-ki chaah-ri-kaah ni-thah-rah thi-yeh-dhah?
අපට යා හැකි චාරිකා නිතර තියේද?

Can we hire a guide?
gaid ke-nek ah-pah-tah lah-baah gah-thah ha-ki-veh-dhah?
ගයිඩ් කෙනෙක් අපට ලබා ගත හැකිවේද?

How much is (the tour; a guide)?
(san-chaah-rah-yah-tah; gaid ke-nek-tah) kee-yahk ge-vahn-nah oh-ne-dhah?
(සංචාරයට; ගයිඩ් කෙනෙක්ට) කීයක් ගෙවන්න ඕනෙද?

How long is the tour?
san-chaah-rah-yah-tah ko-pah-mah-nah veh-laah gah-thah-veh-dhah?
සංචාරයට කොපමණ වේලා ගතවේද?

Will we have free time?
ah-pah-tah vi-veh-kah kaah-lah-yahk thi-yeh-dhah? — අපට විවේක කාලයක් තියේද?

What time should we be back?
ah-pi aah-pah-su en-nah oh-neh kee-yah-tah-dhah? — අපි ආපසු එන්න ඕනේ කීයටද?

The guide (has paid; will pay).
gaid gev-vaah/ge-vai — ගයිඩ් ගෙව්වා/ගෙවයි.

I'm with them.
mah-mah eh ah-yah ek-kai — මම ඒ අය එක්කයි.

I've lost my group.
mah-mah kahn-daah-yah-men mah-gah ha-ri-lah — මම කණ්ඩායමෙන් මග හැරිල.

Have you seen a group of (Australians)?
o-bah (ohs-treh-li-yaah-nu) kahn-daah-yah-mahk dhak-kah-dhah? — ඔබ (ඕස්ට්‍රේලියානු) කණ්ඩායමක් දැක්කද?

PAPERWORK

කඩදාසි සම්පූර්ණ කිරීම

Most of the paperwork in Sri Lanka is trilingual (Sinhala, Tamil and English), but you may need to be familiar with the following terms and phrases:

name	nah-mah	නම
address	li-pi-nah-yah	ලිපිනය
date of birth	u-pahn dhi-nah-yah	උපන් දිනය
place of birth	u-pahn sthaah-nah-yah	උපන් ස්ථානය
age	vah-yah-sah	වයස
sex	sthree/pu-ru-shah bhaah-vah-yah	ස්ත්‍රීශ්‍රීපුරුෂ භාවය
nationality	jaah-thi-kahth-vah-yah	ජාතිකත්වය
religion	aah-gah-mah	ආගම
profession/work	vruth-thee-yah/ ra-ki-yaah-vah	වෘත්තිය/ රැකියාව
marital status	vi-vaah-hah-kah thahth-vah-yah	විවාහක තත්වය
single	ah-vi-vaah-hah-kai	අවිවාහකයි
married	vi-vaah-hah-kai	විවාහකයි
divorced	dhik-kah-saah-dhai	දික්කසාදයි
widow/widower	van-dhah-bu-wah	වැන්දඹුව
identification	han-dhu-nu-mah	හැඳුනුම
passport number	gah-mahn bah-lah-path-rah ahn-kah-yah	ගමන් බලපත්‍ර අංකය
visa	aah-gah-mah-nah ah-vah-sah-rah-yah; vee-saah	ආගමන අවසරය; වීසා
baptismal certificate	bau-this-mah sah-hah-thi-kah-yah	බෞතිස්ම සහතිකය
driver's licence	ri-yah-dhu-ru bah-lah-pahth-rah-yah	රියදුරු බලපත්‍රය
customs	reh-gu kah-tah-yu-thu	රේගු කටයුතු

immigration	aah-gah-mah-nah kah-tah-yu-thu	ආගමන කටයුතු
purpose of visit	(me-rah-tah-tah) eh-mah-tah heh-thu	(මෙරටට) ඒමට හේතු
reason for travel	gah-mah-nah-tah heh-thu	ගමනට හේතු
business	bis-nahs vah-lah-tah	බිස්නස් වලට
holiday	ni-vaah-du	නිවාඩු
visiting relatives	naa-dhaa-yahn bah-lahn-nah	නෑදෑයන් බලන්න
visiting the homeland	mau-rah-tah-tah yaah-mah	මව්රටට යාම

☑ $#@*?!

Swearing isn't as common in Sri Lanka as it is in Western countries, so it generally has a greater impact. Some swear words, which correspond to the more common English swear words, are:

Bastard!
ah-vah-jaah-thah-kah-yaah — අවජාතකයා

Son of a bitch!
bal-li-geh pu-thaah — බැල්ලිගේ පුතා

Shopping

සාප්පු සවාරි

Sri Lanka offers various shopping experiences, from tiny corner stores to vast malls. Look out for the street vendors set up along the pavements – they're a colourful and popular part of Sri Lankan culture.

LOOKING FOR ...

... සොයා යාම

Where can I buy ...?
mah-tah ... gahn-nah pu-lu-vahn ko-hen-dhah?
මට ... ගන්න පුළුවන් කොහෙන්ද?

Where's the nearest ...?
lahn-gah-mah a-thi ... ko-heh-dhah thi-yehn-neh?
ළඟම ඇති ... කොහේද තියෙන්නේ?

bank	ban-ku-wah	බැංකුව
barber	baah-bahr saahp-pu-wah	බාබර් සාප්පු
bookshop	poth kah-dah-yah	පොත් කඩය
camera shop	ka-mah-raah kah-dah-yah; shop e-kah	කැමරා කඩය; ෂොප් එක
clothing store	an-dhum saahp-pu-wah	ඇඳුම් සාප්පුව
craft shop	ahth-va-dah saahp-pu-wah	අත්වැඩ සාප්පුව
department store	di-paah-mahnt stoh	ඩිපාමන්ට් ස්ටෝ
grocery store	gro-sah-ri stoh e-kah	ග්‍රොසරි ස්ටෝ එක
launderette	lon-dah-ri-yah	ලොන්ඩරිය
market	maah-kaht e-kah	මාකට් එක
music shop	sahn-gee-thah tha-ti saahp-pu-wah	සංගීත තැටි සාප්පුව

optician	as kahn-naah-di saah-dhahn-naah	ඇස් කන්නාඩි සාදන්නා
pharmacy	faah-mah-si e-kah	ෆාමසි එක
shoe shop	sah-pahth-thu kah-dah-yah	සපත්තු කඩය
souvenir shop	su-vah-ni-yah shop	සුවනිය ෂොප්
stationers	li-pi-dhrah-vyah kah-dah-yah	ලිපිද්‍රව්‍ය කඩය
supermarket	su-pah maah-kaht e-kah	සුපර් මාකට් එක
travel agency	sahn-chaah-rah-kah eh-jahn-si-yah	සංචාරක ඒජන්සිය

MAKING A PURCHASE

යමක් මිළට ගැනීම

I'm just looking.
mah-mah ni-kahng bah-lah-nah-vaah — මම නිකං බලනවා.

How much is this?
meh-kah kee-yah-dhah? — මේක කීයද?

Can you write down the price?
gah-nah-nah li-yaah dhen-nah pu-lu-vahn-dhah? — ගණන ලියා දෙන්න පුළුවන්ද?

I'd like to buy ...
mah-mah ka-mah-thiy ... gahn-nah — මම කැමතියි ... ගන්න.

Do you have any others?
ve-nah mo-nah-vaah-dhah thi-yen-neh? — වෙන මොනවද තියෙන්නේ?

Can I look at it?
mah-tah eh-kah bah-lahn-nah pu-lu-vahn-dhah? — මට ඒක බලන්න පුළුවන්ද?

I don't like it.
mah-mah eh-kah-tah ka-mah-thi na-ha
මම ඒකට කැමති නැහැ.

Do you accept credit cards?
kaahd e-ken ge-vahn-nah pu-lu-vahn-dhah?
කාඩ් එකෙන් ගෙවන්න පුළුවන්ද?

Could I have a receipt please?
mah-tah ri-seet e-kahk gahn-nah ha-ki-dhah?
මට රිසීට් එකක් ගන්න හැකිද?

Does it have a guarantee?
eh-kah vah-gah-kee-mahk ek-kah-dhah en-neh?
ඒක වගකීමක් එක්කද එන්නේ?

Can I have it sent overseas?
mah-tah eh-kah pi-tah-rah-tah yah-vahn-nah pu-lu-vahn-dhah?
මට ඒක පිටරට යවන්න පුළුවන්ද?

Please wrap it.
kah-ru-naah-kah-rah-lah mah-tah eh-kah o-thah-lah dhe-nah-vaah-dhah?
කරුණාකරල මට ඒක ඔතල දෙනවාද?

I'd like to return this please.
meh-kah aah-pah-su dhen-nah ge-naah-veh
මේක ආපසු දෙන්න ගෙනාවේ.

It's faulty.
eh-keh vah-rah-dhahk thi-yah-nah-vaah
ඒකෙ වරදක් තියනවා.

It's broken.
eh-kah ka-di-laah
ඒක කැඩිල.

I'd like my money back.
mah-geh sahl-li mah-tah aah-pah-su oh-neh
මගේ සල්ලි මට ආපසු ඕනේ.

BARGAINING

කෙවල් කිරීම

Bargaining works in roadside stalls and some large open marketplaces, where shoppers are expected to haggle. In malls, however, bargaining is generally not welcome.

I think it's too expensive.
mah-mah hi-thahn-neh eh-kah gah-nahn va-di ki-yah-laah — මම හිතන්නේ ඒක ගණන් වැඩි කියල.

The price is too high.
gah-nah-nah hun-gaahk va-diy — ගණන හුඟාක් වැඩියි.

It's too much for us.
ah-pi-tah eh-kah gah-nahn va-di — අපිට ඒක ගණන් වැඩියි.

Can you lower the price?
gah-nah-nah ti-kahk ah-du kah-rahn-nah pu-lu-vahn-dhah? — ගණන ටිකක් අඩු කරන්න පුළුවන්ද?

Do you have something cheaper?
mee-tah vah-daah laah-bhah e-kahk thi-yah-nah-vaah-dhah? — මීට වඩා ලාභ එකක් තියනවාද?

Really?
ath-thah-tah? — ඇත්තට?

I'll give you ...
mah-mah o-bah-tah ... dhen-nahm — මම ඔබට ... දෙන්නම්.

No more than ...
...-tah va-di-yah ne-mei — ...ට වැඩිය නෙමෙයි.

ESSENTIAL GROCERIES

අත්‍යාවශ්‍ය සිල්ලර බඩු

Where can I find ...?	... gahn-nah pu-lu-vahn ko-hen-dhah?	... ගන්න පුළුවන් කොහෙන්ද?
I'd like (a/some) ...	mah-tah oh-neh ...	මට ඕනේ ...
batteries	ba-tah-ri	බැටරි
bread	paahn	පාන්
butter	bah-tah	බටර්
candles	i-ti-pahn-dhahm	ඉටිපන්දම්
cheese	chees	චීස්
chocolate	chok-laht	චොක්ලට්

eggs	bith-thah-rah	බිත්තර
flour	pi-ti	පිටි
gas cylinder	gaas si-lin-dah-rah-yah	ගෑස් සිලින්ඩරය
ham	ham	හැම්
honey	pa-ni	පැණි
margarine	maah-jah-reen	මාජරීන්
matches	gi-ni-pet-ti	ගිනිපෙට්ටි
milk	ki-ri	කිරි
mosquito coil	mah-dhu-ru koil/ dhahn-gah-rah	මදුරු දඟර/ කොයිල්
pepper	gahm-mi-ris	ගම්මිරිස්
salt	lu-nu	ලුණු
shampoo	sham-poo	ෂැම්පූ
soap	sah-bahn	සබන්
sugar	see-ni	සීනි
toilet paper	toi-laht kah-dah-dhaah-si	ටොයිලට් කඩදාසි
toothpaste	dhath-be-heth	දත්බෙහෙත්
washing powder	sah-bahn ku-du	සබන් කුඩු
yogurt	yoh-gaht	යෝගට්

CLOTHING

ඇඟලුම්

boots	boot sah-pahth-thu	බූට් සපත්තු
clothing	re-di	රෙදි
coat	koht e-kah; kah-baah-yah	කෝට් එකක කබාය
dress	gah-vu-mah	ගවුම
jacket	ja-kaht koht e-kah	ජැකට් කෝට් එක
jeans	jeens/kah-li-sah-mah	ජීන්ස්/කලිසම
jumper (sweater)	jam-pah-rah-yah (swee-tah-rah-yah)	ජම්පරය (ස්වීටරය)
raincoat	wa-hi kah-baah-yah	වැහි කබාය

shirt	kah-mi-sah-yah	කමිසය
shoes	sah-pahth-thu	සපත්තු
socks	mehs	මේස්
swimsuit	swim soot e-kah	ස්විම් සූට් එක
trousers	kah-li-sah-mah	කලිසම
T-shirt	tee shaht e-kah	ටී ෂර්ට් එක
underwear	yah-tah an-dhum	යට ඇඳුම්

Can I try it on?
mah-mah an-dhah-lah bah-lahn-nah-dhah? — මම ඇඳල බලන්නද?

My size is ...
mah-geh sais e-kah ... — මගේ සයිස් එක ...

It doesn't fit.
meh-kah hah-ri na-ha — මෙක හරි නැහැ.

It's too ...	meh-kah hun-gaahk ...	මෙක හුගාක් ...
big	lo-kuy	ලොකුයි
small	po-diy	පොඩියි
short	ko-tai	කොටයි
long	dhi-gai	දිගයි
tight	thah-dhai	තදයි
loose	bu-rul	බුරුල්

SOUVENIRS

සිහිවටන

batiks	bah-thik	බතික්
brassware	pith-thah-lah bah-du	පිත්තල බඩු
cane ware/ furniture	weh-wal [bah-du; gru-hah bhaahn-dah]	වේවැල් බඩු ගෘහ භාණ්ඩ
handicraft	ahth-va-dah	අත් වැඩ
items made of ...	... vah-lin saa-doo bah-du	... වලින් සෑදූ බඩු
bamboo	u-nah	උණ
ebony	kah-lu-vah-rah	කළුවර
satin	bu-ru-thah	බුරුත
shell	sip-pi kah-tu	සිප්පි කටු
straw	pi-du-ru	පිදුරු
wood	lee	ලී
Sri Lankan tea	sree lahn-kaah theh	ශ්‍රී ලංකා තේ
woodcarved figure	lee ka-tah-yahm roo-pah	ලී කැටයම් රූප

MATERIALS

ද්‍රව්‍ය

brass	pith-thah-lah	පිත්තල
ceramic	pi-gahn gah-dol	පිඟන් ගඩොල්
cotton	kah-pu	කපු
glass	vee-dhu-ru	වීදුරු
gold	rahth-rahn	රත්තරන්
handmade	ah-thin ni-mah voo	අතින් නිමවූ
leather	hahm	හම්
lycra	lik-raah	ලික්රා
metal	loh-hah	ලෝහ
plastic	plaahs-tik	ප්ලාස්ටික්
silk	silk	සිල්ක්
silver	ri-dee	රිදී
stainless steel	su-dhu yah-kah-dah	සුදු යකඩ

synthetic	kru-three-mah	කෘතිම
wood	lee	ලී
wool	loh-mah	ලෝම

COLOURS

පාට

dark ...	thah-dhah ...	තද ...
light ...	laah ...	ලා ...
black	kah-lu	කළු
blue	nil	නිල්
brown	dhum-bu-ru	දුඹුරු
green	ko-lah	කොළ
grey	ah-lu	අළු
orange	tham-bi-li	තැඹිලි
pink	roh-sah	රෝස
purple	dhahm	දම්
red	rah-thu	රතු
white	su-dhu	සුදු
yellow	kah-hah	කහ

TOILETRIES

සනීපාරක්ෂක ද්‍රව්‍ය

bath/shower gel	baahth/shah-wah jel	බාත්/ෂවර් ජෙල්
comb	pah-naah-wah	පනාව
condoms	kon-dom pah-thah	කොන්ඩොම් පත
dental floss	den-tahl flos	ඩෙන්ටල් ෆ්ලොස්
deodorant	di-yod-rahnt	ඩියොඩ්රන්ට්
hairbrush	kon-daah bu-ru-su-wah	කොණ්ඩා බුරුසුව
moisturiser	mois-chah-rah-yi-sah e-kah	මොයිස්චරයිස එක

pregnancy test kit	ghahr-bhah-nee pah-reek-shah-nah kaht-tah-lah-yah	ගර්භණී පරීක්ෂණ කට්ටලය
razor	dha-li-pi-hi-yah	දැලිපිහිය
razor blades	blehd thah-lah	බ්ලේඩ් තල
sanitary napkins	sa-ni-tah-ri paads	සැනිටරි පෑඩ්ස්
shampoo	sham-poo	ෂැම්පු
shaving cream	shehv kreem; ra-vu-lah kah-pah-nah kreem	ෂේව් ක්‍රීම්ෂ රැවුල කපන ක්‍රීම්
soap	sah-bahn	සබන්
sunblock	sahn-blok e-kah	සන්බ්ලොක් එක
tissues	ti-shoo	ටිෂූ
toilet paper	toi-laht kah-dah-dhaah-si	ටොයිලට් කඩදාසි
toothbrush	dhahth bu-ru-su-wah	දත් බුරුසුව
toothpaste	dhahth be-he-th	දත් බෙහෙත්

FOR THE BABY

ළදරුවාට

baby powder	lah-dhah-ru pi-ti	ළදරු පිටි
bib	bib e-kah	බිබ් එක
disposable nappies/diapers	i-vah-thah-lah-nah na-pi	ඉවතලන නැපි
dummy/pacifier	soop-pu-wah	සූප්පුව
feeding bottle	ki-ri boh-thah-lah-yah	කිරි බෝතලය
nappies/diapers	na-pi	නැපි
nappy rash cream	na-pi dhah-dhah kreem e-kah	නැපි දද ක්‍රීම් එක
powdered milk	pi-ti ki-ri	පිටි කිරි
rubber duck	rah-bahr thaah-raah-wah	රබර් තාරාවා
teat	soop-pu	සූප්පු
tinned baby food	tin kah-lah lah-dhah-ru aah-haah-rah	ටින් කළ ළදරු ආහාර

STATIONERY & PUBLICATIONS

ලිපිද්‍රව්‍ය හා ප්‍රකාශන

Is there an English-language bookshop nearby?

in-gree-si poth kah-dah-yahk meh lahn-gah pah-hah-thah ath-dhah? — ඉංග්‍රීසි පොත් කඩයක් මේ ළඟ පහත ඇත්ද?

Is there an English-language section?

in-gree-si bhaah-shaah-wah-tah ve-nah-mah ko-tah-sahk thi-yeh-dhah? — ඉංග්‍රීසි භාෂාවට වෙනම කොටසක් තියේද?

Do you sell ...?	o-bah ... vi-ku-nah-nah-vaah-dhah?	ඔබ ... විකුණනවාද?
dictionaries	shahb-dhah-koh-shah	ශබ්දකෝෂ
envelopes	li-pi kah-vah-rah	ලිපි කවර
maps...	... si-thi-yahm	... සිතියම්
city	nah-gah-rah-yeh	නගරයේ
regional	praah-dheh-shee-yah	ප්‍රාදේශීය
road	maahr-gah	මාර්ග
magazines	sahn-gah-raah	සඟරා
newspapers (in English)	(in-gree-si) pu-wahth-pahth	(ඉංග්‍රීසි) පුවත්පත්
paper	kah-dah-dhaah-si	කඩදාසි
pens	paan	පෑන්
postcards	pohst kaahd	පෝස්ට් කාඩ්
stamps	mudh-dhah-rah	මුද්දර

MUSIC

සංගීතය

Do you have any (traditional) songs?

o-bah lahn-gah (sahm-prah-dhaah-yee) sin-dhu mu-kuth thi-ye-nah-vaah-dhah?

ඔබ ළඟ (සම්ප්‍රදායී) සිංදු මුකුත් තියෙනවාද?

I heard a band/singer called ...

mah-mah ... ki-yah-laah vaah-dhah-kah-yek-tah/ sahn-gee-thah kahn-daah-yah-mah-kah-tah a-hum-kahn dun-naah

මම ... කියලා වාදකයෙක්ට / සංගීත කණ්ඩායමකට ඇහුම්කන් දුන්නා

SMOKING

දුම්බීම

A packet of cigarettes, please.

kah-ru-naah-kah-rah-lah si-gah-raht pa-kaht e-kahk dhen-nah

කරුණාකරල සිගරට් පැකට් එකක් දෙන්න.

Do you have a light?

o-bah lahn-gah gi-ni pet-ti-yahk thi-yeh-dhah?

ඔබ ළඟ ගිනි පෙට්ටියක් තියේද?

Do you mind if I smoke?

mah-mah dhum biv-vaah-tah kah-mahk nadh-dhah?

මම දුම් බිව්වාට කමක් නැද්ද?

Please don't smoke.

kah-ru-naah-kah-rah lah dhum bon-nah e-paah

කරුණාකරල දුම් බොන්න එපා.

SIZES & COMPARISONS

ප්‍රමාණ සහ සැසඳුම්

a little bit	ti-kahk	ටිකක්
also	thah-vah-dhah	තවද
big	lo-kuy	ලොකුයි
enough	a-thi	ඇති
heavy	bah-rai	බරයි
light	sa-hal-luy	සැහැල්ලුයි
little (amount)	pod-dai/ti-kai	පොඩ්ඩයි/ටිකයි
many	go-dai	ගොඩයි
more	thah-vahth	තවත්
small	pun-chi	පුංචි
too much/many	go-daahk; bo-hoh va-di	ගොඩාක්; බොහෝ වැඩි

WEIGHTS & MEASURES

කිරුම් සහ මිනුම්

millimetre	mi-li-mee-tah-rah-yah	මිලිමීටරය
centimetre	sen-ti-mee-tah-rah-yah	සෙන්ටිමීටරය
metre	mee-tah-rah-yah	මීටරය
kilometre	ki-loh-mee-tah-rah-yah	කිලෝමීටරය
litre	ee-tah-rah-yah	ලීටරය
gram	graam e-kah	ග්‍රෑම් එක
100 grams	graam see-yahk	ග්‍රෑම් සීයක්
kilogram	ki-loh-graam e-kah	කිලෝග්‍රෑම් එක
half a kilogram	ki-loh-graam baah-gah-yahk	කිලෝග්‍රෑම් භාගයක්

Specific Needs

විශේෂ අවශ්‍යතා

TRAVELLERS WITH DISABILITIES

ආබාදිත සංචාරකයන්

I have a disability.
mah-mah aah-baah-dhi-thah-yek — මම ආබාදිතයෙක්.

I need assistance.
mah-tah u-dhahv u-pah-kaah-rah oh-neh — මට උදව් උපකාර ඕනේ.

What services do you have for people with disabilities?
aah-baah-dhi-thah-yahn-tah mo-nah seh-vaah-vahn-dhah ath-theh? — ආබාදිතයන්ට මොන සේවාද ඇත්තේ?

Is there wheelchair access?
roh-dhah pu-tu sah-dhah-haah pah-hah-su-kahm thi-yeh-dhah? — රෝද පුටු සඳහා පහසුකම් තියේද?

I'm deaf.
mah-mah bi-hi-riy — මම බිහිරියි.

I have a hearing aid.
kahn a-see-mah-tah mah-mah u-pah-kah-rah-nah-yahk paah-vich-chi kah-rah-nah-vaah — කන් ඇසීමට මම උපකරණයක් පාවිච්චි කරනවා.

Speak more loudly, please.
kah-ru-naah-kah-rah hai-yen kah-thaah kah-rahn-nah — කරුණාකර හයියෙන් කතා කරන්න.

Are guide dogs permitted?
mah-gah pen-vah-nah bahl-lahn sah-dhah-haah ah-vah-sah-rah ath-dhah? — මඟ පෙන්වන බල්ලන් සඳහා අවසර ඇත්ද?

braille library	brehl pus-thah-kaah-lah-yah	බ්‍රේල් පුස්තකාලය
guide dog	mah-gah pen-vah-nah bahl-lahn	මඟ පෙන්වන බල්ලන්
wheelchair	roh-dhah pu-tu-wah	රෝද පුටුව

TRAVELLING WITH THE FAMILY

පවුල් පිටින් ගමන් යාම

Are there facilities for babies?
lah-dhah-ru-wahn sah-dah-haah pah-hah-su-kahm ath-dhah?
ළදරුවන් සඳහා පහසුකම් ඇත්ද?

Do you have a child-minding service?
lah-mun bah-laah ga-nee-meh seh-vaah-vahk thi-yeh-dhah?
ළමුන් බලා ගැනීමේ සේවාවක් තියේද?

Where can I find an (English-speaking) babysitter?
(in-gree-si kah-thaah kah-rah-nah) lah-mun bah-laah gahn-naah ke-nek mah-mah so-yaah gahn-neh ko-hen-dhah?
(ඉංග්‍රීසි කතා කරන) ළමුන් බලා ගන්නා කෙනෙක් මම සොයා ගන්නේ කොහෙන්ද?

Can you put an (extra) bed/ cot in the room?
(va-di-pu-rah) an-dahk/ tho-til-lahk kaah-mah-rah-yeh dhah-mahn-nah pu-lu-vahn-dhah?
(වැඩිපුර) ඇඳක්/ තොටිල්ලක් කාමරයේ දමන්න පුළුවන්ද?

Is there a family discount?
pah-vu-lah-kah-tah mi-lah ah-du-dhah?
පවුලකට මිළ අඩුද?

Are children allowed?
lah-mah-yin-tah yahn-nah pu-lu-vahn-dhah?
ළමයින්ට යන්න පුළුවන්ද?

Do you have a children's menu?
lah-mah-yin-tah ve-nah-mah aah-haah-rah thi-yeh-dhah?
ළමයින්ට වෙනම ආහාර තියේද?

Are there any activities for children?

lah-mah-yin-tah ve-nah-mah kri-yaah-kaah-rah-kahm thi-yeh-dhah? — ළමයින්ට වෙනම ක්‍රියාකාරකම් තියේද?

Is there a playground nearby?

sel-lahm pi-ti-yahk lahn-gah thi-yeh-dhah? — සෙල්ලම් පිටියක් ළඟ තියේද?

PILGRIMAGE & RELIGION

වන්දනා සහ ආගම

What's your religion?	o-bah mo-nah aah-gah-meh-dhah?	ඔබ මොන ආගමේද?
I'm ...	mah-mah ...	මම ...
Buddhist	budh-dhaah-gah-meh	බුද්ධාගමේ
Christian	kris-thi-yaah-ni aah-gah-meh	ක්‍රිස්තියානි ආගමේ
Hindu	hin-du aah-gah-meh	හින්දු ආගමේ
Jewish	yu-dhev aah-gah-meh	යුදෙව් ආගමේ
Muslim	mus-lim aah-gah-meh	මුස්ලිම් ආගමේ

I believe in God.

mah-mah dhe-vi-yahn vish-vaah-sah kah-rah-nah-vaah — මම දෙවියන් විශ්වාස කරනවා

I don't believe in God.

mah-mah dhe-vi-yahn vish-vaah-sah kah-rahn na-ha — මම දෙවියන් විශ්වාස කරන් නැහැ

I believe in rebirth.

mah-mah pu-nah-ruth-pahth-thi-yah vish-vaah-sah kah-rahn-nah-vaah — මම අනරුත්පත්තිය විශ්වාස කරනවා

I don't believe in rebirth.

mah-mah pu-nah-ruth-pahth-thi-yah vish-vaah-sah kah-rahn na-ha — මම පුනරුත්පත්තිය විශ්වාස කරන් නෑ

I am religious.

mah-mah aah-gah-mah-tah la-dhiy

මම ආගමට ලැදියි.

I am not religious.

mah-mah aah-gah-mah-tah la-dhi na-ha

මම ආගමට ලැදි නැහැ.

> ☑ **DREAMS OF THE EAST**
>
> When sleeping, people generally lie with their heads to the east (the direction Buddha is believed to have come from). The dead, however, are placed with their heads to the west as it's thought they shouldn't lie in the same direction as the living.

Can I attend this service/mass?

meh dheh-vah me-he-yah/ poo-jaah-vah-tah mah-tah sah-hah-baah-gi ven-nah pu-lu-vahn-dhah?

මේ දේව මෙහෙයට/ පූජාවට මට සහභාගි වෙන්න පුළුවන්ද?

Can I pray here?

mah-tah me-thah-nah yaahk-gnaah kah-rahn-nah pu-lu-vahn-dhah?

මට මෙතන යාච්නා කරන්න පුළුවන්ද?

Where can I pray/worship?

mah-tah yaahk-gnaah/ van-dhah-naah kah-rahn-nah pu-lu-vahn ko-heh-dhah?

මට යාච්නා/ වන්දනා කරන්න පුළුවන් කොහේද?

SOCIAL

Meeting People

පුද්ගලයන් හමුවීම්

You'll find that a few well-chosen words in Sinhala will go a long way towards enriching your travels in Sri Lanka.

YOU SHOULD KNOW

ඔබ දැන ගත යුතු දේ

Hello.	aah-yu-boh-wahn	ආයුබෝවන්.

While 'aah-yu-boh-wahn' is the traditional greeting, it's more common now for Sri Lankans to greet each other using 'good morning,' 'good afternoon,' 'hello' and similar phrases.

Yes.	o-vu	ඔව්.
No.	na-ha	නැහැ.
Excuse me.	sah-maah-vahn-nah	සමාවන්න.
Excuse me. (to a Buddhist priest)	ah-vah-sah-rah	අවසර.
Please.	kah-ru-naah-kah-rah-lah	කරුණාකරල.

Although the Sinhala translation of 'please' is kah-ru-naah-kah-rah-laah, it's more common for Sri Lankans to use the English term (plees/ප්ලීස්). The English phrases 'thank you' and 'thanks' are also used just as often as the equivalent Sinhala phrases.

Thank you.	sthoo-thiy	ස්තූතියි.
Thank you very much.	bo-ho-mah sthoo-thiy	බොහොම ස්තූතියි.
Sorry.	kah-nah-gaah-tuy	කණගාටුයි.

GREETINGS & GOODBYES

සුභ පැතීම් සහ සමුගැනීම්

People often greet each other with just a friendly smile – there's no particular word for 'hello' in Sinhala. The nearest equivalent is aah-yu-boh-wahn (ආයුබෝවන්), which is now mostly only reserved for official greetings and departures, and literally means 'may you live long'. This is usually accompanied by a slight bow, with the hands joined together in front. If you're greeted in this way, simply return the gesture.

Good morning.	su-bhah u-dhaa-sah-nahk	සුභ උදෑසනක්.
Good afternoon.	su-bhah dhah-vaah-lahk	සුභ දවාලක්.
Good evening.	su-bhah san-dhaa-vahk	සුභ සැන්දෑවක්.
Good night.	su-bhah raahth-ri-yahk	සුභ රාත්‍රියක්.

FORMS OF ADDRESS

ආමන්ත්‍රණය කිරීම

There are many different ways of saying 'you' in Sinhala, such as:

o-bah (ඔබ)	**written Sinhala, and official/formal settings, also found in verse and prose; when addressing the person in front of you, it's common to use the informal** o-yaah **(ඔයා).**
num-bah (නුඹ)	**old-fashioned**
o-yaah (ඔයා)	**more familiar and colloquial**
um-bah (උඹ)	**usually used when in anger; also used among close friends**

It can be difficult to know which form to use – there are many to choose from and the one you select will convey how you feel about the person you're talking to. The all-purpose o-yaah can be used fairly safely, but it's generally best to stick to names or avoid saying 'you' altogether. Close friends and children often call each other by their first names.

☑ HOW TO HELLO

In more informal situations, you can greet people by asking ko-ho-mah-dhah? (කොහොමද?), meaning 'How are you?' The Sinhalese never say 'goodbye' – instead, use gi-hin en-nahm (ගිහින් එන්නම්), literally 'I'll go and come back'.

Useful titles to be familiar with are:

Mr/Sir	mah-hahth-mah-yaah/ mah-hah-thaah (inf)	මහත්මයා/ මහතා
Mrs	mah-hahth-mi-yah	මහත්මිය
Miss	me-nah-vi-yah	මෙනවිය
Master	po-di mah-hahth-mah-yaah	පොඩි මහත්මයා
Your Honour	gah-u-rah-vaahn-vi-thah	ගෞරවාන්විත
thera (Buddhist priest/monks)	swaah-meen-wah-hahn-sah	ස්වාමීන්වහන්ස
police officer	raah-lah-haah-mi	රාළහාමි
shopkeeper	mu-dhah-laah-li	මුදලාලි

Sinhala titles follow a person's name:

Mr Carl Young
kaahl yahng mah-hah-thaah (lit: Carl Young Mr) — කාල් යං මහතා

Miss Mary Richards
meh-ri ri-chahds me-nah-vi-yah (lit: Mary Richards Miss) — මේරි රිචඩ්ස් මෙනවිය

TALKING TO MONKS

පැවිදි අය ආමන්ත්‍රණය කිරීමේදී

When greeting or farewelling Buddhist priests or monks, join your hands together (as if in prayer) and with a bow say: ah-vah-sah-rah swaah-meen-wah-hahn-sah (අවසර ස්වාමීන්වහන්ස), which means 'Excuse me, priest/monk'. If in conversation you need to say 'yes', use e-hei (එහෙයි) – not the more usual word o-vu (ඔව්).

Here is a list of other key words used when speaking with monks.

Word	Temple Vocabulary	Standard Sinhala
bathing (wash)	pan sa-nah-he-nah-vaah පැන් සැනහෙනව	naah-nah-vaah නානවා
breakfast	heel dhaah-nah-dyah හීල් දානය	u-dheh kaa-mah උදේ කෑම
coming/ going	vah-di-nah-vaah වඩිනව	e-nah-vaah එනවා
die	ah-pah-vahth ve-nah-vaah අපවත් වෙනව	ma-re-nah-vaah මැරෙනවා
drinks	gi-lahn pah-sah ගිලන් පස	bee-mah බීම
eating	vah-lahn-dhi-nah-vaah වළඳිනව	kah-nah-vaah කනවා
food	dhaah-nah-yah දානය	kaa-mah කෑම
garden	mah-lu-wah මළුව	mi-dhu-lah මිදුල
lunch	dhah-vahl dhaah-nah-yah දවල් දානය	dhah-vahl kaa-mah දවල් කෑම
saying	vah-dhaah-rah-nah-vaah වදාරනව	ki-yah-nah-vaah කියනවා
sleeping	sa-thah-pe-nah-vaah සැතපෙනව	ni-dhah-nah-vaah නිදනවා
sweep	ah-mah-dhi-nah-vah අමදිනව	ah-thu-gaah-nah-vah අතුගානව
wash	dhoh-wah-nah-yah kah-rah-nah-vaah දෝවනය කරනව	soh-dhah-nah-vah සෝදනව
water	pan පැන්	wah-thu-rah වතුර
yes	e-hei එහෙයි	o-vu ඔව්
you	o-bah vah-hahn-seh ඔබ වහන්සේ	o-bah; o-yaah ඔබ; ඔයා

BODY LANGUAGE

ශාරීරික ඉඟියන්

Body language plays an important part in Sinhala communication. Even the eyes convey meaning – particularly 'thank you' and 'sorry' – far more expressively than words do.

One important gesture not to misunderstand is the shaking of the head from side to side – this is not a negative sign but, in fact, indicates approval of something or a 'yes'.

Waving a hand towards oneself with the palm down signals 'come here'. When the gesture is made in an outward manner, it signals 'go away'.

Generally speaking, public displays of affection between couples are not appreciated, especially by older members of the community.

Avoid blowing your nose in public where possible – Sri Lankans would rather sniff incessantly than blow into a handkerchief.

FIRST ENCOUNTERS

පළමු හමුවීම්

When first making conversation with someone, an effective 'kick start' to the process is to ask their name:

What's your name?
o-beh nah-mah mo-kahk-dhah? ඔබේ නම මොකක්ද?

A more conversational way to address the other person is to use o-yaah (you/ඔයා) and o-yaah-geh (yours/ඔයාගේ).

My name is ...
mah-geh nah-mah ... මගේ නම ...

I'm pleased to meet you.
o-bah dha-nah-gan-nah la-bee-mah sah-thu-tahk ඔබ දැනගන්න ලැබීම සතුටක්.

I'd like to introduce you to ...
...-tah o-bah hah-dhu-naah dhen-nah mah-mah ka-mah-thiy ...ට ඔබ හඳුනා දෙන්න මම කැමතියි.

How are you?	ko-ho-mah-dhah?	කොහොමද?
Good, thank you.	hon-dhin in-nah-waah	හොඳින් ඉන්නවා.
Not too bad.	wah-rah-dhahk na-ha	වරදක් නැහැ.
Not too good.	e-thah-rahm hon-dhah na-ha	එතරම් හොඳ නැහැ.

MAKING CONVERSATION

කතාවට මුලපිරීම

Do you live here?
o-bah me-heh-dhah in-neh? — ඔබ මෙහේද ඉන්නේ?

Where are you going?
o-bah ko-heh-dhah yahn-neh? — ඔබ කොහේද යන්නේ?

What are you doing?
o-bah mo-kahk-dhah kah-rahn-neh? — ඔබ මොකක්ද කරන්නේ?

Can I take a photo (of you)?
mah-tah (o-beh) fo-toh e-kahk gahn-nah pu-lu-vahn-dhah? — මට (ඔබේ) ෆොටෝ එකක් ගන්න පුළුවන්ද?

Are you here on holiday?
o-bah ni-vaah-du-vah-tah a-vith-dhah? — ඔබ නිවාඩුවට ඇවිත්ද?

I'm here ...	mah-mah me-heh in-neh ...	මම මෙහේ ඉන්නේ ...
for a holiday	ni-vaah-du-vah-kah-tah	නිවාඩුවකට
on business	bis-nahs vah-lah-tah	බිස්නස් වලට
to study	i-ge-nah gahn-nah	ඉගෙන ගන්න

How long are you here for?
o-bah koch-chah-rah kah-lahk in-nah-vaah-dhah? — ඔබ කොච්චර කලක් ඉන්නවාද?

I'm/We're here for ... weeks/days.
mah-mah/ah-pi sah-thi/dhah-vahs ...-k in-nah-vaah — මම/අපි සති/දවස් ...ක් ඉන්නවා.

Do you like it here?
o-bah me-heh-tah ka-mah-thi-dhah? ඔබ මෙහෙට කැමතිද?

I/We like it here very much.
mah-mah/ah-pi me-heh-tah hah-ri ka-mah-thiy මම/අපි මෙහෙට හරි කැමතියි.

I'm here with my partner.
mah-mah me-heh in-neh mah-geh sah-hah-kah-ru/ sah-hah-kaah-ri-yah ek-kah (m/f) මම මෙහේ ඉන්නේ මගේ සහකරු/ සහකාරිය එක්ක.

NATIONALITIES

ජාතීන්

When meeting someone, especially for the first time, you're bound to be asked where you come from.

Where are you from?
o-bah ko-hen-dhah? ඔබ කොහෙන්ද?

Which country are you from?
o-bah mo-nah rah-ten-dhah? ඔබ මොන රටෙන්ද?

I'm from ...	mah-mah ...	මම ...
We're from ...	ah-pi ...	අපි ...
America	ah-meh-ri-kaah-ven	අමෙරිකාවෙන්
Argentina	aahr-jahn-tee-naah-ven	ආර්ජන්ටිනාවෙන්
Australia	ohs-treh-li-yaah-ven	ඕස්ට්‍රේලියාවෙන්
Canada	ka-nah-daah-ven	කැනඩාවෙන්
Dubai	du-bai vah-lin	ඩුබායි වලින්
England	en-gah-lahn-thah-yen	එංගලන්තයෙන්
France	prahn-shah-yen	ප්‍රංශයෙන්
Germany	jahr-mah-ni-yen	ජර්මනියෙන්
Holland	oh-lahn-dhah-yen	ඕලන්දයෙන්
India	in-dhi-yaah-ven	ඉන්දියාවෙන්
Ireland	ah-yahr-lahn-thah-yen	අයර්ලන්තයෙන්

Italy	i-thaah-li-yen	ඉතාලියෙන්
Japan	jah-paah-nah-yen	ජපානයෙන්
Malaysia	mah-lah-yah- aah-si-yaah-ven	මලයාසියාවෙන්
New Zealand	nah-vah-see- lahn-thah-yen	නවසී- ලන්තයෙන්
Russia	ru-si-yaah-ven	රුසියාවෙන්
Scotland	s-kot-lahn-thah-yen	ස්කොට්ලන්තයෙන්
South America	dhah-ku-nu ah-meh-ri-kaah-ven	දකුණු අමෙරිකාවෙන්
Spain	spaahn-gna-yen	ස්පාන්නයෙන්
Thailand	thaai-lahn-thah-yen	තායිලන්තයෙන්
Wales	wehls vah-lin	වේල්ස් වලින්

I live in/at the/a ... mah-mah in-neh ... මම ඉන්නේ ...

city	nah-gah-rah-yeh	නගරයේ
countryside	gah-meh/ gahm-bah-dhah	ගමේ/ගම්බද
mountains	kahn-dhu-kah-rah-yeh	කඳුකරයේ
seaside	mu-hu-dhu-bah-dah	මුහුදුබඩ
village	gah-meh	ගමේ

CULTURAL DIFFERENCES

සංස්කෘතික වෙනස්කම්

Is this a custom in your country?
meh o-beh rah-teh chaah-ri-thrah-yak-dhah? — මේ ඔබේ රටේ චාරිත්‍රයක්ද?

How do you do this in your country?
meh-kah o-beh rah-teh kah-rahn-neh ko-ho-mah-dhah? — මේක ඔබේ රටේ කරන්නේ කොහොමද?

I'm not accustomed to this.
mah-tah meh-kah pu-ru-dhu na-ha — මට මේක පුරුදු නැහැ.

I don't mind watching but I'd prefer not to participate.
mah-mah sah-hah-baah-gee ven-neh na-ha, nah-muth bah-laah in-nahm — මම සහභාගී වෙන්නේ නැහැ, නමුත් බලා ඉන්නම්.

I don't want to offend you.
o-beh hi-thah ri-dhah-vahn-nah mah-mah ka-mah-thi na-ha — ඔබේ හිත රිදවන්න මම කැමති නැහැ.

I'm sorry, it's not the custom in my country.
kah-nah-gaah-tuy, mah-geh rah-te si-ri-thah eh-kah no-veh — කණගාටුයි, මගේ රටේ සිරිත ඒක නොවේ.

I'm sorry, it's against my ...	mah-tah kah-nah-gaah-tuy eh-kah, mah-geh ...-tah vi-rudh-dhai	මට කණගාටුයි ඒක, මගේ ...ට විරුද්ධයි.
beliefs	a-dhah-heem	ඇදහීම්
culture	sahns-kru-thi-yah	සංස්කෘතිය
religion	aah-gah-mah	ආගම

I'll give it a go.
mah-mah eh-kah kah-rah-lah bah-lahn-nahm — මම ඒක කරල බලන්නම්.

I'll watch.
mah-mah bah-laah in-nahm — මම බලා ඉන්නම්.

AGE

වයස

How old ...?	... vah-yah-sah kee-yah-dhah?	... වයස කීයද?
are you	o-bah-geh	ඔබගේ
is your son/daughter	o-bah-geh pu-thaah-geh/dhu-wah-geh	ඔබගේ පුතාගේ/දුවගේ

I'm ... years old.
mah-geh vah-yah-sah ah-vu-ru-dhu ... — මගේ වයස අවුරුදු ...

For numbers, see p43.

OCCUPATIONS

රැකියාවන්

What (work) do you do?	o-beh ra-ki-yaah-wah mo-kahk-dhah?	ඔබේ රැකියාව මොකක්ද?
I am a/an ...	mah-mah ...	මම ...
artist	chith-rah shil-pi-yek/ shil-pi-ni-yahk (m/f)	චිත්‍ර ශිල්පියෙක්/ ශිල්පිනියක්
author	kah-thu vah-rah-yek/ vah-ri-yahk (m/f)	කතු වරයෙක්/ වරියක්
business-person	ve-lahn-dhah vyaah-paah-ri-kah-yek/vyaah-paah-ri-kaah-vahk (m/f)	වෙළඳ ව්‍යාපාරිකයෙක්/ ව්‍යාපාරිකාවක්
doctor	vai-dhyah-vah-rah-yek/ vai-dhyah-vah-ri-yahk (m/f)	වෛද්‍යවරයෙක්/ වෛද්‍යවරියක්
engineer	inji-neh-ru-vek/ inji-neh-ru-vah-ri-yahk (m/f)	ඉංජිනේරුවෙක්/ ඉංජිනේරුවරියක්
factory worker	kahm-hahl kah-ru-vek/ kaah-ri-yak (m/f)	කම්හල් කරුවෙක්/කාරියක්
farmer	go-vi-yek/go-vi kaahn-thaah-wahk (m/f)	ගොවියෙක්/ ගොවි කාන්තාවක්
journalist	leh-khah-kah-yek/leh-khah-kaah-vi-yahk (m/f)	ලේඛකයෙක්/ ලේඛකාවියක්
lawyer	nee-thee-gnah vah-rah-yek/ vah-ri-yahk (m/f)	නීතිඥ වරයෙක්/ වරියක්
mechanic	kaahr-mi-kah shil-pi-yek/ shil-pi-ni-yahk (m/f)	කාර්මික ශිල්පියෙක්/ ශිල්පිනියක්
musician	sahn-gee-thah-gna-yek/ sahn-gee-thah-gna-vah-ri-yahk (m/f)	සංගීතඥයෙක්/ සංගීතඥවරියක්
nurse	saahth-thu seh-vah-kah-yek/ seh-vi-kaah-vahk (m/f)	සාත්තු සේවකයෙක්/ සේවිකාවක්

office worker	kaahr-yaah-lah seh-vah-kah-yek/ seh-vi-kaah-vahk (m/f)	කාර්යාල සේවකයෙක්/ සේවිකාවක්
scientist	vi-dhyaah-gnah vah-rah-yek/ vah-ri-yahk (m/f)	විද්‍යාඥවරයෙක් වරයෙක්/ වරියක්
secretary	leh-khahm vah-rah-yek/ vah-ri-yahk (m/f)	ලේකම් වරයෙක්/ වරියක්
student	shish-yah-yek/ shish-yaah-wahk (m/f)	ශිෂ්‍යයෙක්/ ශිෂ්‍යාවක්
teacher	guru-vah-rah-yek/ guru-vah-ri-yahk (m/f)	ගුරුවරයෙක්/ ගුරුවරියක්
waiter	u-pah-tan veh-tah ke-nek	වේට කෙනෙක්

I'm retired.
mah-mah vish-raah-mi-kai — මම විශ්‍රාමිකයි

I'm unemployed.
mah-mah ra-ki-yaah-vahk kah-rahn-neh na-ha — මම රැකියාවක් කරන්නේ නැහැ.

I'm self-employed.
mah-mah swah-yahn ra-ki-yaah kah-rahn-neh — මම ස්වයං රැකියා කරන්නේ.

I stay home doing the housework.
mah-mah ge-dhah-rah va-dah kah-rah-ge-nah ge-dhah-rah in-nah-vaah — මම ගෙදර වැඩ කරගෙන ගෙදර ඉන්නවා.

Do you enjoy your work?
o-beh kah-rah-nah ra-ki-yaah-vah hon-dhah-dhah? — ඔබ කරන රැකියාව හොඳද?

How long have you been in the job?
o-bah koch-chah-rah kaah-lah-yak in-dhahn-dha va-dah kah-rahn-neh? — ඔබ කොච්චර කාලයක් ඉඳන්ද වැඩ කරන්නේ?

What are you studying?
o-bah mo-nah-wah-dhah i-ge-nah gahn-neh? — ඔබ මොනවද ඉගෙන ගන්නේ?

I'm studying ...	mah-mah kah-rahn-neh ...	මම කරන්නේ ...
art	chi-thra shil-pah-yah	චිත්‍ර ශිල්පය
business studies	vyaah-paah-ri-kah ah-dhyah-yah-nah-yah	ව්‍යාපාරික අධ්‍යයනය
education	ah-dhyaah-pah-nah-yah	අධ්‍යාපනය
engineering	in-ji-neh-ru vi-dhyaah-vah	ඉංජිනේරු විද්‍යාව
hospitality	aah-gahn-thu-kah sahth-kah-rah-nah-yah	ආගන්තුක සත්කරණය
languages	bhaah-shaah-vahn	භාෂාවන්
law	nee-thi vi-dhyaah-vah	නීති විද්‍යාව
medicine	vai-dhyah vi-dhyaah-vah	වෛද්‍ය විද්‍යාව
science	vi-dhyaah-vah	විද්‍යාව

FEELINGS

හැඟීම්

I'm ...	mah-mah ... in-neh	මම ... ඉන්නේ.
afraid	bhah-yen	බයෙන්
angry	thah-rah-hen	තරහෙන්
cold	see-thah-len	සීතලෙන්
happy	sah-thu-tin	සතුටින්
hot	rahs-nen	රස්නෙන්
hungry	bah-dah-gin-neh	බඩගින්නේ
in a hurry	hah-dhis-si-yen	හදිස්සියෙන්
sad	dhu-kin	දුකින්
sleepy	ni-dhi-mah-then	නිදිමතෙන්
thirsty	thi-bah-hen	තිබහෙන්
tired	mah-han-si-yen	මහන්සියෙන්
well	sah-nee-pen	සනීපෙන්
worried	sith tha-vu-len	සිත් තැවුලෙන්

I'm sorry. (apology)
mah-tah sah-maah-ven-nah	මට සමාවෙන්න.

I'm grateful (to you).
mah-mah o-bah-tah kru-thah-gnah ve-nah-vaah	මම ඔබට කෘතඥ වෙනවා.

Instead of saying 'I'm grateful (to you)', it's common to say mah-tah o-yaah lo-ku u-dahv-vahk kah-leh (මට ඔයා ලොකු උදව්වක් කලේ), which stands for 'you did a great help for me'.

I'm happy for you.
o-bah ga-nah mah-tah sahn-thoh-sai	ඔබ ගැන මට සන්තෝෂයි.

I'm worried about you.
o-bah ga-nah mah-tah bhah-yai	ඔබ ගැන මට බයයි.

I'm sorry (for you).
o-bah ga-nah mah-tah dhu-kai	ඔබ ගැන මට දුකයි.

BREAKING THE LANGUAGE BARRIER

භාෂාව පිලිබඳ බාධක මඟ හැරීම

Do you speak English?
o-bah in-gree-si kah-thaah kau-rah-nah-vaah-dhah?	ඔබ ඉංග්‍රීසි කතා කරනවාද?

Does anyone speak English?
kau-ru hah-ri in-gree-si kah-thaah kah-rah-nah-vaah-dhah?	කව්රු හරි ඉංග්‍රීසි කතා කරනවාද?

I am still learning.
mah-mah eh-kah thah-vah-mah i-ge-nah gahn-nah-vaah	මම ඒක තවම ඉගෙන ගන්නවා.

My Sinhala is not that good.
mah-geh sin-hah-lah e-chchah-rah hon-dhah nee	මගේ සිංහල එච්චර හොඳ නෑ.

I don't understand you.

mah-tah o-bah-vah theh-rum gahn-nah ba-ha	මට ඔබව තේරුම් ගන්න බැහැ.

Could you please repeat that?

kah-ru-naah-kah-rah-lah eh-kah na-vah-thah ki-yahn-nah pu-lu-vahn-dhah?	කරුණාකරල ඒක නැවත කියන්න පුළුවන්ද?

Could you please write that for me?

kah-ru-naah-kah-rah-lah mah-tah eh-kah li-yah-lah dhen-nah pu-lu-vahn-dhah ?	කරුණාකරල මට ඒක ලියලා දෙන්න පුළුවන්ද?

How would you say ...?

... ki-yahn-neh ko-ho-mah-dhah?	... කියන්නේ කොහොමද?

What does ... mean?

... theh-ru-mah mo-kahk-dhah?	... තේරුම මොකක්ද?

How do you say this word?

meh vah-chah-nah-yah ki-yahn-neh ko-ho-mah-dhah?	මේ වචනය කියන්නේ කොහොමද?

What's this called?

meh-kah-tah mo-kahk-dhah ki-yahn-neh?	මේකට මොකක්ද කියන්නේ?

STAYING IN TOUCH

ඇසුරේ සිටිම

When you're about to leave the country, you may need the following phrases to help you stay in touch:

... is my last day.
... mah-geh ahn-thi-mah dhah-vah-sah
... මගේ අන්තිම දවස.

I'll be leaving on ...
mah-mah ... yah-nah-vaah
මම ... යනවා.

For Days of the Week, see p39.

If you ever visit ..., you must come and visit me.
o-bah kah-vah-dhaah hah-ri ... aah-voth maah ha-mu ven-nah en-nah oh-neh
ඔබ කවදා හරි ... ආවොත් මා හමු වෙන්න එන්න ඕනේ.

Do you have an email address?
o-bah-tah e-mehl li-pi-nah-yahk thi-yeh-dhah?
ඔබට ඊමේල් ලිපිනයක් තියේද?

Do you have WhatsApp/Instagram?
o-yaah-tah vahts-ap/ ins-tah-graam thi-ye-nah-vah-dhah?
ඔයාට වට්ස්ඇප්/ ඉන්ස්ටග්‍රෑම් තියෙනවද?

Don't forget to write.
li-yum li-yahn-nah ah-mah-thah-kah kah-rahn-nah e-paah
ලියුම් ලියන්න අමතක කරන්න එපා.

It's been great meeting you.
o-bah hah-mu-vee-mah lo-ku de-yahk
ඔබ හමුවීම ලොකු දෙයක්.

Text me.
mah-tah teks kah-rahn-nah
මට ටෙක්ස් කරන්න.

ONCE YOU RETURN HOME ගෙදර ගිය පසු

Once you get back home, you may want to write to or email the people you met. Here are a few lines to help you:

Dear ...
හිතවත් ...

I'm sorry it's taken me so long to write.
මෙපමණ කලකට ලියන්න බැරි වීම ගැන කණගාටුයි.

It was great to meet you.
ඔබ හමුවීම ගැන මම හරි සන්තෝෂයි.

Thank you so much for your hospitality.
ඔබ දැක්වූ සත්කාර වලට බොහොම ස්තූතියි.

I miss you. (sg)
ඔබ නැතුව මට පාළු දැනෙනවා.

I miss you. (pl)
ඔබලා නැතුව මට පාළු දැනෙනවා.

I had a fantastic time in ...
... මම රසවත් කාලයක් ගත කලා.

My favourite place was ...
ගිය තැන් වලින් මම හුගාක්ම ආශා වුනේ ...

I hope to visit ... again.
...ට යන්න මා නැවත එන්න බලාපොරොත්තු වෙනවා.

Say 'hi' to ... and ... for me.
...ට හා ...ට කියන්න මම මතක් කළ බව.

I'd love to see you again.
මට නැවත ඔබලා බලන්න ආසයි.

Write soon!
ඉක්මණට ලියුමක් එවන්න!

With love,
ආදරයෙන්,

Regards,
සමරනුයේ,

For Addresses, see p49.

☑ SAY WHAT?

When translated into Sinhala, the expression 'I beg your pardon', becomes a question, mo-kahk-dhah kiv-veh? (මොකක්ද කිව්වේ?), literally meaning 'What did you say?'. Alternatively, you could say sa-maah-ven-nah (සමාවෙන්න), meaning 'sorry'.

USEFUL PHRASES

ප්‍රයෝජනවත් වාක්‍යපද

OK.	hon-dhai	හොඳයි.
Sure.	hah-ri	හරි.
Let's go.	yah-mu	යමු.
Careful!	bah-laah-ge-nai!	බලාගෙනයි!
Wait!	oh-ho-mah in-nah!	ඔහොම ඉන්න!
Just a minute.	vi-naah-di-yahk in-nah	විනාඩියක් ඉන්න.
Are you ready?	o-bah laas-thi-dhah?	ඔබ ලෑස්තිද?
I'm ready.	mah-mah laas-thiy	මම ලෑස්තියි.
No problem.	prash-nah-yahk na-ha	ප්‍රශ්නයක් නැහැ.

FESTIVALS & NATIONAL HOLIDAYS

උත්සව සහ ජාතික නිවාඩු

With a diversity of cultural and religious festivals, Sri Lankans have developed a flair for pageantry and ceremony – almost every month brings with it a celebration. Certain festival dates may vary as they are governed by the lunar calendar.

FESTIVALS

Dhuruthu Perahera දුරුතු පෙරහැර
a religious pageant in January at the Kelaniya Temple, commemorating the first visit of Lord Buddha to Sri Lanka

Thai Pongal තායි පොන්ගල්
a Hindu festival celebrating the harvest, and offering thanks giving to the Sun God, held on 14 or 15 January

Independence Day නිදහස් සමරු උළෙළ
celebrated on 4 February, commemorating the end of 450 years of colonial rule in 1948

Ramzan Festival රාම්සාන් උත්සවය
also known as Id-Ul-Fitr, this Islamic celebration, usually celebrated in March, marks the end of Ramadan fasting

Sinhalese & Hindu New Year සිංහල සහ හින්දු අළුත් අවුරුද්ද
celebrated on 13 and 14 April, marking the end of harvest and the start of the southwest monsoon

Vesak Full Moon Day වෙසක් පුර පසළොස්වක දින
a two-day celebration in May, commemorating the birth, enlightenment and death of Buddha

Poson Full Moon Day පොසොන් පුර පසළොස්වක දින
held in June, commemorating the arrival of Buddhism to Sri Lanka in the 3rd century BCE

The Kandy Perahera නුවර පෙරහැර
a spectacular pageant and festival honouring the Sacred Tooth Relic of Buddha, held over 10 days in July / August

Kataragama Festival කතරගම උත්සවය
an August festival honouring a shrine dedicated to the god Kataragama, located in the southeast of the island

The Dondra Festival දෙවුන්දර උත්සවය
another August festival, held in Dondra, south of Colombo, around a shrine dedicated to the Hindu god, Vishnu

Sri Pada ශ්‍රී පාද වන්දනාව
a multi-denominational pilgrimage in December, venerating a footprint, believed to be Buddha's, located at the summit of Sri Pada, also known as Adam's Peak

CELEBRATIONS

උත්සව

When's your birthday?
o-beh u-pahn dhi-nah-yah kah-vah-dhaah-dhah? — ඔබේ උපන් දිනය කවදාද?

My birthday is on (25 January).
mah-geh u-pahn dhi-nah-yah (jah-nah-vaah-ri 25) — මගේ උපන් දිනය (ජනවාරි 25).

Happy birthday!
su-bhah u-pahn dhi-nah-yahk! — සුභ උපන් දිනයක්!

☑ PLANETARY PLANNING

Horoscopes carry a lot of weight in Sri Lanka – even cutting a child's hair for the first time or introducing them to solids is done in consultation with their horoscope.

Christmas Day	nath-thahl dhah-va-sah	නතතල් දවස
Christmas Eve	nath-thahl dhi-nah-tah pe-rah dhi-nah	නතතල් දිනට පෙර දින
Happy Christmas!	su-bhah nath-thah-lak!	සුභ නත්තලක්!
New Year's Eve	ah-luth ahv-rudh-dhah-tah pe-rah dhi-nah	අළුත් අවුරුද්දට පෙර දින
New Year's Day	ah-luth ahv-ru-dhu dhaah	අළුත් අවුරුදු දා
Happy New Year!	su-bhah ah-luth ahv-rudh-dhahk!	සුභ අළුත් අවුරුද්දක්!
Easter	paahs-ku	පාස්කු
Happy Easter!	su-bhah paahs-ku dhi-nah-yahk!	සුභ පාස්කු දිනයක්!

TOASTS & CONDOLENCES

සව්දිය පිරවීම හා අනුශෝචනය

Bon voyage!	su-bhah gah-mahn!	සුභ ගමන්!
Cheers!	waah-sah-naah-vahn!	වාසනාවන්!
Congratulations!	su-bhah ah-shin-sah-nah!	සුභ ආශිංසන!
Get well soon.	ik-mah-nin su-wah veh-vah	ඉක්මණින් සුව වේවා.
Good luck!	waah-sah-naah veh-waah!	වාසනා වේවා!
I'm very sorry.	mah-tah bo-hoh-mah kah-nah-gaah-tuy	මට බොහෝම කණගාටුයි.
My deepest sympathy.	mah-geh dha-di show-kah-yah	මගේ දැඩි ශෝකය.
My thoughts are with you.	mah-tah o-bah ni-thah-rah mah-thahk ve-nah-vaah	මට ඔබ නිතර මතක් වෙනවා

Going Out

විනෝද ගමන්

There are various cinemas and theatres in Sri Lanka, catering for all tastes. Concerts and operas are also popular and the nightlife is fast catching up with that of European countries.

WHERE TO GO

යා හැකි තැන්

What's there to do in the evenings?

han-dhaa-veh mo-nah-vaah-dhah kah-rahn-nah pu-lu-wahn?	හැන්දෑවේ මොනවාද කරන්න පුළුවන්?

Where can I find out what's on?

mah-mah dha-nah-gahn-ne ko-ho-mah-dhah mo-nah-vah-dhah thi-yen-neh ki-yah-laah?	මම දැනගන්නෙ කොහොමද මොනවද තියෙන්නේ කියලා

What's on tonight?

ah-dhah raa-tah mo-nah-vah-dhah thi-yehn-neh?	අද රෑට මොනවද තියෙන්නේ?

I feel like going to a/the ...	mah-tah hi-the-nah-vaah ... yahn-nah	මට හිතෙනවා ... යන්න.
bar/pub	baahr e-kah-tah; tha-baa-ru-mah-tah	බාර් එකට; තැබෑරුමට
concert	kon-sahrt e-kah-kah-tah	කොන්සර්ට් එකකට
nightclub	raah-three sah-maah-jah shaah-laah-vah-kah-tah/ nah-it klahb e-kah-tah	රාත්‍රී සමාජ ශාලාවකට/ නයිට් ක්ලබ් එකට
restaurant	aah-pah-nah shaah-laah-vah-kah-tah	ආපන ශාලාවකට

I feel like ...	mah-tah ... hi-the-nah-vaah	මට හිතෙනවා ...
a stroll	a-vi-din-nah yahn-nah	ඇවිදින්න යන්න
dancing	baahl na-tu-mah-kah-tah yahn-nah	බාල් නැටුමකට යන්න
going for a coffee/drink	koh-pi/bee-mah e-kahk bon-nah yahn-nah	කෝපි/බීම එකක් බොන්න යන්න

INVITATIONS

ආරධනා

What are you doing this evening/weekend?
ah-dhah hah-vah-sah/sah-thi ahn-thah-yeh o-bah mo-kah-dhah kah-rahn-neh?
අද හවස/සති අන්තයේ ඔබ මොකද කරන්නේ?

Shall [we] go for a drink/meal?
bon-nah/kahn-nah yah-mu-dhah?
බොන්න/කන්න යමුද?

It's my shout. (I'll buy)
mah-geh vaah-rah-yah
මගේ වාරය.

Do you want to come to the variety show with me?
maah ek-kah vi-vi-dhah prah-sahn-gah-yah-tah yahn-nah o-bah ka-mah-thi-dhah?
මා එක්ක විවිධ ප්‍රසංගයට යන්න ඔබ කැමතිද?

RESPONDING TO INVITATIONS

ආරාධනා සඳහා ප්‍රතිචාරය දැක්ම

Yes, I'd love to.
o-vu. mah-mah hah-ri aah-sai
ඔව්. මම හරි ආසයි.

Where shall we go?
ah-pi ko-heh-dhah yahn-neh?
අපි කොහේද යන්නේ?

No, I'm afraid I can't.
ba-ha. mah-tah ba-ri-ve-yi
බැහැ. මට බැරිවෙයි.

What about tomorrow?
he-tah ko-ho-mah-dhah? හෙට කොහොමද?

NIGHTCLUBS & BARS

රාත්‍රී සමාජ ශාලා සහ තැබෑරුම්

Are there any good nightclubs?
hon-dhah nah-it klahb thi-yah-nah-vaah-dhah? හොඳ රාත්‍රී නයිට් කලබ් තියනවාද?

Do you want to dance?
o-yaah-tah nah-tan-nah ka-mah-thi-dhah? ඔයාට නටන්න කැමතිද?

Do you want to go to a karaoke bar?
ka-ri-oh-ki sahn-gee-thah-yah a-thi tha-nah-kah-tah o-yaah yahn-nah ka-mah-thi-dhah? කැරිඕකි සංගීතය ඇති තැනකට ඔයා යන්න කැමතිද?

Do you have to pay to enter?
a-thul vee-mah-tah ge-vahn-nah oh-neh-dhah? ඇතුල් වීමට ගෙවන්න ඕනේද?

No, it's free.
na-ha. e-kah no-mi-leh. නැහැ. ඒක නොමිලේ.

Yes, it's ...
o-vu. e-kah ... ඔව්. ඒක ...

I'm having a great time!
mah-tah hah-ri vi-noh-dhai! මට හරි විනෝදයි!

I don't like the music here.
me-thah-nah sahn-gee-thah-yah-tah mah-mah ka-mah-thi na-ha මෙතන සංගීතයට මම කැමති නැහැ.

It's great here.
ni-yah-mai me-thah-nah නියමයි මෙතන.

Shall we go somewhere else?
ah-pi ve-nah tha-nah-kah-tah yah-mu-dhah? අපි වෙන තැනකට යමුද?

☑ STATEMENT TO QUESTION

Adding -dhah (ද) to the end of a statement, transforms it into a question.

ARRANGING TO MEET

හමුවීමට යොදා ගැනීම

What time shall we meet?
ah-pi kee-yah-tah-dhah hahm-bah vahn-neh? — අපි කීයටද හම්බ වන්නේ?

Where will we meet?
ah-pi ko-heh-dhah hahm-bah vahn-neh? — අපි කොහේද හම්බ වන්නේ?

Let's meet at (eight o'clock) at the (...).
ah-pi (ah-tah-tah) hahm-bah-ve-mu (...-dhee) — අපි (අටට) හම්බවෙමු (...දී).

OK. I'll see you then.
hon-dhai. e-thah-ko-tah hahm-bah-ve-mu — හොඳයි. එතකොට හම්බවෙමු.

I'll come over at (six).
mah-mah (hah-yah-tah) en-nahm — මම (හයට) එන්නම්.

I'll try to make it.
mah-mah en-nah bah-lahn-nahm — මම එන්න බලන්නම්.

See you later/tomorrow.
pahs-seh/he-tah hahm-bah-ve-mu — පස්සේ/හෙට හම්බවෙමු.

Sorry I'm late.
kah-nah-gaah-tuy mah-mah pah-rahk-kuy — කණගාටුයි මම පරක්කුයි.

Never mind.
kah-mahk na-ha — කමක් නැහැ.

Family

පවුල්

In Sri Lanka, people place great importance on family life. When visiting friends or relatives, the whole family goes together.

QUESTIONS

ප්‍රශ්න

Are you married?	
o-bah vi-vaah-hah-kah-dhah?	ඔබ විවාහකද?
Do you have a girlfriend/boyfriend?	
o-bah-tah pem-vah-thi-yahk/ pem-vah-thek si-tee-dhah?	ඔබට පෙම්වතියක්/ පෙම්වතෙක් සිටීද?
How many children do you have?	
o-bah-tah lah-mai kee dhe-nek in-nah-vaah-dhah?	ඔබට ළමයි කී දෙනෙක් ඉන්වාද?
How many brothers/sisters do you have?	
o-bah-tah sah-hoh-dhah-rah/ sah-hoh-dhah-ri-yahn kee dhe-nek in-nah-vaah-dhah?	ඔබට සහෝදර/ සහෝදරියන් කී දෙනෙක් ඉන්නවාද?
How old are they?	
e-yaah-lah-geh yah-sah kee-yah-dhah?	එයාලගේ වයස කීයද?
Do you live with your family?	
o-bah jee-vahth vehn-neh o-beh pah-vu-leh ah-yah ek-kah-dhah?	ඔබ ජීවත් වෙන්නේ ඔබේ පවුලේ අය එක්කද?

REPLIES

පිළිතුරු

I'm ...	mah-mah ...	මම ...
single	ah-vi-vaah-hah-kai	අවිවාහකයි
married	vi-vaah-hah-kai	විවාහකයි
separated	ven-ve-laah	වෙන්වෙලා
divorced	dhik-kah-saah-dhai	දික්කසාදයි
widowed	van-dhah-bhu-yi	වැන්දඹුයි

I have a partner.

mah-tah sah-hah-kah-ru-vek/ sah-hah-kaah-ri-yahk **(m/f)** in-nah-vaah	මට සහකරුවෙක්/ සහකාරියක් ඉන්නවා.

We live together but we're not married.

ah-pi e-kah-tah jee-vahth ve-nah-vaah nah-muth ah-pi kah-saah-dhah ban-dhah-laah na-ha	අපි එකට ජීවත් වෙනවා නමුත්, අපි කසාද බැඳල නැහැ.

I don't have any children.

mah-tah lah-mai kah-vu-ruth na-ha	මට ළමයි කවුරුත් නැහැ.

I have a daughter/son.

mah-tah e-kah dhu-wek/ pu-thek in-nah-vaah	මට එක දුවෙක්/ පුතෙක් ඉන්නවා.

I live with my family.

mah-geh pah-vu-leh ah-yah ek-kai mah-mah in-neh	මගේ පවුලේ අය එක්කයි මම ඉන්නේ.

☑ 'TIL DEATH DO US PART

In the past, unless horoscopes could confirm a couple's compatibility, it was thought their marriage would not last.

FAMILY

පවුල

aunt	nan-dhaah (father's sister)	නැන්දා
	lo-ku ahm-maah (mother's older sister)	ලොකු අම්මා
	pun-chi ahm-maah (mother's younger sister)	පුංචි අම්මා
baby	lah-dhah-ru-waah/ bah-baah	ළදරුවා/ බබා
boy	pi-ri-mi lah-mah-yaah	පිරිමි ළමයා
brother	ai-yaah (older)	අයියා
	mahl-lee (younger)	මල්ලී
	so-ho-yu-raah (refers to either)	සොහොයුරා
brother-in-law	mahs-si-naah	මස්සිනා
dad	thaahth-thaah	තාත්තා
daughter	dhu-wah	දුව
daughter-in-law	leh-lee	ලේලී
family	pah-vu-lah	පවුල
family name	vaah-sah-gah-mah	වාසගම
father	pi-yaah	පියා
father-in-law	maah-maah	මාමා
girl	ga-ha-nu lah-mah-yaah	ගැහැණු ළමයා
given name	pah-lah-mu nah-mah	පළමු නම
grandfather	see-yaah	සීයා
grandmother	aahch-chee	ආච්චී
husband	sa-mi-yaah/ swaah-mi-yaah	සැමියා/ ස්වාමියා

mother	mah-vah	මව
mother-in-law	nan-dhahm-maah	නැන්දම්මා
mum	ahm-maah/ahm-mee	අම්මා/අම්මී
nickname	vi-kah-tah nah-mah	විකට නම
sister	ak-kaah (older)	අක්කා
	nahn-gee (younger)	නංගී
	so-ho-yu-ri-yah (refers to either)	සොහොයුරිය
sister-in-law	naa-naah	නෑනා
son	pu-thaah	පුතා
son-in-law	baa-naah	බෑනා
uncle	maah-maah (mother's brother)	මාමා
	mah-hap-paah (father's older brother)	මහප්පා
	baahp-paah (father's younger brother)	බාප්පා
wife	bi-rin-dhah/ bhaahr-yaah-wah	බිරිඳ/ භාර්යාාව

Interests & Activities

විනෝදාංශ සහ ක්‍රියාකාරකම්

COMMON INTERESTS

පොදු විනෝදාංශ

What do you do in your spare time?

o-beh vi-veh-kah kaah-lah-yeh o-bah mo-kah-dhah kah-rahn-neh?	ඔබේ විවේක කාලයේ ඔබ මොකද කරන්නේ?

Do you like ...?	o-bah ka-mah-thi-dhah ... vah-lah-tah?	ඔබ කැමතිද ... වලට?
I (don't) like ...	mah-mah ... vah-lah-tah ka-mah-thi (na-ha)	මම ... වලට කැමති (නැහැ).
dancing	na-tum	නැටුම්
gardening	wahth-theh va-dah-tah	වත්තේ වැඩට
travelling	gah-mahn yahn-nah	ගමන් යන්න
I like to ...	mah-mah ka-mah-thiy ...	මම කැමතියි ...
cook	u-yahn-nah	උයන්න
draw	an-dhee-mah-tah	ඇඳීමට
paint	pin-thaah-ru kah-rahn-nah	පින්තාරු කරන්න
take photographs	chaah-yaah-roo-pah gahn-nah	චායාරූප ගන්න

MUSIC

සංගීතය

Do you like listening to music?

sahn-gee-thah-yah-tah	සංගීතයට
sah-vahn dhee-mah-tah	සවන් දීම ඔබ
o-bah ka-mah-thi-dhah?	කැමතිද?

What music do you like?

o-bah mo-nah	ඔබ මොන
sahn-gee-thah-yah-tah-dhah	සංගීතයටද
ka-mah-thi?	කැමති?

I really like (reggae).

mah-mah hun-gaahk ka-mah-thiy	මම හුඟාක් කැමතියි
(re-geh) sahn-gee-thah-yah-tah	(රෙගේ) සංගීතයට.

Which bands do you like?

o-bah mo-nah vaah-dhah-kah	ඔබ මොන වාදක
mahn-dah-lah vah-lah-tah-dhah	මණ්ඩල වලටද
ka-mah-thi?	කැමති?

I like ...

mah-mah ka-mah-thi ...	මම කැමති ...

Have you heard the latest record by ...?

...-geh ah-luth tha-ti-yah	... ගේ අළුත්
a hu-vaah-dhah?	තැටිය ඇහුවද?

Where can you hear traditional music around here?

sahm-prah-dhaah-yee	සම්ප්‍රදායී සංගීතය
sahn-gee-thah-yah	අහන්න පුළුවන්
ah-hahn-nah pu-lu-vahn	කොහේද?
ko-heh-dhah?	

Shall we sit or stand?

ah-pi in-dhah-gahn-nah-dhah	අපි ඉඳගන්නද
hi-tah gahn-nah-dhah?	හිට ගන්නද?

What a fantastic concert!

is-thah-rahm kon-saht e-kah!	ඉස්තරම් කොන්සට් එක!

It's terrible!
hah-ri-mah pahl eh-kah! හරිම පල් ඒක!

This singer is brilliant.
gaah-yah-kah-yaah vi-shish-tai ගායකයා විශිෂ්ටයි.

CINEMA & THEATRE

සිනමාව සහ තියටරය

I feel like going to a/an/the ... ... mah-tah yahn-nah hi-the-nah-vaah ... මට යන්න හිතෙනවා.

- **ballet** ba-leh e-kah-kah-tah; na-tu-mah-kah-tah බැලේ එකකට; නැටුමකට
- **comedy** haahs-yah jah-nah-kah naah-tyah-kah-tah හාස්‍ය ජනක නාට්‍යයකට
- **film** chi-thrah-pah-ti-yah-kah-tah චිත්‍රපටියකට
- **opera** or-pah-raah e-kah-kah-tah ඔපෙරා එකකට
- **play** naah-tyah-kah-tah නාට්‍යයකට

What's on at the cinema tonight?
si-nah-maah shaah-laah-vah-lah ah-dhah pen-vahn-neh mo-nah-vaah-dhah? සිනමා ශාලාවල අද පෙන්වන්නේ මොනවාද?

Are there any tickets for ...?
...-tah ti-kaht thi-yeh-dhah? ...ට ටිකට් තියේද?

Sorry, we're sold out.
kah-nah-gaah-tuy, ti-kaht na-ha කණගාටුයි, ටිකට් නැහැ.

Is it in English?
eh-kah in-gree-si-yen-dhah? ඒක ඉංග්‍රීසියෙන්ද?

Does it have English subtitles?
eh-keh in-gree-si sahb-tah-i-tahls thi-yeh-dhah? ඒකෙ ඉංග්‍රීසි සබ්ටයිටල්ස් තියේද?

OPINIONS

අදහස්

Did you like the ...?	...-tah o-bah ka-mah-thi vu-naah-dhah?	...ට ඔබ කැමති වුනාද?
film	chi-thrah-pah-ti-yah	චිත්‍රපටිය
performance	rahn-gah dhak-mah	රඟ දැක්ම
play	naaht-yah-yah	නාට්‍යය

I liked it very much.
mah-mah eh-kah-tah hun-gaahk ka-mah-thi vu-naah
මම ඒකට හුඟාක් කැමති වුනා.

I didn't like it very much.
mah-mah eh-kah-tah va-di-yah ka-mah-thi vu-neh na-ha
මම ඒකට වැඩිය කැමති වුනේ නැහැ.

I thought it was ...	mah-mah hi-thu-veh eh-kah ... ki-yah-lah	මම හිතුවේ ඒක ... කියල.
It's ...	eh-kah ...	ඒක ...
awful	ahn-thi-mai	අන්තිමයි
beautiful	lahs-sah-nai	ලස්සණයි
boring	nee-rah-sai	නීරසයි
dramatic	vish-mah-yah jah-nah-kai	විශ්මය ජනකයි
entertaining	vi-noh-dhaath-mah-kai	විනෝදාත්මකයි
excellent	hun-gaahk hon-dhai	හුඟාක් හොඳයි
great	bo-ho-mah hon-dhai	බොහොම හොඳයි
incomprehensible	theh-rum gah-thah no-ha-ki	තේරුම් ගත නොහැකි
interesting	sith gahn-naah su-luy	සිත් ගනනා සුළුයි
OK	hon-dhai	හොඳයි
too expensive	mi-lah va-di	මිළ වැඩි
unusual	ah-saah-maahn-yai	අසාමාන්‍යයි

TYPES OF SPORT

ක්‍රීඩා

What sport do you play?

o-bah mo-nah kree-daah-dhah sel-lahm kah-rahn-neh? — ඔබ මොන ක්‍රීඩාද සෙල්ලම් කරන්නේ?

I play/practise ...	mah-mah kah-rahn-neh ...	මම ... කරන්නේ
aerobics	ridh-mah-yaah-nu-koo-lah vi-yaah-yaah-mah	රිද්ම-යානුකූල ව්‍යායාම
athletics	vi-yaah-yaah-mi-kah kree-dhaah	ව්‍යායාමික ක්‍රීඩා
basketball	baahs-kaht-bawl	බාස්කට්බෝල්
cricket	kri-kaht	ක්‍රිකට්
cycling	bai-si-kaahl pa-dee-mah	බයිසිකල් පැදීම
diving	ki-mi-dee-mah	කිමිදීම
football (soccer)	paah-pahn-du	පාපන්දු
hockey	hoh-ki	හොකි
rowing	o-ru pa-dhee-mah	ඔරු පැදීම
rugby	rah-gah	රගර්
swimming	pi-hi-nee-mah	පිහිනීම
tennis	te-nis	ටෙනිස්
volleyball	vo-li-bawl	වොලිබෝල්

For hiking terms, see p142.

CALMER ACTIVITIES

සන්සුන් ක්‍රියාකාරකම්

meditation	bhaa-vah-naah ki-ree-mah	භාවනා කිරීම
Tai Chi	taai chi	ටායි චි
yoga	yoh-gaah	යෝගා

TALKING ABOUT SPORT

ක්‍රීඩා ගැන කතා කිරීම

Do you like sport?
o-bah kree-dhaah vah-lah-tah ka-mah-thi-dhah? — ඔබ ක්‍රීඩා වලට කැමතිද?

Yes, very much.
o-vu, bo-hoh-mah ka-mah-thiy — ඔව්, බොහොම කැමතියි.

No, not at all.
na-ha, ko-hehth-mah na-ha — නැහැ, කොහේත්ම නැහැ.

I like watching it.
mah-mah ka-mah-thiy eh-kah bah-lahn-nah — මම කැමතියි ඒක බලන්න.

What sports do you follow?
o-bah bah-lahn-neh mo-nah kree-dhaah-vah-dhah? — ඔබ බලන්නේ මොන ක්‍රීඩාවද?

I follow ...
mah-mah bah-lahn-neh ... — මම බලන්නේ ...

Who's your favourite ...?	o-beh pri-yah-thah-mah ... kau-dhah?	ඔබේ ප්‍රියතම ... කවුද?
player	kree-dhah-kah-yaah	ක්‍රීඩකයා
sportsperson	kree-dhaah shil-pi-yah	ක්‍රීඩා ශිල්පියා

Which team do you support?
o-bah koi kahn-dhaah-yah-mah-dhah sah-poht kah-rahn-neh? — ඔබ කොයි කණ්ඩායමද සපෝට් කරන්නේ?

I support ...
mah-mah sah-poht kah-rahn-neh ... — මම සපෝට් කරන්නේ ...

Do you play (tennis)?
o-bah (te-nis) gah-hah-nah-vaah-dhah? — ඔබ (ටෙනිස්) ගහනවාද?

GOING TO A MATCH

තරඟයක් බලන්නට යෑම

Would you like to go to a (cricket) match?
o-bah (cri-kaht) thah-rahn-gah-yahk bah-lahn-nah-tah yahn-nah ka-mah-thi-dhah?
ඔබ (ක්‍රිකට්) තරඟයක් බලන්නට යන්න කැමතිද?

Where is it being held?
ko-heh-dhah eh-kah thi-yen-neh?
කොහේද ඒක තියෙන්නේ?

How much are the tickets?
ti-kaht mi-lah kee-yah-dhah?
ටිකට් මිළ කීයද?

What time does it start?
eh-kah pah-tan gahn-neh kee-yah-tah-dhah?
ඒක පටන් ගන්නේ කීයටද?

Who's playing?
kau-dhah gah-hahn-neh?
කව්ද ගහන්නේ?

Who do you think will win?
kau-ru dhi-nai ki-yaah-dhah hi-then-neh?
කව්රු දිනයි කියාද හිතන්නේ?

Which team is winning/losing?
koi kahn-daah-yah-mah-dhah dhi-nahn-neh/pah-rah-dhin-neh?
කොයි කණ්ඩායමද දිනන්නේ/පරදින්නේ?

What's the score?
lah-ku-nu thahth-vah-yah ko-ho-mah-dhah?
ලකුණු තත්වය කොහොමද?

What a great performance!
hah-ri is-thah-rahm!
හරි ඉස්තරම්!

KEEPING FIT

ශරීර යෝග්‍යතාව

Where's the best place to jog/run around here?

jog kah-rahn-nah/ dhu-wahn-nah hon-dhah-mah tha-nah meh kit-tu-wah ko-heh-dhah thi-yen-neh?

ජොග් කරන්න/දුවන්න හොඳම තැන මේ කිට්ටුව කොහේද තියෙන්නේ?

Do you feel like (going for a run)?

o-bah-tah (dhu-wahn-nah) yahn-nah hi-the-nah-vaah-dhah?

ඔබට (දුවන්න) යන්න හිතෙනවාද?

Would you like to play (tennis)?

o-bah (te-nis) gah-hahn-nah ka-mah-thi-dhah?

ඔබ (ටෙනිස්) ගහන්න කැමතිද?

Where's the nearest ...?	lahn-gah-mah a-thi ... ko-heh-dhah thi-yen-neh?	ළඟම ඇති ... කොහේද තියෙන්නේ?
gym	jim e-kah	ජිම් එක
(swimming) pool	(swi-ming) pool e-kah	(ස්විමිං) පූල් එක
tennis court	te-nis pit-tah-ni-yah	ටෙනිස් පිට්ටනිය

☑ GIVE IT SOME STICK!

Long before present-day sports became popular, Sri Lankans enjoyed other sporting activities, such as gu-du (ගුඩු). This game involves two or more players and two sticks - one short and one long. The short stick is placed on two blocks or stones and the long stick is used to hit the short one as far as possible. The long stick is then used to score by measuring the distance the short stick has been hit. In villages and more rural areas, gu-du is still popular.

Do I have to be a member to attend?
sah-hah-bhaah-gi ven-nah mah-mah saah-maah-ji-kah-yah-ku ven-nah oh-ne-dhah?
සහභාගි වෙන්න මම සාමාජිකයකු වෙන්න ඕනෙද?

Where are the changing rooms?
an-dhum maah-ru kah-rah-nah kaah-mah-rah ko-heh-dhah thi-yen-neh?
ඇඳුම් මාරු කරන කාමර කොහේද තියෙන්නේ?

TALKING ABOUT TRAVELLING

ගමන්-බිමන් ගැන කතා කිරීම

Have you travelled much?
o-bah hun-gahk gah-mahn kah-rah thi-ye-nah-vah-dhah?
ඔබ හුගාක් ගමන් තියෙනවද?

How long have you been travelling?
o-bah koch-chah-rah kah-lahk this-seh sahn-chaah-rah-yah kah-rah-nah-vaah-dhah?
ඔබ කොච්චර කලක් තිස්සේ සංචාරය කරනවාද?

I've been travelling for (two) months.
mah-mah maah-sah (dhe-kahk) this-seh sahn-chaah-rah-yah kah-rah-nah-vaah
මම මාස (දෙකක්) තිස්සේ සංචාරය කරනවා.

Where have you been?
o-bah ko-heh ko-heh-dhah gi-yeh?
ඔබ කොහේ කොහේද ගියේ?

I've been to ...
mah-mah ...-tah gi-yaah
මම ...ට ගියා.

What did you think of (Athens)?
o-bah (a-thahns) ga-nah mo-nah-vah-dhah hi-thu-veh?
ඔබ (ඇතන්ස්) ගැන මොනවද හිතුවේ?

People are really friendly there.
e-heh mi-nis-su hah-ri yah-hah-luy
එහේ මිනිස්සු හරි යහළුයි.

There are too many tourists there.
e-heh sahn-chaah-rah-kah-yin bo-hoh-mah va-diy
එහි සංචාරකයින් බොහොම වැඩියි.

Not many people speak (English).

(in-gree-si) kah-thaah
kah-rahn-neh bo-ho-ma
ti-kah dhe-nai

(ඉංග්‍රීසි) කතා
කරන්නේ බොහොම
ටික දෙනයි.

I was ripped off in (...).

(...) vah-lah maah-vah
gah-saah kaa-vaah

(...) වල
මාව ගසා කෑවා.

What's there to do in (Brussels)?

(brah-sahls)-vah-lah
mo-nah-vah-dhah
kah-rahn-nah thi-yen-neh?

(බ්‍රසල්ස්)වල
මොනවද කරන්න
තියෙන්නේ?

The best time to go is in (December).

e-heh yahn-nah hon-dhah-mah
kaah-lah-yah (dhe-sam-bahr)
vah-lah

එහෙ යන්න හොඳම
කාලය (දෙසැම්බර්)
වල.

Is it safe for women travellers on their own?

ga-ha-nu ah-yah thah-ni-vah
yaa-mah aah-rahk-shaah
sah-hi-thah-dhah?

ගැහැණු අය තනිව
යෑම ආරක්ෂා
සහිතද?

Social Issues

සමාජ ගැටලු

POLITICS

දේශපාලනය

Although Sri Lankans enjoy discussing politics, they're very cautious about where they speak and with whom.

Did you hear about ...?
... ga-nah aah-rahn-chi-dhah? ... ගැන ආරංචිද?

What do you think of the current government?
dhan pah-vah-thi-nah rah-jah-yah ga-nah o-bah mo-na-vaah-dhah hi-thahn-neh?
දැන් පවතින රජය ගැන ඔබ මොනවද හිතන්නේ?

I (don't) agree with their policy on (the) ...	... ga-nah o-vun-geh prah-thi-pahth-thi ek-kah mah-mah e-kahn-gah ven-neh (na-ha)	... ගැන ඔවුන්ගේ ප්‍රතිපත්ති එක්ක මම එකඟ වෙන්නේ (නැහැ).
drugs	mahth-dhrah-vyah	මත්ද්‍රව්‍ය
economy	aahr-thi-kah-yah	ආර්ථිකය
education	ah-dhyaah-pah-nah-yah	අධ්‍යාපනය
environment	pah-ri-sah-rah-yah	පරිසරය
globalisation	goh-lee-kah-rah-nah-yah	ගෝලීකරණය
military service	hah-mu-dhaah seh-vah-yah	හමුදා සේවය
privatisation	pudh-gah-lee-kah-rah-nah-yah	පුද්ගලී-කරණය
social welfare	sah-maah-jah su-bhah saah-dhah-nah-yah	සමාජ සුභ සාධනය

I support the ... party.	mah-mah ... pahk-shah-yah path-theh	මම ... පක්ෂය පැත්තේ.
I'm a member of the ... party.	mah-mah ... pahk-shah-yeh saah-maah-ji-kah-yek	මම ... පක්ෂයේ සාමාජිකයෙක්.
Communist	kah-mu-nist	කොමියුනිස්ට්
National People's Power	jaah-thi-kah jah-nah bah-lah-veh-gah-yah	ජාතික ජන බලවේගය
People's Front	po-dhu-jah-nah pe-rah-mu-nah	පොදුජන පෙරමුණ
People's Liberation Front	jaah-thi-kah vi-muk-thi pe-rah-mu-nah	ජාතික විමුක්ති පෙරමුණ
Socialist	sah-maah-jah-vaah-dhee	සමාජවාදී
Sri Lanka Freedom	sree lahn-kaah ni-dhah-hahs pahk-shah-yah	ශ්‍රී ලංකා නිදහස් පක්ෂය
United National	ek-sath jaah-thi-kah	එක්සත් ජාතික

I'm an abstainer.

mah-mah chahn-dha-yah daahn-neh naa — මම ඡන්දය දානනේ නෑ

In my country we have a (socialist) government.

ah-peh rah-teh ath-theh (sah-maah-jah-vaah-dhi) rah-jah-yahk — අපේ රටේ ඇත්තේ (සමාජවාදී) රජයක්.

candidate's speech	chahn-dhah dhaah-yah-kah-yaah-geh kah-thaah-vah	ඡන්ද දායකයාගේ කතාව
corrupt	dhoo-shah-nah	දූෂණ
counting of votes	chahn-dhah gah-nahn ki-ree-mah	ඡන්ද ගණන් කිරීම
democracy	prah-jaah-thahn-thrah-vaah-dhah-yah	ප්‍රජාතන්-ත්‍රවාදය
demonstration	pe-lah-paah-li-yah	පෙළපාලිය
election	chahn-dhah vi-mah-see-mah	ඡන්ද විමසීම
legislation	vyaah-vahs-thah	ව්‍යවස්ථා
legalisation	nee-thyaah-nu-koo-lah ki-ree-mah	නීත්‍යානුකූල කිරීම
parliament	paahr-li-mehn-thu-wah	පාර්-ලිමේන්තුව
policy	pra-thi-pahth-thi	ප්‍රතිපත්ති
polls	chahn-dhah vi-mah-see-mah	ඡන්ද විමසීම
president	jah-naah-dhi-pah-thi	ජනාදිපති
prime minister	ah-gah-ma-thi	අගමැති
rally	ras-vee-mah	රැස්වීම
sexism	lin-gi-kahth-vah-yah	ලිංගිකත්වය
strike	va-dah vahr-jah-nah-yah	වැඩ වර්ජනය
term of office	ni-lah kaah-lah-yah	නිල කාලය
trade union	vruth-thee-yah sah-mi thi-yah	වෘත්තීය සමිතිය
unemployment	ra-ki-yaah vi-rah-hi-tha kah-mah	රැකියා විරහිත කම
vote	chahn-dhah-yah	ඡන්දය

SOCIAL ISSUES

සමාජීය ගැටළු

How do people feel about ...?
... ga-nah mah-hah-jah-nah-yaah-geh ha-geem mo-nah-vaah-dhah?
... ගැන මහජනයාගේ හැනීම් මොනවාද?

What do you think about ...?
... ga-nah o-bah mo-nah-vaah-dhah hi-thahn-neh?
... ගැන ඔබ මොනවාද හිතන්නේ?

I'm (in favour of/against) ...	... ga-nah mah-mah e-kahn-gai/ vi-rudh-dhai	... ගැන මම එකඟයි/ විරුද්ධයි.
abortion	gahb-saah ki-ree-mah	ගබ්සා කිරීම
animal rights	sahth-vah hi-mi-kahm	සත්ව හිමිකම්
equal opportunity	sah-maah-nah ah-vahs-thaah-wah	සමාන අවස්තාව
euthanasia	ah-naah-yaah-sah mah-rah-nah-yah	අනායාස මරණය
immigration	aah-gah-mah-ni-kah	ආගමනික
racism	jaah-thi bheh-dhah-yah	ජාති භේදය
tax	bah-dhu	බදු
unions	sah-mi-thi	සමිති

In the Country

ගම්බද පළාත් වලදී

Some of Sri Lanka's most beautiful spots are in the country – if you have the time, head out of the cities and into nature.

CAMPING

කඳවුරු

Is there a campsite nearby?
kaamp gah-hahn-nah tha-nahk lahn-gah thi-ye-nah-vah-dhah?
කැම්ප් ගහන්න තැනක් ළඟ තියෙනවද?

Do you have any sites available?
i-dah-kah-dah a-thi than thi-ye-nah-vah-dhah?
ඉඩකඩ ඇති තැන් තියෙනවද?

How much is it per ...?	... kee-yahk veh-dhah?	... කීයක් වේද?
person	ek ke-ne-ku-tah	එක් කෙනෙකුට
tent	tent e-kah-tah	ටෙන්ට් එකට
vehicle	vaah-hah-nah-yah-kah-tah	වාහනයකට

Where can I hire a tent?
tent e-kahk ku-li-yah-tah gahn-nah pu-lu-vahn ko-hen-dhah?
ටෙන්ට් එකක් කුලියට ගන්න පුළුවන් කොහෙන්ද?

Are there shower facilities?
naahn-nah pah-hah-su-kahm thi-yeh-dhah?
නාන්න පහසුකම් තියේද?

Can we camp here?
ah-pah-tah me-thah-nah kaamp gah-hahn-nah pu-lu-vahn-dhah?
අපට මෙතන කැම්ප් ගහන්න පුළුවන්ද?

HIKING

කඳු නැගීම

Although there was no thriving outdoor culture in the past, trekking and hiking are now increasingly popular with locals as well as tourists who visit the country.

GETTING INFORMATION තොරතුරු ලබාගැනීම

Where can I find out about hiking trails in the region?
pah-laah-theh hah-yik ga-nah mah-mah dha-nah-gahn-neh ko-hen-dhah?
පළාතේ හයික් ගැන මම දැනගන්නේ කොහෙන්ද?

Do we need a guide?
gaid ke-nek ah-pah-tah oh-neh veh-dhah?
ගයිඩ් කෙනෙක් අපට ඕනේ වේද?

How long is the trail?
meh maahr-gah-yah koch-chah-rah dhu-rah-dhah?
මේ මාර්ගය කොච්චර දුරද?

Is the track (well-)marked?
mah-gah sah-lah-ku-nu (hon-dhah-tah) kah-rah ath-dhah?
මග සලකුණු (හොඳට) කර ඇත්ද?

How high (is the climb)?
koch-chah-rah u-sah-dhah?
කොච්චර උසද?

Which is the easiest route?
leh-si-mah maahr-gah-yah mo-kahk-dhah?
ලේසිම මාර්ගය මොකක්ද?

Is the path open?
eh paah-rah a-rah-lah-dhah?
ඒ පාර ඇරලද?

When does it get dark?
kah-lu-vah-rah ven-neh koi veh-laah-vah-tah-dhah?
කළුවර වෙන්නේ කොයි වේලාවටද?

Where can we buy supplies?
ah-pah-tah ah-vahsh-yah bah-du gahn-neh ko-hen-dhah? — අපට අවශ්‍ය බඩු ගන්නේ කොහෙන්ද?

ON THE PATH මඟ තොටදී

Where have you come from?
o-bah ko-heh si-tah-dhah aah-veh? — ඔබ කොහේ සිටද ආවේ?

How long did it take you?
o-bah-tah koch-chah-rah ve-laah gahth-thah-dhah? — ඔබට කොච්චර වෙලා ගත්තද?

Does this path go to ...?
meh paah-rah ...-tah yah-nah-vah-dhah? — මේ පාර ...ට යනවද?

I'm lost.
mah-mah ah-thah-rah-mahn ve-laah — මම අතරමං වෙලා.

☑ NEEDLES & PINS

Don't pass pins or needles directly to anyone, as it's believed it will affect your friendship adversely. If you need to give anyone a pin or a needle, just place it in front of them.

Where can we spend the night?
ah-pi raa gah-thah kah-rahn-neh ko-heh-dhah? — අප රෑ ගත කරන්නේ කොහේද?

Can I leave some things here for a while?
mah-geh bah-du ti-kahk ti-kah ve-laah-vah-kah-tah me-heh thi-yahn-nah pu-lu-vahn-dhah? — මගේ බඩු ටිකක් ටික වෙලාවකට මෙහේ තියන්න පුළුවන්ද?

Can we go through here?
meh hah-rah-haah ah-pi-tah yahn-nah pu-lu-vahn-dhah? — මේ හරහා අපට යන්න පුළුවන්ද?

Is the water OK to drink?
meh wah-thu-rah bon-nah hon-dhah-dhah? — මේ වතුර බොන්න හොඳද?

AT THE BEACH

මුහුදු වෙරළේදී

Can we swim here?
ah-pah-tah me-thah-nah pi-hi-nahn-nah pu-lu-vahn-dhah? — අපට මෙතන පිහිනන්න පුළුවන්ද?

Is it safe to swim here?
me-thah-nah pi-hi-nahn-nah aah-rahk-shaah sah-hi-thah-dhah? — මෙතන පිහිනන්න ආරක්ෂා සහිතද?

What time is high/low tide?
wah-dah-dhi-yah/baah-dhi-yah a-thi vahn-neh koi veh-laah-vah-lah-dhah? — වඩදිය/බාදිය ඇති වන්නේ කොයි වේලාවලද?

Is there a beach near here?
mu-hu-du ve-rah-lahk meh kit-tu-wah ath-dhah? — මුහුදු වෙරළක් මේ කිට්ටුව ඇත්ද?

How much for a/an ...?	...-tah gah-nah-nah kee-yah-dhah?	...ට ගණන කීයද?
chair	pu-tu-wah	පුටුව
hut	pal-pah-thah	පැල්පත
umbrella	ku-dah-yah	කුඩය

beach	ve-rah-lah	වෙරළ
coast	ve-rah-lah-bah-dah	වෙරළබඩ
coral	hi-ri-gahl	හිරිගල්
fishing	maah-lu baa-ma	මාළු බෑම
lagoon	kah-lah-pu-wah	කලපුව
ocean	saah-gah-rah-yah	සාගරය
reef	gahl pah-rah	ගල් පර
rock	gahl pahr-wah-thah	ගල් පර්වත
sand	wa-li	වැලි
sea	mu-hu-dhah	මුහුද
sunglasses	ahv-kahn-naah-di	අව්කන්නාඩි

surf	rah-la pe-nah	රළ පෙණ
surfing	rah-lah pa-dhee-mah	රළ පැදීම
swimming	pi-hi-nee-mah	පිහිනීම
towel	thu-waah-yah	තුවාය
waves	rah-lah	රළ

DIVING කිමිදීම

Are there good diving sites here?
ki-mi-dhen-nah hon-dah thahn me-heh thi-yeh-dhah?
කිමිදෙන්න හොඳ තැන් මෙහේ තියේද?

Can we hire a diving boat/guide?
ki-mi-dhen-nah yahn-nah boht-tu-wahk/ gah-yid ke-nek ah-pah-tah gahn-nah pu-lu-vahn-dhah?
කිමිදෙන්න යන්න බෝට්ටුවක්/ ගයිඩ් කෙනෙක් අපට ගන්න පුළුවන්ද?

We'd like to hire diving equipment.
ki-mi-dhum u-pah-kah-rah-nah ku-li-yah-tah gahn-nah ah-pah-tah pu-lu-vahn-dhah?
කිමිදුම් උපකරණ කුලියට ගන්න අපට පුළුවන්ද?

I'm interested in exploring wrecks.
sun-bun gah-veh-shah-nah-yah kah-rahn-nah mah-mah ka-mah-thiy
සුන්බුන් ගවේෂණය කරන්න මම කැමතියි.

AQUATIC CREATURES ජලජ සත්වයන්

crab	kah-ku-lu-waah	කකුළුවා
dolphin	dol-fin mahth-syah-yaah	ඩොල්ෆින් මත්සයයා
eel	aahn-dhaah	ආඳා
fish (pl)	maah-lu	මාළු
lobster	po-ki-ris-sa	පොකිරිස්සා
ray	reh mahth-syah-yaah	රේ මත්සයයා
seal	seel mahth-syah-yaah	සීල් මත්සයයා
shark	moh-raah	මෝරා
shellfish	kah-bah-lu mahth-syah-yaah	කබලු මත්සයයා
turtle	kas-baa-waah	කැස්බෑවා
whale	thahl-mah-hah	තල්මහ

WEATHER

කාලගුණය

What's the weather like?
kah-lah-gu-nah-yah ko-ho-mah-dhah? — කාලගුණය කොහොමද?

Today it's ...	ah-dhah nahm ...	අද නම් ...
cloudy	kah-lu kah-rah-lah	කළු කරල
cold	see-thah-lai	සීතලයි
hot	rahs-nei	රස්නෙයි
warm	ush-nai	උෂ්ණයි
windy	hu-lahn-gai	හුළඟයි
Will it be ... tomorrow?	he-tah ...-dhah?	හෙට ...ද?
cloudy	kah-lu kah-raah-vi	කළු කරාවි
cold	see-thah-lah-veh	සීතලවේ
hot	rahs-neh-veh	රස්නේ
warm	ush-nah-veh	උෂ්ණවේ
windy	hu-lahn-gah thi-yeh	හුළඟ තියේ

It's raining.
dhan vah-hi-nah-vaah — දැන් වහිනවා.

The weather is fine/bad today.
ah-dhah kaah-lah-gu-nah-yah hon-dhai/nah-rah-kai — අද කාලගුණය හොඳයි/නරකයි.

It's sunny.
dhan av-vai — දැන් අව්වයි.

Tomorrow it's supposed to be cooler.
he-tah vah-daahth see-thah-lai-lu — හෙට වඩාත් සීතලයිලු.

bright	hah-ri e-li-yai	හරි එලියයි
cold	see-thah-lai	සීතලයි
cloudy	vah-laah-ku-len va-hi-laah	වළාකුළෙන් වැහිලා
dry season	vi-yah-li kaah-lah-yah	වියලි කාලය
floods	gahn wah-thu-rah	ගං වතුර
foggy	mee-dhu-men va-hi-laah	මීදුමෙන් වැහිලා
frosty	hi-mah sah-hi-thai	හිම සහිතයි
misty	mee-dhum sah-hi-thai	මීදුම් සහිතයි
monsoon season	moh-sahm kaah-lah-yah	මෝසම් කාලය
overcast	ah-hah-sah kah-lu kah-rah-lah	අහස කළු කරල
raining	vah-hi-nah-vaah	වහිනවා
rainy season	vas-sah kaah-leh	වැස්ස කාලේ
snowing	hi-mah va-te-nah-vaah	හිම වැටෙනවා
spitting	po-dah gah-hah-nah-vaah/ ku-naah-tu-wah	පොද ගහනවා/ කුණාටුව
sun/sunny	av-wah/av-vai	අව්ව/අව්වයි
typhoon	su-li-su-lahng	සුළිසුළං
windy	hu-lahn-gai	හුළඟයි

GEOGRAPHICAL TERMS

භූගෝලික වචන

bridge	paah-lah-mah	පාලම
cave	gu-haah-wah	ගුහාව
cliff	kahn-du prah-paah-thah-yah	කඳු ප්‍රපාතය
earthquake	bhoo-mi kahm-paah-wah	භූමි කම්පාව
farm	go-vi-pah-lah	ගොවිපළ
footpath	ah-di paah-rah	අඩි පාර
forest	ka-laa-wah	කැලෑව
harbour	wah-raah-yah	වරාය
hill	kahn-dhah	කන්ද
hot springs	u-nu dhi-yah ling	උණු දිය ලිං
island	dhi-vah-yi-nah	දිවයින
lake	wa-wah	වැව
mountain	kahn-dhah	කන්ද
peak	mu-dhu-nah	මුදුන
river	gahn-gah	ගඟ
sea	mu-hu-dhah	මුහුද
valley	tha-ni-thah-laah-wah	තැනිතලාව
waterfall	dhi-yah al-lah	දිය ඇල්ල

FAUNA

සත්ව වර්ගයා

What animal is that?
ah-rah mo-nah sah-thaah-dhah? අර මොන සතාද?

What do you call that animal?
ah-rah sah-thaah-tah mo-kaahk-dhah ki-yahn-neh? අර සතාට මොකක්ද කියන්නේ?

DOMESTTC CREATURES ගෘහස්ත සජීන්

bird	ku-rul-laah	කුරුල්ලා
buffalo	mee hah-rah-kaah	මී හරකා
calf	wah-hu pa-ti-yaah	වහු පැටියා
cat	bah-lah-laah/poo-saah	බළලා/පූසා
chicken	ku-ku-lu pa-ti-yaah	කුකුළු පැටියා
cow	e-lah-dhe-nah	එළදෙන
dog	bahl-laah	බල්ලා
donkey	boo-ru-waah	බූරුවා
duck	thaah-raah-waah	තාරාවා
goat	e-lu-waah	එළුවා
hen	ki-ki-lee	කිකිළි
horse	ahsh-wah-yaah	අශ්වයා
ox	hah-rah-kaah/go-naah	හරකා/ගොනා
pig	oo-raah	ඌරා
rooster	ku-ku-laah	කුකුළා
sheep	ba-tah-lu-waah	බැටළුවා

WILDLIFE වන් සජීන්

ant	koom-bi-yaah	කුම්බියා
bee	mee mas-saah	මී මැස්සා
bird	ku-rul-laah	කුරුල්ලා
butterfly	sah-mah-nah-lah-yaah	සමනළයා
cockroach	ka-rah-poth-thaah	කැරපොත්තා
crocodile	kim-bu-laah	කිබුලා
deer	mu-vaah	මුවා
elephant	ah-li-yaah	අලියා
elk	goh-naah	ගෝනා
fish	maah-lu	මාළු
fly	mas-saah	මැස්සා
frog	gem-baah	ගෙම්බා
game (animals)	dha-dah mas	දඩ මස්

hare	haah-vaah	හාවා
iguana	thah-lah-go-yaah	තලගොයා
leech	koo-dal-laah	කූඩැල්ලා
leopard	dhi-vi-yaah	දිවියා
lion	sin-hah-yaah	සිංහයා
monkey	wahn-dhu-raah	වඳුරා
mosquito	mah-dhu-ru-waah	මදුරුවා
mouse	mee-yaah	මීයා
snail	go-lu-bel-laah	ගොළුබෙල්ලා
snake	nah-yaah	නයා
spider	mah-ku-lu-waah	මකුළුවා
squirrel	leh-naah	ලේනා
tiger	ko-ti-yaah	කොටියා
wild boar	vahl-oo-raah	වල් ඌරා

FLORA & AGRICULTURE

ගස් කොළං සහ කෘෂිකර්මය

What tree/plant/flower is that?
eh mo-nah gah-hahk-dhah/ pa-lah-yahk-dhah/mah-lahk-dhah? — ඒ මොන ගහක්ද/ පැලයක්ද/මලක්ද?

What's it used for?
eh-kah paah-vich-chi kah-rahn-neh mo-kah-tah-dhah? — ඒක පාවිච්චි කරන්නේ මොකටද?

Can you eat the fruit?
eh ge-di kahn-nah pu-lu-vahn-dhah? — ඒ ගෙඩි කන්න පුළුවන්ද?

coconut	pol	පොල්
date	rah-tah in-di	රට ඉරි
eucalyptus	yoo-kah-lip-tahs	යූකලිප්ටස්
camphor	kah-pu-ru	කපුරු
oak	sin-doo-rah	සින්දූර
palm	thahl	තල්
pine	pain gahs	පයින් ගස්

HFRBS, FLOWERS & CROPS ඖෂධ, මල් සහ වගා

agriculture	kru-shi-kahr-mah-yah	කෘෂිකර්මය
areca nut	pu-wahk	පුවක්
bougainvillea	boh-gahn-wi-laah	බෝගන්විලා
cardamom	e-nah-saahl	එනසාල්
cinnamon	ku-run-dhu	කුරුඳු
cloves	kah-raah-bu na-ti	කරාබු නැටි
cocoa	ko-koh	කොකෝ
coconut palm	pol	පොල්
coffee	koh-pi	කෝපි
corn	i-rin-gu	ඉරිඟු
crops	vah-gaah	වගා
flower	mahl	මල්
grapevine	mi-dhi va-lah	මිදි වැල
harvest (noun)	ahs-van-nah	අස්වැන්න
irrigation	vaah-ri-maahr-gah	වාරිමාර්ග
jasmine	pich-chah	පිච්ච
kitul palm	ki-thul	කිතුල්
lavender	sa-van-dhah-raah	සැවැන්දරා
leaf	ko-lah-yah	කොළය
lemon tree	dhe-hi gah-hah	දෙහි ගහ
orchard	pah-lah-thu-ru vah-thu	පළතුරු වතු
orange tree	dho-dhahm gah-hah	දොඩම් ගහ
planting/sowing	si-tu-vee-mah/ va-pi-ree-mah	සිටුවීම/ වැපිරීම

☑ MILK OF THE GODS

When planted in the front garden, trees that release milky substances are said to bring good fortune to the house and its inhabitants.

palm trees	thaah-lah vahr-gah-yeh gahs	තාල වර්ගයේ ගස්
pepper	gahm-mi-ris	ගම්මිරිස්
rice field/paddy	kum-bu-rah	කුඹුර
sunflower	soo-ri-yah kaahn-thah	සූරිය කාන්ත
sugar cane	uk-gahs	උක්ගස්
talipot palm	thahl	තල්
tea	theh	තේ
tea estate	theh wahth-thah	තේ වත්ත
terraced land	te-rahs i-dahm	ටෙරස් ඉඩම්
tobacco	dhum-ko-lah	දුම්කොළ
tree	gah-hah	ගහ
vineyard	mi-dhi wahth-thah	මිදි වත්ත
wheat	thi-rin-gu	තිරිඟු

Health

සෞඛ්‍ය

Western-style medicine is practised throughout Sri Lanka and public hospitals offer free service to all. Private hospitals can also be found, and some hospitals function both privately and publicly.

AT THE DOCTOR

වෛද්‍යවරයා ළඟදී

I'm sick.

mah-tah sah-nee-pah na-ha (lit: to-me well not) — මට සනීප නැහැ.

My friend is sick.

mah-geh yah-hah-lu-waah-tah sah-nee-pah na-ha — මගේ යහළුවාට සනීප නැහැ.

I need a doctor (who speaks English).

(in-gree-si kah-thaah kah-rah-nah) dhos-thah-rah ke-nek mah-tah oh-neh — (ඉංග්‍රීසි කතා කරනා) දොස්තර කෙනෙක් මට ඕනේ.

Could the doctor come here?

dhos-thah-rah-tah me-heh en-nah pu-lu-vahn-dhah? — දොස්තරට මෙහේ එන්න පුළුවන්ද?

Whero's the nearest ...?	lahn-gah-mah a-thi ... ko-heh-dhah thi-yen-neh?	ළඟම ඇති ... කොහේද තියෙන්නේ?
dentist	dhahth dos-thah-rah	දත් දොස්තර
dispensary	dis-pen-sah-ri-yah	ඩිස්පෙන්සරිය
doctor	dhos-thah-rah	දොස්තර
hospital	roh-hah-lah	රෝහල
pharmacist	in-gree-si be-heth saahp-pu-wah	ඉංග්‍රීසි බෙහෙත් සාප්පුව

AILMENTS

අසනීප

I'm ill.
mah-tah ah-sah-nee-pai
මට අසනීපයි.

I've been vomiting.
mah-tah vah-mah-nah-yah yah-nah-vaah
මට වමනය යනවා.

I can't sleep.
mah-tah nin-dhah yahn-neh na-ha
මට නින්ද යන්නේ නැහැ.

It hurts here.
me-thah-nah ri-dhe-nah-vaah
මෙතන රිදෙනව.

I have (a/an) ...	mah-tah ... thi-ye-nah-vaah	මට ... තියෙනවා.
I've had (a/an) ...	mah-tah ... thi-bu-naah	මට ... තිබුණා.
allergy	a-lah-ji e-kahk	ඇලජී එකක්
anaemia	leh ah-du kah-mahk	ලේ අඩු කමක්
blister	bi-bi-lah	බිබිළ
bronchitis	bron-kah-yi-tis	බ්‍රොන්කයිටිස්
burn	dha-vil-lah	දැවිල්ල
cancer	pi-li-kaah-wah	පිලිකාව
chicken pox	pa-po-lah	පැපොල
cold	hem-bi-ris-saah-wah	හෙම්බිරිස්සාව
constipation	bah-dhah veh-lee-mah	බඩ වේලීම
cough	kas-sah	කැස්ස
cramp	ken-dah pe-rah-lee-mah	කෙණ්ඩ පෙරලීම
diarrhoea	bah-dah bu-rul vee-mah	බඩ බුරුල් වීම
fever	u-nah	උණ
gastroenteritis	bah-dah-val i-dhi-mu-mah	බඩවැල් ඉදුමුම
glandular fever	grahn-thee-yah u-nah	ග්‍රන්ථිය උණ
hayfever	pee-nahs roh-gah-yah	පීනස් රෝගය
headache	hi-sah rah-dhah-yah	හිස රදය
heart condition	pa-pu-weh ah-maah-ru-wah	පපුවේ අමාරුව
hepatitis	he-pah-tai-tis	හෙපටයිටිස්
indigestion	ah-jeer-nah-yah	අජීර්ණය

infection	bo-we-nah yah-mahk	බෝවෙන යමක්
inflammation	dha-vil-lah sah-hi-thah i-dhi-mu-mah	දැවිල්ල සහිත ඉදිමුම
influenza	sem-prah-thish-yaah u-nah	සෙම්ප්‍රතිශ්‍යා උණ
lice	u-ku-nahn	උකුණන්
lump	gu-li-yahk	ගුලියක්
migraine	mai-grehn hi-sah-rah-dhah-yah	මයිග්‍රෙන් හිසරදය
pain	kahk-ku-mah	කැක්කුම
rash	raahsh e-kah; dhah-dhah	රැෂ් එක; දද
sore throat	u-gu-reh ah-maah-ru-vah	උගුරේ අමාරුව
sprain	u-luk-ku-wah	උළුක්කුව
stomachache	bah-deh kak-ku-mah	බඩේ කැක්කුම
sunburn	av-vah-tah pich-chee-mah	අව්වට පිච්චීම
travel sickness	gah-mahn ki-ree-meh-dee a-thi-wah-nah vah-mah-nah-yah	ගමන් කිරීමේදී ඇතිවන වමනය
urinary infection	mu-thraah roh-gah	මුත්‍රා රෝග
venereal disease	lin-gaah-shri-thah roh-gah	ලිංගාශ්‍රිත රෝග
worms	pah-nu ah-maah-ru-wah	පණු අමාරුව
I feel ...	mah-tah ...	මට ...
dizzy	ka-rah-kil-lai	කැරකිල්ලයි
shivery	vev-lah-nah-vaah	වෙව්ලනවා
nauseous	ok-kaah-rah-yah vah-geh	ඔක්කාරය වගේ
weak	dhur-vah-lai vah-geh	දුර්වලයි වගේ

I feel better/worse.
dhan mah-tah hon-dhai/ an-thai vah-geh — දැන් මට හොඳයි/ අන්තයි වගේ.

This is my usual medicine.
meh mah-geh saah-maahn-yah be-he-thah — මේ මගේ සාමාන්‍ය බෙහෙත.

I don't want a blood transfusion.
mah-tah leh dhen-nah oh-neh na-ha — මට ලේ දෙන්න ඕනේ නැහැ.

Can I have a receipt for my insurance?
mah-geh rahk-shah-nah-yah-tah ri-seet e-kahk gahn-nah pu-lu-vahn-dhah?
මගේ රක්ෂණයට රිසීට් එකක් ගන්න පුළුවන්ද?

LISTEN FOR

mo-kah-dhah vu-neh? — මොකද වුනේ?
What's the matter?

o-bah-tah kak-ku-mah dha-ne-nah-vaah-dhah? — ඔබට කැක්කුම දැනෙනවාද?
Do you feel any pain?

ko-heh-dhah ri-dhen-neh? — කොහේද රිදෙන්නේ?
Where does it hurt?

o-bah-tah u-nah thi-yeh-dhah? — ඔබට උණ තියේද?
Do you have a temperature?

me-heh-mah ve-laah dhan koch-chah-rah kahl-dhah? — මෙහෙම වෙලා දැන් කොච්චර කල්ද?
How long have you been like this?

mee-tah kah-lin meh-kah ha-di-lah thi-yeh-dhah? — මීට කලින් මේක හැදිල තියේද?
Have you had this before?

o-bah dhan be-heth bo-nah-vaah-dhah? — ඔබ දැන් බෙහෙත් බොනවාද?
Are you on medication?

o-bah dhum bo-nah-vaah-dhah? — ඔබ දුම් බොනවාද?
Do you smoke?

o-bah mahth-pan paah-vich-chi kah-rah-nah-vaah-dhah? — ඔබ මත්පැන් පාවිච්චි කරනවාද?
Do you drink?

o-bah mahth drahv-yah paah-vich-chi kah-rah-nah-vaah-dhah? — ඔබ මත් ද්‍රව්‍ය පාවිච්චි කරනවාද?
Do you take drugs?

o-bah mo-nah-vaah-tah hah-ri a-lah-jik-dhah? — ඔබ මොනවට හරි ඇලර්ජික්ද?
Are you allergic to anything?

WOMEN'S HEALTH

කාන්තා සෞඛ්‍ය

Could I see a female doctor?

mah-tah ga-ha-nu dhos-thah-rah ke-nek bah-lahn-nah pu-lu-vahn-dhah?

මට ගැහැණු දොස්තර කෙනෙක් බලන්න පුළුවන්ද?

I'm pregnant.

mah-mah ga-bi-niy

මම ගැබිණියි.

I think I'm pregnant.

mah-mah hi-thahn-neh mah-mah ga-bi-niy ki-yaah

මම හිතන්නේ මම ගැබිණියි කියා.

I'm on the pill.

mah-mah pe-thi paah-vich-chi kah-rah-nah-vaah

මම පෙති පාවිච්චි කරනවා.

I haven't had my period for ... weeks.

sah-thi ...-tah mah-tah o-sahp vee-mah thi-bu-neh na-ha

සති ...ට මට ඔසප් වීම තිබුණේ නැහැ.

I'd like to use contraception.

pi-li-si-dhee-mah va-lak-vee-meh krah-mah paah-vich-chi kah-rahn-nah mah-mah ka-mah-thiy

පිලිසිදීම වැළැක්වීමේ ක්‍රම පාවිච්චි කරන්න මම කැමතියි.

I'd like to have a pregnancy test.

gab ga-nee-meh pah-reek-shah-nah-yahk mah-tah kah-rah-gahn-nah oh-neh

ගැබ් ගැනීමේ පරීක්ෂණයක් මට කරගන්න ඕනේ.

abortion	gahb-saah-vah	ගබ්සාව
cystitis	oh-jahs sah-hi-thah ge-di ni-saah mu-thraah-shah-yeh i-dhi-mu-mah	ඕජස් සහිත ගෙඩි නිසා මුත්‍රාශයේ ඉදිමුම
diaphragm	mah-haah praah-chee-rah-yah	මහා ප්‍රාචීරය
IUD	ai-yoo-dee e-kah	අයි.යූ.ඩී. එක
mammogram	ma-moh-graam e-kah	මැමෝග්‍රෑම් එක
menstruation	o-sahp vee-mah	ඔසප් වීම
miscarriage	gahb-saah vee-mah	ගබ්සා වීම
pap smear	pap-smi-yah e-kah	පැප්ස්මියා එක
period pain	o-sahp ru-dhaah	ඔසප් රුදා
the Pill	peth-thah	පෙත්ත
premenstrual tension	o-sahp poor-vah kah-lah-hah gah-thi-yah	ඔසප් පූර්ව කලහ ගතිය
thrush	ak-kaah-rah-mah	අක්කාරම
ultrasound	ah-thi dhvah-nee-yah shahb-dhah thah-rahn-gah	අති ද්වනීය ශබ්ද තරංග

LISTEN FOR

o-bah-tah dhan o-sahp vee-mah ath-dhah? — ඔබට දැන් ඔසප් වීම ඇත්ද?
Are you menstruating?

o-bah gahr-bah-nee-dhah? — ඔබ ගර්භනීද?
Are you pregnant?

o-bah pi-li-si-dhee-mah va-lak-vee-mah-tah pe-thi gahn-nah-vaah-dhah? — ඔබ පිලිසිදීම වැළැක්වීමට පෙති ගන්නවාද?
Are you on the Pill?

SPECIAL HEALTH NEEDS

විශේෂ සෞඛ්‍ය අවශ්‍යතා

I'm ...	mah-mah ... ath-thek	මම ... ඇත්තෙක්
anaemic	a-nee-mik	ඇනීමික්
asthmatic	a-dhu-mah	ඇදුම
diabetic	dhi-yah-va-di-yaah-vah	දියවැඩියාව
I'm allergic to ...	mah-tah ... a-lah-jik	මට ... ඇලජික්
antibiotics	an-ti-bah-yah-tik	ඇන්ටිබයටික්
aspirin	as-prin	ඇස්ප්‍රින්
bees	mee mas-soh	මී මැස්සෝ
codeine	koh-deen	කෝඩීන්
dairy products	ki-ri aah-haah-rah	කිරි ආහාර
penicillin	pe-ni-si-lin	පෙනිසිලින්
pollen	mahl reh-nu	මල් රේණු

I have a skin allergy.
mah-geh hah-meh a-lah-jik e-kahk thi-ye-nah-vaah
මගේ හමේ ඇලජික් එකක් තියෙනවා

I have high/low blood pressure.
mah-tah thi-yen-neh ah-dhi-kah/ah-du ru-dhee-rah pee-dah-nah-yah
මට තියෙන්නේ අදික/අඩු රුදිර පීඩනය.

I have a weak heart.
mah-geh hahr-dhah-yah vahs-thu-wah hah-ri dhur-vah-lai
මගේ හෘදය වස්තුව හරි දුර්වලයි.

I've had my vaccinations.
mah-tah vak-seen gah-hah-laah thi-yen-neh
මට වැක්සීන් ගහලා තියෙන්නේ.

Is that a new syringe you're using?
o-bah meh paah-vich-chi kah-rahn-neh ah-luth si-rin-jah-rah-yahk-dhah?
ඔබ මේ පාවිච්චි කරන්නේ අළුත් සිරින්ජරයක්ද?

I have my own syringe.
mah-tah mah-geh si-rin-jah-rah-yah thi-ye-nah-vaah — මට මගේ සිරින්ජරය තියෙනව.

I'm on medication for ...
mah-mah ...-tah be-heth bo-nah-vaah — මම ...ට බෙහෙත් බොනව.

I'm on a special diet.
mah-mah kahn-neh vi-sheh-shah kaa-mah — මම කන්නේ විශේෂ කෑම.

I need a new pair of glasses.
mah-tah ah-luth kahn-naah-di kut-tah-mahk oh-neh — මට අළුත් කන්නාඩි කුට්ටමක් ඕනේ.

addiction	ab-ba-hi vee-mah	ඇබ්බැහි වීම
bite	sah-paah kaa-mah	සපා කෑම
blood test	leh chek kah-rah-nah-vaah	ලේ චෙක් කරනවා
inhaler	in-heh-lah e-kah	ඉන්හේල එක
injection	in-jek-shahn e-kah	ඉන්ජෙක්ෂන් එක
injury	ah-nah-thu-rah	අනතුර
pacemaker	pehs-meh-kah-rah-yah	පේස්මේකරය
wound	thu-waah-lah-yah	තුවාලය

PARTS OF THE BODY

ශාරීරික අවයව

My ... hurts.
mah-geh ... ri-dhe-nah-vaah — මගේ ... රිදෙනවා.

I have a pain in my ...
mah-geh ... kak-ku-mahk thi-ye-nah-vaah — මගේ ... කැක්කුමක් තියෙනවා.

I can't move my ...
mah-geh ... so-lah-vahn-nah ba-ha — මගේ ... සොලවන්න බැහැ.

ankle	vah-lah-lu-kah-rah	වළලුකර
appendix	un-du-kah puch-chah-yah	උණ්ක පුච්චය
arm	ah-thah	අත
back	kon-dhah	කොන්ද
bladder	muth-thraah-shah-yah	මුත්‍රාශය
blood	leh	ලේ
bone	kah-tu	කටු
chest	pa-pu-wah	පපුව
ears	kahn	කන්
eye	a-ha	ඇහැ
finger	an-gil-lah	ඇනිල්ල
foot	paah-dhah-yah	පාදය
hand	ah-thah	අත
head	o-lu-wah	ඔළුව
heart	hah-dhah-wah-thah	හදවත
jaw	hahk-kah	හක්ක
kidney	vah-ku-gah-du	වකුගඩු
knee	dhah-nah-hi-sah	දණහිස
leg	kah-ku-lah	කකුල
liver	ak-maah-wah	අක්මාව
lungs	pe-nah-hah-lu	පෙනහළු
mouth	kah-tah	කට
muscle	maahn-shah peh-sheen	මාංශ පේශීන්
nose	nah-hah-yah/ naah-sah-yah	නහය/ නාසය
ribs	i-lah a-tah	ඉළ ඇට
shoulders	u-rah-his	උරහිස්
skin	hah-mah	හම
spine	kon-dhah	කොන්ද
stomach	bah-dah	බඩ
teeth	dhahth	දත්
throat	u-gu-rah	උගුර
vein	nah-hah-rah	නහර

ALTERNATIVE TREATMENTS

විකල්ප වෙදකම්

Alternative treatments, including homeopathy and Ayurveda, are available at specialist medical clinics.

acupuncture	kah-tu chi-kith-saah-wah	කටු චිකිත්සාව
aromatherapy	a-roh-maah-the-rah-pi	ඇරෝමාතෙරපි
chiropractor	thu-nah-ti-yeh ve-dhah-kahm kah-rahn-naah	තුනටියේ වෙදකම් කරන්නා
faith healer	aah-gahm bhahk-thi-kah he-dhah-kah-mah	ආගම් භක්තික හෙදකම
herbalist	au-shah-dha-veh-dhee	ඖෂධවේදී
homeopathy	hoh-mi-yoh-pah-thy ve-dhah-kah-mah	හෝමියෝපති වෙදකම
massage	mah-saahj e-kah	මසාජ් එක
meditation	bhaah-vah-naah ki-ree-mah	භාවනා කිරීම
naturopathy	swaah-baah-vi-kah krah-mah ve-dhah-kah-mah	ස්වාභාවික ක්‍රම වෙදකම
reflexology	rif-lek-so-lah-ji	රිෆ්ලෙක්සොලජි
yoga	yoh-gaah	යෝගා

AT THE PHARMACY

ඉංග්‍රීසි බෙහෙත් සාප්පුවේදී

Is there an all-night pharmacy nearby?
raah-three be-heth saahp-pu-wahk lahn-gah thi-yeh-dhah? — රාත්‍රී බෙහෙත් සාප්පුවක් ළඟ තියේද?

I need something for ...
mah-tah ...-tah mo-nah-vaah hah-ri oh-neh — මට ...ට මොනවා හරි ඕනේ.

Do I need a prescription for ...?
...-tah be-heth thun-du-vahk oh-ne-dhah? — ...ට බෙහෙත් තුණ්ඩුවක් ඕනෙද?

I have a prescription.
mah-tah be-heth thun-du-vahk thi-yah-nah-vaah — මට බෙහෙත් තුණ්ඩුවක් තියෙනව.

How many times a day?
dhah-vah-sah-tah kee sa-rah-yahk-dhah? — දවසට කී සැරයක්ද?

Twice a day (with food).
dhah-vah-sah-tah dhe-sa-rah-yahk (kaa-mah ek-kah) — දවසට දෙසරයක් (කෑම එක්ක).

Can I drive on this medication?
meh be-heth a-rah-ge-nah mah-tah e-lah-vahn-nah pu-lu-vahn dhah? — මේ බෙහෙත් අරගෙන මට එළවන්න පුළුවන්ද?

Will it make me drowsy?
meh be-he-thah-tah mah-tah ni-dhi-mah-thah ei-dhah? — මේ බෙහෙතට මට නිදිමත එයිද?

antibiotics	an-ti-bah-yah-tiks	ඇන්ටිබයටික්ස්
antiseptic	vi-shah naah-shah-kah	විෂ නාශක
aspirin	as-prin	ඇස්ප්‍රින්
bandage	ban-dehj e-kah	බැන්ඩේජ් එක
Band-Aids	plaahs-tah e-kah	ප්ලාසට එක
condoms	kon-dom e-kah	කොන්ඩොම් එක
contraceptives	pi-li-si-dhee-mah va-lak-vee-meh dheh-vahl	පිලිසිදීම වැළැක්වීමේ දේවල්
cotton balls	pu-lun ka-bah-li boh-lah	පුළුන් කැබලි බෝල
cough medicine	kas-sah-tah gahn-nah be-heth	කැස්සට ගන්න බෙහෙත්
gauze	gors kaa-li	ගෝස් කෑලි
laxatives	vi-reh-kah-yahn	විරේකයන්
painkillers	veh-dhah-naah naah-shah-kah-yahn	වේදනා නාශකයන්
sleeping pills	ni-dhi pe-thi	නිදි පෙති
vitamins	vi-tah-min	විටමින්

See general toiletries, see p90.

AT THE DENTIST

දන්ත වෛද්‍යවරයා ළඟදී

I have a toothache.

mah-tah dhah-theh kak-ku-mahk thi-ye-nah-vaah — මට දතේ කැක්කුමක් තියෙනව.

I have a cavity.

mah-geh dhah-theh ku-hah-rah-yahk thi-ye-nah-vaah — මගේ දතේ කුහරයක් තියෙනව.

I've lost a filling.

mah-geh dhah-theh pi-rah-vee-mah ga-lah-vi-laah — මගේ දතේ පිරවීම ගැලවිල.

I've broken my tooth.

mah-geh dhah-thah ga-lah-vi-laah — මගේ දත ගැලවිල.

My gums hurt.

mah-geh vi-dhu-ru-mahs ri-dhe-nah-vaah — මගේ විදුරුමස් රිදෙනව.

I don't want it extracted.

dhah-thah gah-lah-vahn-nah mah-tah oh-neh na-ha — දත ගලවන්න මට ඕනේ නැහැ.

Please give me an anaesthetic.

kah-ru-naah-kah-rah mah-tah hi-ri waht-tan-nah be-he-thah dhen-nah — කරුණාකර මට හිරි වට්ටන බෙහෙත දෙන්න.

Ouch!

aah-i! — ආයි!

Emergencies

හදිසි අවස්ථා

GENERAL

පොදු

Help!	kau-ruth nadh-dhah? (lit: anyone isn't here?)	කව්රුත් නැද්ද?
Stop!	nah-vah-thin-nah!	නවතින්න!
Go away!	yahn-nah!	යන්න!
Thief!	ho-rek!	හොරෙක්!
Fire!	gin-nahk!	ගින්නක්!
Watch out!	bah-laah-ge-nai!	බලාගෙනයි!
It's an emergency!	meh-kah hah-dhis-si-yahk!	මේක හදිස්සියක්!

Could you help us please?
kah-ru-naah-kah-rah-lah ah-pah-tah u-dhahv kah-rahn-nah pu-lu-vahn-dhah?
කරුණාකරල අපට උදව් කරන්න පුළුවන්ද?

Could I please use the telephone?
kah-ru-naah-kah-rah-lah mah-tah te-li-fohn e-kah paah-vich-chi kah-rahn-nah pu-lu-vahn-dhah?
කරුණාකරල මට ටෙලිෆෝන් එක පාවිච්චි කරන්න පුළුවන්ද?

I'm lost.
mah-mah ah-thah-rah mahn-we-laah
මම අතරමං වෙලා

Where are the toilets?
toi-laht/va-si-ki-li-yah ko-heh-dhah thi-yen-neh?
ටොයිලට්/වැසිකිලිය කොහේද තියෙන්නේ?

HEALTH

සෞඛ්‍ය

Call a doctor!
dhos-thah-rah ke-nek-tah kah-thaah kah-rahn-nah! — දොස්තර කෙනෙක්ට කතා කරන්න!

Call an ambulance!
am-byu-lahns e-kah-kah-tah kah-thaah kah-rahn-nah! — එම්බ්‍යුලන්ස් එකකට කතා කරන්න!

I'm ill.
mah-tah sah-nee-pah na-ha — මට සනීප නැහැ.

My friend is ill.
mah-geh yah-hah-lu-waah-tah sah-nee-pah na-ha — මගේ යහළුවාට සනීප නැහැ.

I have medical insurance.
mah-tah wai-dyah rahk-shah-nah thi-ye-nah-waah — මට වෛද්‍ය රක්ෂණ තියෙනවා.

POLICE

පොලීසිය

Call the police!
po-lee-si-yah-tah kah-thaah kah-rahn-nah! — පොලිසියට කතා කරන්න!

Where's the police station?
po-lee-si-yah ko-heh-dhah thi-yen-neh? — පොලිසිය කොහේද තියෙන්නේ?

We want to report an offence.
va-rah-dhi va-dhahk ga-nah ah-pah-tah pa-mi-ni-li kah-rahn-nah oh-neh — වැරදි වැඩක් ගැන අපට පැමිණිලි කරන්න ඕනේ.

I've been raped/assaulted.
maah-vah dhoo-shah-nah-yah kah-laah; mah-tah ga-hu-vaah — මාව දූෂණය කළා; මට ගැහුවා.

I've been robbed.
mah-gen so-raah gahth-thaah — මගෙන් සොරා ගත්තා.

My ... was/were stolen.	mah-geh ... so-rah-kahm ke-ru-waah	මගේ ... සොරකම් කෙරුවා.
backpack	bak-pak e-kah	බැක්පැක් එක
bags	baag/mahl-lah	බැග්/මල්ල
handbag	ahth baag e-kah	අත් බැග් එක
money	sahl-li	සල්ලි
papers	ko-lah	කොළ
passport	paahs-poht e-kah	පාස්පෝට් එක
wallet	pers e-kah	පර්ස් එක

My possessions are insured.
mah-geh bah-du rahk-shah-nah-yah kah-rah-lai thi-yen-neh — මගේ බඩු රක්ෂණය කරලයි තියෙන්නේ.

I'm sorry; I apologise.
kah-nah-gaah-tuy; mah-tah sah-maah ven-nah — කණගාටුයි; මට සමා වෙන්න.

SORRY!

The English phrase 'I'm sorry' or just 'sorry' is widely used to apologise.

I didn't realise I was doing anything wrong.
mah-mah va-radh-dhak kah-rah-nah-vah ki-yah-laah theh-ru-neh na-ha — මම වැරැද්ද කරනවා කියලා තේරුනේ නැහැ.

I didn't do it.
mah-mah ke-ru-veh na-ha — මම කෙරුවේ නැහැ.

We're innocent.
ah-pi nir-dhoh-shai — අපි නිර්දෝෂයි.

We're foreigners.
ah-pi vi-dheh-shi-kah-yoh — අපි විදේශිකයෝ.

I want to contact my embassy/consulate.
mah-geh thaah-naah-pah-thi/ kon-sahl kahn-thoh-ru-wah-tah mah-tah kah-thaah kah-rahn-nah oh-neh — මගේ තානාපති/ කොන්සල් කන්තෝරුවට මට කතා කරන්න ඕනේ.

Can I call someone?
kaah-tah hah-ri kah-thaah kah-rahn-nah mah-tah pu-lu-vahn-dhah? — කාට හරි කතා කරන්න මට පුළුවන්ද?

Can I have a lawyer who speaks English?
in-gree-si kah-thaah kah-rah-nah nee-theeg-gnah vah-rah-yek mah-tah gahn-nah pu-lu-vahn-dhah? — ඉංග්‍රීසි කතා කරන නීතිඥ වරයෙක් මට ගන්න පුළුවන්ද?

Is there a fine we can pay to clear this?
dhah-dhah mu-dhah-lahk ge-vah-lah ah-pah-tah meh-ken ni-dhah-hahs ven-nah pu-lu-vahn-dhah? — දඩ මුදලක් ගෙවල අපට මේකෙන් නිදහස් වෙන්න පුළුවන්ද?

I (don't) understand.
mah-tah theh-ren-neh (na-ha) — මට තේරෙන්නේ (නැහැ).

I know my rights.
mah-geh hi-mi-kahm ga-nah mah-mah dahn-nah-vaah — මගේ හිමිකම් ගැන මම දන්නවා.

What am I accused of?
mo-nah vah-rah-dhah-kah-tah-dhah mah-tah choh-dhah-naah kah-rahn-neh? — මොන වරදකටද මට චෝදනා කරන්නේ?

arrested	ahth ah-dan- gu-wah-tah gahth	අත් අඩංගුවට- ගත්
cell	si-rah koo-du-wah	සිර කුඩුව
consulate	kon-sahl kahn-thoh-ru-wah	කොන්සල් කන්තෝරුව
embassy	thaah-nah-pah-thi kahn-thoh-ru-wah	තානාපති කන්තෝරුව
fine (payment)	dhah-dah-yah	දඩය
guilty	vah-rah-dhah-kaah-rai	වරදකාරයි
lawyer	nee-theeg-gnah- vah-rah-yaah	නීතිඥවරයා
not guilty	nir-dhoh-shai	නිර්දෝෂයි
police officer	po-lis ni-lah-dhaah-ree	පොලිස් නිළධාරී
police station	po-lis sthaah-nah-yah	පොලිස් ස්ථානය
prison	si-rah ge-dhe-rah	සිර ගෙදර
trial	nah-dhu vi-bhaah-gah-yah	නඩු විභාගය
You'll/He'll/She'll be charged with ...	... ga-nah o-bah/ o-hu/a-yah choh-dhah-naah lah-bah-nu a-thah	... ගැන ඔබ/ඔහු/ඇය චෝදනා ලබනු ඇත.
anti-government activity	rah-jah-yah-tah- vi-rudh-dhah-vah kri-yaah ki-ree-mah	රජයට- විරුද්ධව ක්‍රියා කිරීම
assault	pah-hah-rah dhee-mah	පහර දීම
disturbing the peace	saah-mah-yah kah-dhah ki-ree-mah	සාමය කඩ කිරීම
possession (uf illegal substances)	(nee-thi vi-roh-dhee dheh) lahn-gah thah-baah ga-nee-mah	(නීති විරෝදි දේ) ළඟ තබා ගැනීම
illegal entry	nee-thyaah-nu-koo-lah no-voo pa-mi-nee-mah	නීත්‍යානුකූල නොවු පැමිණීම
laundering	ho-rah mu-dhal noht-tu gah-nu-dhe-nu-wah	හොර මුදල් නෝට්ටු ගනුදෙනුව
murder	mi-nee-ma-ru-mah	මිනීමැරුම

not having a visa	vee-saah e-kahk no-thi-bee-mah	වීසා එකක් නොතිබීම
overstaying your/his/her visa	o-bah-geh/o-hu-geh/ a-yah-geh vee-saah e-kah ik-mah-vaah si-tee-mah	ඔබගේ/ඔහුගේ/ ඇයගේ වීසා එක ඉක්මවා සිටීම
paedophilia	lah-maah ah-pah-chaah-rah	ළමා අපචාර
rape	dhoo-shah-nah-yah	දූෂණය
robbery/theft	so-rah-kah-mah	සොරකම
shoplifting	saahp-pu bah-du ho-ren ga-nee-mah	සාප්පු බඩු හොරෙන් ගැනීම
traffic violation	maahr-gah nee-thi kah-dah ki-ree-mah	මාර්ග නීති කඩ කිරීම
working without a permit	ah-vah-sah-rah-yahk na-thi-wah va-dah ki-ree-mah	අවසරයක් නැතිව වැඩ කිරීම

FOOD

ආහාර

Sri Lankan food is generally hot and spicy, but can be made less so (or even spiceless) on request. Modern Sri Lankan cuisine is largely vegan and vegetarian-friendly thanks to Hindu and Buddhist religious influences. Seafood is abundant, particularly along the coast, and Sri Lankans often like meat dishes such as chicken, beef and pork. Other popular cuisines include adaptations of Chinese, Indian and Western fusion.

BREAKFAST, LUNCH & DINNER

උදේ ආහාරය, දිවා ආහාරය සහ රාත්‍රී ආහාරය

Lunch is the main meal of the day and typically consists of rice and a meat or fish curry with one or two vegetables, a salad and/or a green leafy vegetable. Restaurants often sell vegetarian rice and curry meals, too.

At dinner, the family gets together for a sit-down meal followed by a chat. This may also be a rice and curry meal but people often choose common breakfast foods. Other dinner-time favourites include pasta, noodles and Western cuisine.

breakfast	u-dheh kaa-mah	උදේ කෑම
lunch	dhah-vahl kaa-mah	දවල් කෑම
dinner	raa kaa-mah	රෑ කෑම

BREAKFAST FOOD උදේ කෑමට ගන්නා දේ

Popular breakfast choices include:

hoppers aahp-pah ආප්ප
like a bowl-shaped pancake with crusty edges and a soft centre

kiribath ki-ri-bahth කිරිබත්
rice cooked in coconut milk, often cut into diamond-shaped portions

pittu	pit-tu	පිට්ටු

cylindrical cake of rice flour and grated coconut, steamed (usually in a bamboo mould)

roti	ro-tee	රොටී

doughy pancake that is fried without oil, often served wrapped around a variety of fillings

string hoppers	in-di aahp-pah	ඉඳි ආප්ප

noodle-like strands of dough, tangled up to form a flat circle

Other breakfast food includes:

boiled legumes/ yams	thahm-bah-pu a-tah/ ah-lah jaah-thi	තම්බපු ඇට/ අල ජාති
bread	paahn	පාන්
buns	bah-nis	බනිස්
rolls	rohls	රෝල්ස්

SHORT EATS ශෝට් ඊට්ස්

In Sri Lanka, snacks are called 'short eats,' an umbrella term used for both savoury and sweet snacks eaten between main meals.

biscuits/cookies	vis koh-thu	විස්කෝතු
cake	kehk	කේක්
cutlets (savouries)	kaht-lahs	කට්ලස්
patties	pa-tees	පැටීස්
rice cakes (deep-fried, sweet)	ka-vun	කැවුම්
muscat (sweet, made with ghee)	mahs-kaht	මස්කට්

EATING OUT

කඩෙන් කෑම

Table for (five), please.

kah-ru-naah-kah-rah-lah (pahs) dhe-ne-ku-tah meh-sah-yahk oh-neh	කරුණාකරල (පස්) දෙනෙකුට මේසයක් ඕනේ.

May we see the menu?
mo-noo e-kah bah-lahn-nah pu-lu-vahn-dhah? — මෙනු එක බලන්න පුළුවන්ද?

Could you recommend something?
mo-nah-vah-dhah hon-dhah — මොනවද හොඳ

I'll have what they're having.
eh ah-yah kah-nah dheh mah-mahth gahn-nahm — ඒ අය කන දේ මමත් ගන්නම්.

What's in that dish?
eh dhee-si-yeh mo-nah-vah-dhah thi-yen-neh? — ඒ දීසියේ මොනවද තියෙන්නේ?

Please bring some ...
kah-ru-naah-kah-rah-lah ... ti-kahk gehn-nah — කරුණාකරල ... ටිකක් ගේන්න.

Do I get it myself or do they bring it to us?
e-kah mah-mah ah-rah-ge-nah en-nah oh-ne-dhah, nath-nahm ah-pi lahn-gah-tah geh-nah-vaah-dhah? — ඒක මම අරගෙන එන්න ඕනේද, නැත්නම් අපි ළඟට ගේනවාද?

Please bring a/the ...	kah-ru-naah-kah-rah-lah ...gehn-nah	කරුණාකරල ... ගෙනෙන්න.
bill	bi-lah	බිල
fork	gaa-rahp-pu-vahk	ගෑරප්පුවක්
glass of water	vah-thu-rah vee-dhu-ru-vahk	වතුර වීදුරුවක්
with ice	ais ek-kah	අයිස් එක්ක
without ice	ais na-thu-vah	අයිස් නැතුව
knife	pi-hi-yahk	පිහියක්
plate	pi-gaah-nahk	පිඟානක්

No ice in my drink, please.
kah-ru-naah-kah-rah-lah mah-ghe bee-mah e-kah-tah ais dhah-mahn-nah e-paah — කරුණාකරල මගේ බීම එකට අයිස් දමන්න එපා.

Is service included in the bill?
seh-vaah gaahs-thu bi-lah-tah a-thu-lahth-dhah? — සේවා ගාස්තු බිලට ඇතුළත්ද?

I love this dish.
meh vaahn-jah-nah-yah-tah mah-mah hah-ri ka-mah-thiy — මේ ව්‍යාංජනයට මම හරි කැමතියි.

We love the local cuisine.
me-heh kaa-mah vah-lah-tah ah-pi hah-ri ka-mah-thiy — මෙහේ කෑම වලට අපි හරි කැමතියි.

That was delicious!
eh-kah hah-ri-mah rah-sai! — ඒක හරිම රසයි!

Our compliments to the chef.
shef-geh kaa-mah ni-yah-mahy — ෂෙෆ්ගේ කෑම නියමයි.

CELEBRATORY DISHES උත්සව ආහාර

kah-hah bahth කහ බත්
'yellow rice', as it is commonly known, is rice cooked in a spicy coconut milk broth with a pinch of saffron or turmeric

bah-tu moh-ju බටු මෝජු
fried eggplant, diced onion and green chillies cooked in a moderately sweet ground mustard vinaigrette

kah-ju kah-ri-yah කජු කරිය
cashew nuts cooked in a thick white coconut sauce

po-los kah-ri-yah පොලොස් කරිය
jackfruit cooked in a spicy coconut sauce

am-bul-thi-yahl ඇඹුල් තියල්
tuna braised in a gravy with go-rah-kaah (ගොරකා, an acidic fruit), which adds a tangy flavour

mahs ba-du-mah මස් බැදුම
sliced beef boiled in vinaigrette, shallow-fried and served with onion rings and slit green chillies in a broth

mahs kah-ri-yah මස් කරිය
diced meat (any type) in a rich, hot and spicy coconut sauce with lemongrass

ba-dhah-pu maah-lu බැදපු මාළු
deep-fried fish, particularly Spanish mackerel, served with a dash of fresh lime / lemon juice

VEGETARIAN & SPECIAL MEALS

එළවළුමය සහ විශේෂ කෑම

I'm vegetarian.

mah-mah e-lah-vah-lu
vi-thah-rai kahn-neh

මම එළවළු
විතරයි කන්නේ.

I don't eat meat.

mah-mah mahs kahn-neh na-ha

මම මස් කන්නේ නැහැ.

I can't eat dairy products.

mah-tah ki-ri vah-lin ha-doo
kaa-mah kahn-nah ba-ha

මට කිරි වලින් හැදූ
කෑම කන්න බැහැ.

I don't eat chicken, fish or ham.

mah-mah ku-kul mahs,
maah-lu, hoh ham
kahn-neh na-ha

මම කුකුල් මස්,
මාළු හෝ හැම්
කන්නේ නැහැ.

Do you have any vegetarian dishes?

e-lah-vah-lu kaa-mah mu-kuth
thi-yeh-dhah?

එළවළු කෑම මුකුත්
තියේද?

Does this dish contain eggs/meat?

meh-keh bith-thah-rah/mahs
thi-ye-nah-vaah-dhah?

මේකේ බිත්තර/මස්
තියෙනවාද?

Can I get this without meat?

meh-kah mahs na-thu-vah
mah-tah gahn-nah ba-ri-dhah?

මේක මස් නැතුව
මට ගන්න බැරිද?

I'm allergic to (peanuts).

mah-tah (rah-tah-kah-ju)
a-lah-jik

මට (රටකජු)
ඇලජික්.

☑ DON'T GO EMPTY-HANDED

When people visit each other in Sri Lanka, they take something along, eg, cake, biscuits or chocolate, or a gift for the child of the family – they never go empty-handed. Foreign visitiors should do the same.

SELF-CATERING

ස්වයං සේවා

IN THE DELICATESSEN හීතකළ මස් මාංශ ංලෙමු හළ

Deli products, including local varieties of cheese and butter, are usually available in supermarkets. Some pharmacies and grocery shops carry a limited range as well.

How much is (a kilo of cheese)?
(chees ki-loh e-kahk) kee-yah-dhah? — (චීස් කිලෝ එකක්) කීයද?

Do you have anything cheaper?
mee-tah vah-daah mi-lah ah-du yah-mahk thi-ye-nah-vaah-dhah? — මීට වඩා මිළ අඩු යමක් තියෙනවාද?

What's the local speciality?
me-heh vi-sheh-shah-yen hah-dhah-nah dheh mo-nah-vaah-dhah? — මෙහේ විශේෂයෙන් හදන දේ මොනවාද?

Can I taste it?
mah-mah rah-sah bah-lahn-nah-dhah? — මම රස බලන්නද?

Give me (half) a kilo please.
kah-ru-naah-kah-rah mah-tah ki-loh (baah-gah-yahk) dhen-nah — කරුණාකර මට කිලෝ (භාගයක්) දෙන්න.

I'd like (six slices of ham).
mah-tah (ham kaa-li hah-yahk) gahn-nah pu-lu-vahn-dhah? — මට (හැම් කෑලි) ගන්න පුළුවන්ද?

AT THE MARKET

මාකට් එකේදී

MEAT & POULTRY මස් සහ කුකුළු මස්

beef	hah-rahk mahs	හරක් මස්
chicken	ku-kul mahs	කුකුල් මස්
chop	mahs pe-thi	මස් පෙති
cured ham	pah-dahm kah-lah ham	පදම් කළ හැම්
elk meat	goh-nah mahs	ගෝන මස්
goat	e-lu mahs	එළු මස්
lamb	ba-tah-lu mahs	බැටළු මස්
meat	hah-rahk mahs	හරක් මස්
meatballs	meet-bohls	මීට් බෝල්ස්
pork	oo-ru mahs	ඌරු මස්
rabbit	haah mahs	හා මස්
sausage	lin-gus	ලිංගුස්
steak	ba-dhu-mah-tah mahs pe-thi	බැදුමට මස් පෙති
turkey	kah-lu-ku-maah	කලුකුමා
veal	vah-hu mahs	වහු මස්
venison	mu-wah mahs	මුව මස්
wild boar	vahl oo-ru mahs	වල් ඌරු මස්

SEAFOOD මුහුදු මත්ස්‍යයන්

clams	bel-laah	බෙල්ලා
fish	maah-lu	මාළු
lobster	po-ki-ris-saah	පොකිරිස්සා
mussels	math-ti-yaah	මට්ටියා
oysters	mu-thu bel-laah	මුතු බෙල්ලා
prawns	is-saah	ඉස්සා
shrimp	koo-nis-saah	කූනිස්සා

VEG OUT!

dhahm-bah-lah දඹල
dambala, frilled beans

go-tu-ko-lah ගොටුකොළ
gotu kola, leafy, similar to watercress

kahn-kun කන්කුන්
kankun, similar to watercress, but with long slim leaves

kah-thu-ru mu-run-gaah කතුරු මුරුංගා
katuru murunga, leafy vegetable

kah-thu-ru mu-run-gaah mahl කතුරු මුරුංගා මල්
katuru murunga mal, flower of katuru murunga

ko-hi-lah කොහිල
kohila, stringy root vegetable

ko-hi-lah dhah-lu කොහිල දළු
kohila, leaf of kotila dalu

mahn-gnok-kaah මන්නොක්කා
manioc, yam, similar to sweet potato

mu-ku-nu-wan-nah මුකුනුවැන්න
mukunuwenna, very similar to watercress

thahm-pah-laah තම්පලා
thampala, leafy vegetable, like spinach

VEGETABLES එළවළු

artichoke	ah-lu	අළු
	soo-ri-yah-kaahn-thah	සූරියකාන්ත
ash plantain	a-lu ke-sel	අළු කෙසෙල්
asparagus	as-pa-rah-gahs	එස්පැරගස්
aubergine	wahm-bah-tu	වම්බටු
(green) beans	bohn-chi	බෝංචි
	(ko-lah paah-tah)	(කොළ පාට)
beetroot	beet-root	බීට්රූට්
bitter gourd	kah-rah-wi-lah	කරවිල
breadfruit	dhel	දෙල්
butter beans	bah-tahr bohn-chi	බටර් බෝංචි
cabbage	goh-waah	ගෝවා

carrot	ka-raht	කැරට්
cauliflower	mahl goh-waah	මල් ගෝවා
celery	sal-dhi-ri	සැල්දිරි
cucumber	pi-pin-gnaah	පිපින්නා
drumsticks	mu-run-gaah	මුරුංගා
eggplant	wam-bah-tu	වම්බටු
leeks	leeks	ලීක්ස්
lettuce	sah-laah-dhah ko-lah	සලාද කොළ
long beans	maa-kah-tah	මෑකරල්
mushrooms	hah-thu	හතු
okra	bahn-dahk-kaah	බන්ඩක්කා
onion	loo-nu	ලූනු
peas	pees-a-tah	පීස් ඇට
(red/green) pepper	(rah-thu/ko-lah) maah-lu mi-ris	(රතු/කොළ) මාළු මිරිස්
potato	ah-lah	අල
snake gourd	pah-thoh-lah	පතෝල
spinach	ni-vi-thi	නිවිති
spring onion	loo-nu-ko-lah	ලූණුකොළ
sweet potato	bah-thah-lah	බතල
tomato	thahk-kaah-li	තක්කාලි
zucchini/courgette	su-kee-ni	සුකීනි

FRUIT පළතුරු

Tropical fruits are in abundance in Sri Lanka and are enjoyed by both locals and visitors.

apple	a-pahl	ඇපල්
avocado	ah-li-peh-rah	අලිපේර
banana	ke-sel	කෙසෙල්
coconut	pol	පොල්
grapes	mi-dhi	මිදි
lemon	dhe-hi	දෙහි
mango	am-bah	අඹ
mangosteen	man-gos-teen	මැන්ගොස්ටින්
melon	ko-mah-du	කොමඩු

orange	dho-dham	දොඩම්
pear	pe-yaahs	පෙයාස්
pineapple	an-naah-si	අන්නාසි
sapodilla	sa-pah-dhil-laah	සැපදිල්ලා
strawberry	straw-be-rees	ස්ට්‍රෝබෙරීස්
watermelon	pa-ni ko-mo-du	පැණි කොමඩු

NUTS ඇට වර්ග

almond	rah-tah kot-than	රට කොට්ටන්
blanched	sud-dah kah-rah, ka-abh-li vah-lah-tah	සුද්ධ කර, කැබලි වලට
raw	ah-mu	අමු
roasted	rohst kah-lah	රෝස්ට් කළ
cashew nut	kah-ju pu-hu-lahn	කජු පුහුලන්
peanut	rah-tah kah-ju	රට කජු

GOING BANANAS!

Don't go ape over the many varieties of banana in Sri Lanka:

aah-nah-maah-lu ආනමාළු
long, dark green and not very sweet

koh-li-kut-tu කෝලිකුට්ටු
short, fat and yellow

am-bun ඇම්බුන්
long, light green and not very sweet

see-ni සීනි
small, yellow and very sweet (most common)

rah-bahr රබර්
similar to see-ni, but rubbery

su-vahn-del සුවඳැල්
tiny and yellow, with medicinal properties

poo-vaah-lu පූවාලු
medium, yellow and not very sweet

am-bul ඇඹුල්
medium, yellow and sweet-sour

rath ke-hel රත් කෙහෙල්
red in colour, thick and not very sweet

PULSES ධාන්‍ය වර්ග

cereal	see-ri-yahl	සීරියල්
chickpeas	kah-dah-lah	කඩල
kidney beans	maa a-tah	මෑ ඇට
lentils	pah-rip-pu	පරිප්පු
lima beans	lee-mah bohn-chi	ලීමා බෝංචි
rice	haahl	හාල්

SPICES & CONDIMENTS කුළු බඩු සහ පිත්පත

chillies	mi-ris	මිරිස්
coriander	koth-thah-mahl-lee	කොත්තමල්ලි
cummin	soo-dhu-ru	සූදුරු
fennel	mah-hah-dhu-ru	මහදුරු
fenugreek	u-lu-haahl	උළුහාල්
garlic	su-dhu-loo-nu	සුදුළූණු
ginger	in-gu-ru	ඉඟුරු
salt	lu-nu	ලුනු

DRINKS

බීම වර්ග

NON-ALCOHOLIC DRINKS මද්‍යප බීම වර්ග

Sri Lankans are great tea-drinkers and are renowned for having many cups of tea throughout the day.

coffee	koh-pi	කෝපි
cocoa	ko-koh	කොකෝ
ginger beer	jin-jah bi-yah	ජින්ජර් බියර්
lemonade	le-mah-nehd	ලෙමනේඩ්
orange barley	or-rehn-j baah-li	ඔරේන්ජ් බාර්ලි
portello (fizzy drink)	poh-te-loh	පෝටෙලෝ

(cup of) tea	theh (kohp-pah-yahk)	තේ (කෝප්පයක්)
with/without milk	ki-ri ek-kah/ na-thu-wah	කිරි එක්ක/ නැතුව
with/without sugar	see-ni ek-kah/ na-thu-wah	සීනි එක්ක/ නැතුව

PLAIN TEA

At restaurants, you'll often see Sri Lankans order 'plain tea', which is black tea served without milk. 'Tea' often comes with milk.

water	wah-thu-rah	වතුර
boiled water	u-thu-raah-gahth wah-thu-rah	උතුරාගත් වතුර
mineral water	si-sil bee-mah	සිසිල් බීම

ALCOHOLIC DRINKS මද්‍යසාර බීම වර්ග

beer	bi-yahr	බියර්
brandy	bran-di	බ්‍රැන්ඩි
champagne	sham-pehn	ෂැම්පේන්
cocktail	kok-tehl	කොක්ටේල්
rum	rahm	රම්
toddy	raah	රා
whisky	wis-ki	විස්කි
a bottle/glass of ... wine	... wain boh-thah-lah-yahk/ vee-du-ru-wahk	... වයින් බෝතලයක්/ වීදුරුවක්
red	rah-thu	රතු
rose	rohs	රෝස්
sparkling	bu-bu-lu nahn-vah-nah	බුබුළු නංවන
sweet	pa-ni rah-sah	පැණි රස
white	su-dhu	සුදු
a ... of beer	bi-yahr ...	බියර් ...
small bottle	po-di boh-thah-lah-yahk	පොඩි බෝතලයක්
large bottle	lo-ku boh-thah-layahk	ලොකු බෝතලයක්
small glass	po-di vee-dhu-ru-wahk	පොඩි වීදුරුවක්
tall glass	u-sah vee-dhu-ru-vahhk	උස වීදුරුවක්
jug	jog-gu-waks	ජොග්ගුවක්
a shot of whisky	wis-ki ah-di-yahk	විස්කි අඩියක්

Dictionary

ENGLISH – SINHALA

Where there's more than one Sinhala entry for an English word, the alternatives are separated by a bullet:

difficult	ah-maah-ru • ah-pah-hah-su

Where two words are interchangeable, they're separated by a slash:

double bed (meaning either lo-ku an-dhah or dah-bahl an-dhah)	lo-ku/dah-bahl an-dhah

Masculine and feminine forms of the same word are also separated by a slash:

artist	chith-rah shil-pi-yek/ shil-pi-ni-yahk (m/f)

All verbs are listed in the present/future tense, which is the dictionary form in Sinhala, and are followed by '(v)'. Nouns are not indicated.

A

be able (can, v)	ha-ki ve-nah-vaah	හැකි වෙනවා
abortion	gab-saah-vah	ගබ්සාව
above	u-dah	උඩ
abroad	pi-tah-rah-tah	පිටරට
accept (v)	pi-li-gahn-nah-vaah	පිලිගන්නවා
accident	ah-nah-thu-rah	අනතුර
accommodation	i-dhum hi-tum	ඉදුම් හිටුම්
across	hah-rah-haah	හරහා
activist	kri-yaah-kaah-ri saah-maah-ji-kah-yah	ක්‍රියාකාරී සමාජිකයා
adaptor	a-dahp-tah-rah-yah	ඇඩප්ටරය
addiction	ah-ha-hi-vee-mah	ඇබ්බැහිවීම
address	li-pi-nah-yah	ලිපිනය
admission	a-thul-vee-mah	ඇතුල්වීම
adult	va-di-hi-ti	වැඩිහිටි
advantage	va-dah-dhaah-yee	වැඩදායි
advice	ah-vah-vaah-dhah	අවවාද
aeroplane	ah-hahs yaah-nah-yah	අහස් යානය
be afraid of (v)	bah-yah ve-nah-vaah	භය වෙනවා
after	pah-su-wah	පසුව

afternoon	dhah-vahl	දවල්
in the afternoon	dhah-vaah-leh (spoken language)	දවාලේ
again	na-vah-thah	නැවත
against	vi-rudh-dhah-vah	විරුද්ධව
age	vah-yah-sah	වයස
aggressive	kah-lah-hah-kaah-ree	කලහකාරී
(a while) ago	(kah-lah-kah-tah) u-dah-dhee	(කලකට) උඩදී
agree (v)	e-kahn-gah ve-nah-vaah	එකඟ වෙනවා
I don't agree.	mah-mah e-kahn-gah ven-neh na-ha	මම එකඟ වෙන්නේ නැහැ.
Agreed!	e-kahn-gai!	එකඟයි!
agriculture	kru-shi-kar-mah	කෘෂිකර්ම
ahead	kah-lin • is-sah-rah ve-laah	කලින් • ඉස්සර වෙලා
aid (help)	aah-dhaah-rah	ආධාර
AIDS	ehds roh-gah-yah	ඒඩ්ස් රෝගය
air	vaah-thah-yah	වාතය
air-conditioning	vaah-yu sah-mee-kah-rah-nah-yah kah-rah-nah lah-dhah	වායු සමීකරණය කරන ලද
air mail	gu-wahn tha-pal	ගුවන් තැපැල්
airport	gu-wahn tho-tu-pah-lah	ගුවන් තොටුපළ
alarm clock	ah-vah-dhi kah-rah-vah-nah o-rah-loh-su-wah	අවදි කරවන ඔරලෝසුව
all	si-yahl-lah • ok-ko-mah	සියල්ල • ඔක්කොම
allergy	a-lah-ji e-kahk • ah-saahth-mi-kah	ඇලජි එකක් • අසාත්මික
allow (v)	i-dah dhee-mah • ah-vah-sah-rah dhee-mah	ඉඩ දීම • අවසර දීම
It's not allowed.	ah-vah-sah-rah (na-ha)	අවසර (නැහැ).
almost	on-nah-men-nah	ඔන්න-මෙන්න
alone	thah-ni-vah	තනිව
already	dha-nah-tah-mahth	දැනටමත්
also	thah-vah-dhah	තවද
altitude	u-sah prah-maah-nah-yah	උස ප්‍රමාණය
always	sa-mah-vi-tah-mah	සැමවිටම
among	ah-thah-rah	අතර
ancient	aah-dhi-kaah-lee-nah / pu-raah-nah	ආදිකාලීන / පුරාණ
and	sah-hah	සහ
angry	thah-rah-hah • kehn-thi	තරහ • කේන්ති
animals	sah-thun	සතුන්
answer	pi-li-thu-rah	පිළිතුර
antibiotics	an-ti-bah-yah-tik	ඇන්ටිබයටික්

antique	i-pa-rah-ni	ඉපැරණි
antiseptic	vi-shah naah-shah-kah	විෂ නාශක
any	oh-naa-mah	ඕනෑම
appointment	dhi-nah yo-dhaah-gahth	දින යොදාගත්
archaeological	pu-raah-vahs-thu-kah	පුරාවස්තුක
architecture	gru-hah nir-maah-nah shil-pah-yah	ගෘහ නිර්මාණ ශිල්පය
argue (v)	vaah-dhah kah-rah-nah-vaah	වාද කරනවා
arm	baah-hu-wah	බාහුව
arrivals	pa-mi-neem	පැමිණීම්
arrive (v)	pa-mi-ne-nah-vaah	පැමිණෙනවා
art	kah-laah-wah	කලාව
art gallery	kah-laah bhah-vah-nah-yah	කලා භවනය
artist	chith-rah shil-pi-yek / shil-pi-ni-yahk (m/f)	චිත්‍ර ශිල්පියෙක් / ශිල්පිනියක්
ask (for something, v)	il-lah-nah-vah	ඉල්ලනවා
ask (a question, v)	ah-hah-nah-vah	අහනවා
aspirin	as-prin	ඇස්ප්‍රින්
atmosphere	vaah-thaah-vah-rah-nah-yah	වාතාවරණය
aunt	nan-dhaah • (father's sister)	නැන්දා •
	lo-ku ahm-maah • (mother's older sister)	ලොකු අම්මා •
	pun-chi ahm-maah • (mother's younger sister)	පුංචි අම්මා •
automatic teller (ATM)	eh-tee-em e-kah	ඒ.ටී.එම්. එක
autumn	sah-rahth ir-thu-wah	සරත් ඍතුව
awful	ahn-thi-mai	අන්තිමයි

B

baby	lah-dhah-ru-waah	ළදරුවා
baby food	lah-dhah-ru aah-haah-rah	ළදරු ආහාර
baby powder	lah-dhah-ru pu-yah-rah	ළදරු පුයර
babysitter	lah-mun bah-laah gahn-naah ah-yah	ළමුන් බලා ගන්නා අය
back (body)	pi-tah	පිට
at the back (behind)	pi-tu-pah-sah	පිටුපස
backpack	bak-pak e-kah	බැක්පැක් එක
bad	nah-rah-kah	නරක
bag	baag e-kah	බෑග් එක
baggage	bah-du mah-lu	බඩු මළු
baggage claim	bah-du mah-lu bhaah-rah ga-nee-mah	බඩු මළු භාර ගැනීම
bakery	beh-kah-ri-yah	බේකරිය
balcony	sah-dhah-lu-thah-lah-yah	සඳළුතලය
ball (game)	boh-lah-yah	බෝලය
ball (dance)	baahl na-tu-mah	බාල් නැටුම

ballet	nruth-thyah • rahn-gah-nah	නෘත්‍ය • රංගන
band (music)	vaah-dhah-kah mahn-dah-lah-yah • baand e-kah	වාදක මණ්ඩලය • බෑන්ඩ් එක
bandage	ve-lum pah-ti • ban-dehj e-kah	වෙළුම් පටි • බැන්ඩේජ් එක
bank	ban-ku-wah	බැංකුව
baptism	bau-thees-mah	බෞතීස්ම
basket	koo-dah-yah	කූඩය
bath	naa-mah	නෑම
bathroom	naah-nah kaah-mah-rah-yah	නාන කාමරය
battery	ba-tah-ri-yah	බැටරිය
beach	mu-hu-dhu ve-rah-lah	මුහුදු වෙරළ
beautiful	lahs-sah-nah	ලස්සණ
because	ni-saah	නිසා
bed	an-dhah	ඇඳ
bedroom	ni-dhah-nah kaah-mah-rah-yah	නිදන කාමරය
before	kah-lin	කලින්
beggar	si-gahn-naah	සිගන්නා
begin	pah-tahn gahn-nah	පටන් ගන්න
behind	pah-su-pah-sah	පසුපස
below	yah-tah	යට
beside	ai-neh	අයිනේ
best	i-thaah-mahth hon-dhah	ඉතාමත් හොඳ
bet	ot-tu-wah	ඔට්ටුව
better	i-thaah hon-dah	ඉතා හොඳ
between	ah-thah-rah-thu-rah	අතරතුර
bicycle	bai-si-kah-lah-yah	බයිසිකලය
big	lo-ku	ලොකු
bill (account)	bi-lah	බිල
binoculars	dhoo-rah-dhahr-shah kahn-naah-di-yah	දුරදර්ශ කන්නාඩිය
biodegradable	jee-vah naah-shah-kah	ජීව නාශක
bird	ku-rul-laah	කුරුල්ලා
birthday	u-pahn dhi-nah-yah	උපන් දිනය
bite (dog)	sah-paah kaa-mah	සපා කෑම
bite (insect)	vi-dhee-mah (kroo-mi)	විදීම (කෘමි)
black	kah-lu	කළු
blanket	blan-kaht-tu-vah	බ්ලැන්කට්ටුව
bless (v)	aah-sheer-vaah-dhah kah-rah-nah-vaah	ආශීර්වාද කරනවා

Bless you! (when sneezing)	dhe-vi pi-hi-tai!	දෙවි පිහිටයි!

blind	ahn-dhah	අන්ධ
blood	leh	ලේ
blood group	leh kaahn-dah-yah	ලේ කාණ්ඩය
blood pressure	ru-dhi-rah pee-dah-nah-yah	රුදිර පීඩනය
blood test	leh pah-reek-shah-nah-yah	ලේ පරීක්ෂණය
blue	nil	නිල්
board (ship, etc, v)	na-gee-mah	නැගීම
boarding pass	boh-din paahs e-kah	බෝඩිං පාස් එක
boat	boht-tu-wah	බෝට්ටුව
body	an-gah	ඇඟ
Bon voyage!	su-bhah gah-mahn!	සුබ ගමන්!
bone	kah-tu-wah	කටුව
book (n)	po-thah	පොත
book (v)	kah-lin ven kah-rah-vaah gahn-nah-vaah	කලින් වෙන් කරවා ගන්නවා
bookshop	poth saahp-pu-wah	පොත් සාප්පුව
boots	boot sah-path-thu	බූට් සපත්තු
bored	kaahn-si-yah	කාන්සිය
boring	kaahn-si-mahth	කාන්සිමත්
borrow (v)	nah-yah-tah gahn-nah-vaah	ණයට ගන්නවා
both (inanimate)	dhe-kah-mah	දෙකම
both (animate)	dhen-nah-mah	දෙන්නම
bottle	boh-thah-lah-yah	බෝතලය
bottle opener	boh-thahl ari-nah-yah	බෝතල් අරිනය
(at the) bottom	yah-tah	යට
box	pet-ti-yah	පෙට්ටිය
boy	pi-ri-mi lah-mah-yaah	පිරිමි ළමයා
boyfriend	pem-wah-thaah	පෙම්වතා
brave	nir-bhee-thah	නිර්භීත
bread	paahn	පාන්
break (v)	kah-dah-nah-vaah	කඩනවා
breakfast	u-dheh kaa-mah	උදේ කෑම
breathe (v)	hus-mah gahn-nah-vaah	හුස්ම ගන්නවා
bribe	ahl-lah-sah	අල්ලස
bridge	paah-lah-mah	පාලම
brilliant	is-thah-rahm	ඉස්තරම්
bring (v)	go-ne-nah-vaah	ගෙනෙනවා
broken	ka-du-nu	කැඩුණු
brother	ai-yaah (older) mahl-lee (younger) so-ho-yu-raah (refers to either)	අයියා මල්ලී සොහොයුරා
brown	dhum-bu-ru paah-tah	දුඹුරු පාට
bruise	see-ree-mah	සීරීම
bucket	pah-nit-tu-wah	පනිට්ටුව
building	go-dah-na-gil-lah	ගොඩනැගිල්ල

bus (city)	bahs e-kah	බස් එක
bus (intercity)	nah-gah-rah ahn-thah-rah bahs e-kah	නගර අන්තර බස් එක
bus stop	bahs staand e-kah • bahs na-vah-thum po-la	බස් ස්ටෑන්ඩ් එක • බස් නැවතුම් පොළ
business	vyaah-paah-rah-yah	ව්‍යාපාරය
businessperson	paah-ri-kah-yek / vyaah-paah-ri-kaah-vak (m / f)	ව්‍යාපාරිකයෙක් / ව්‍යාපාරිකාවක්
busy	va-dah ah-di-kah	වැඩ අදික
but	nah-muth	නමුත්
butterfly	sah-mah-nah-lah-yaah	සමනළයා
button	both-thah-mah	බොත්තම
buy (v)	gahn-nah-vaah	ගන්නවා

I'd like to buy ...	mah-tah ... gahn-nah ka-mah-thiy	මට ... ගන්න කැමතියි.
Where can I buy a ticket?	mah-mah ti-kaht e-kahk gahn-neh ko-hen-dhah?	මම ටිකට් එකක් ගන්නේ කොහෙන්ද?

C

cafe	ka-feh e-kah	කැෆේ එක
calendar	ka-lahn-da-rah-yah	කැලැන්ඩරය
camera	ka-mah-raah-vah	කැමරාව
camera shop	ka-mah-raah saahp-pu-wah / shop e-kah	කැමරා සාප්පුව / ෂොප් එක
can (be able, v**)**	ha-ki ve-nah-vaah / pu-lu-vahn (spoken)	හැකි වෙනවා / පුළුවන්
can (aluminium)	tin	ටින්
can opener	tin ah-ri-nah e-kah	ටින් අරින එක
cancel (v)	ah-vah-lahn-gu kah-rah-nah-vaah	අවලංගු කරනවා
candle	i-ti-pahn-dhah-mah	ඉටිපන්දම
car	kaahr e-kah	කාර් එක
cards	kaahd	කාඩ්
care (about, v**)**	sa-lah-ki-li-mahth ve-nah-vaah	සැලකිලිමත් වෙනවා
care (for someone, v**)**	bah-laah gahn-nah-vaah	බලා ගන්නවා

Careful!	prah-veh-sah-min!	ප්‍රවේසමින්!

carry (v)	o-sah-vah-nah-vaah	ඔසවනවා
cashier	ah-yah-ka-mi-yaah	අයකැමියා
cat	bah-lah-laah	බළලා
cathedral	dhev ma-dhu-rah	දෙව් මැදුර
cave	gu-haah-wah	ගුහාව
celebrate (v)	uth-sah-vah pah-vahth vah-nah-vaah	උත්සව පවත්වනවා

centimetre	sen-ti-mee-tah-rah-yah	සෙන්ටිමීටරය
chair	pu-tu-wah	පුටුව
championships	shoo-rah-taah	ශූරතා
chance	vaah-rah-yah	වාරය
change (v)	ve-nahs kah-rah-nah-vaah	වෙනස් කරනවා
change (coins)	maah-ru sahl-li	මාරු සල්ලි
chat up (v)	kah-thaah-vah-tah mu-lah pu-rah-nah-vaah	කතාවට මුල පුරනවා
cheap	laah-bah	ලාභ
Cheat!	vahn-chaah-kaah-rah-yaah!	වංචාකාරයා!
check-in (desk)	vaahr-thaah ki-ree-mah	වාර්තා කිරීම
cheese	chees	චීස්
chemist	au-shah-dah-veh-dhee	ඖෂධවේදී
chess	ches kree-daah-vah	චෙස් ක්‍රීඩාව
chest	pa-pu-wah	පපුව
chewing gum	chu-wing gahm	චුවිං ගම්
chicken (meat)	ku-kul mahs	කුකුළු මස්
child	lah-mah-yaah	ළමයා
childminding	lah-mun bah-laah ga-nee-mah	ළමුන් බලා ගැනීම
children	lah-mah-yin	ළමයින්
chocolate	cho-co-laht	චොක්ලට්
choose (v)	thoh-rah-nah-vaah	තෝරනවා
Christmas Day	nahth-thahl dhi-nah	නත්තල් දින
Christmas Eve	nahth-thahl dhi-nah-tah pe-rah di-nah	නත්තල් දිනට පෙර දින
church	pahl-li-yah	පල්ලිය
cigarette papers	si-gah-raht ko-lah	සිගරට් කොළ
cigarettes	si-gah-raht	සිගරට්
cinema	si-ni-maah-wah	සිනමාව
citizenship	pu-rah-va-si bhaah-vah-yah	පුරවැසි භාවය
city/city centre	nah-gah-rah-yah	නගරය
clean	pi-ri-si-dhu	පිරිසිදු
cleaning	pi-ri-si-dhu ki-ree-mah	පිරිසිදු කිරීම
client	seh-vaah-dhaah-yah-kah-yaah	සේවාදායකයා
cliff	kahn-dhu prah-paah-thah-yah	කඳු ප්‍රපාතය
climb (v)	nah-gi-nah-vaah	නගිනවා
cloakroom	kah-baah kaah-mah-rah-yah	කබා කාමරය
clock	o-rah-loh-su-wah	ඔරලෝසුව
close (v)	va-hah-nah-vaah	වහනවා
closed	vah-saah a-thah	වසා ඇත
clothing	an-dum	ඇඳුම්

clothing store	an-dum saahp-pu-wah	ඇඳුම් සාප්පුව
cloudy	vah-laah-ku-lu sah-hi-thai	වලාකුළු සහිතයි
coast	mu-hu-dhu-bah-dah	මුහුදුබඩ
coat	kah-baah-yah	කබාය
coins	kaah-si	කාසි
cold	hem-bi-ris-saah-wah	හෙම්බිරිස්සාව
cold (adj)	see-tha-la	සීතල
It's cold.	see-tha-lai	සීතලයි.
cold water	al wha-thu-rah	ඇල් වතුර
colleague	ko-leh-j e-kah	කොලේජ් එක
college	paah-tah-shaah-laah-wah	පාටශාලාව
colour	paah-tah	පාට
comb	pah-naah-wah	පනාව
come (v)	e-nah-vaah	එනවා
comedy	vi-kah-tah	විකට
comfortable	su-wah-dhaah-yah-kai	සුවදායකයි
communion	sam-bahn-dhah-kah-mah • sath-pra-saah-dhah	සම්බන්ධකම • සත්ප්‍රසාද
communist	ko-mu-nis vaah-dhi-yaah	කොමයුනිස් වාදියා
companion	sah-gah-yaah • sah-hah-chah-rah-yaah	සගයා • සහචරයා
company	sah-maah-gah-mah	සමාගම
compass	maah-li-maah yahn-thrah-yah	මාලිමා යන්ත්‍රය
computer	pah-ri-ghah-nah-kah-yah	පරිගනකය
concert	ran-gah dhak-mahk	රග දැක්මක්
confession	paah-poch-chaah-rah-nah-yah (religious)	පාපෝච්චාරණය
confirm (v)	thah-hah-vu ru (a booking)	තහවුරු කරනවා
Congratulations!	su-bhah aah-shin-sah-nah!	සුභ ආශිංසන!
conservative	gah-thaah-nu-gah-thi-kah	ගතානුගතික
be constipated (v)	bah-dah veh-lah-nah-vaah	බඩ වේලනවා
consulate	kon-sahl vah-rah-yaah	කොන්සල් වරයා
contact lenses	kon-tak lens	කොන්ටැක් ලෙන්ස්
contraceptives	pi-li-si-dhee-mah va-lak-vee-meh dheh-vahl • gab ga-nee-mah va-lak-vee-meh u-pahk-krah-mah	පිලිසිදීම වැළැක්වීමේ දේවල් • ගැබ් ගැනීම වැළැක්වීමේ උපක්‍රම
convent	kahn-yaah-raah-mah-yah	කන්‍යාරාමය
cook (v)	u-yah-nah-vaah	උයනවා
cool (colloquial)	shohk	ෂෝක්
corner	ko-nah	කොණ

corrupt	dhoo-shi-thah	දූෂිත
cost (v)	va-yah ve-nah-vaah	වැය වෙනවා
How much does it cost to go to ...?	...-tah yahn-nah kee-yahk vei-dhah?	...ට යන්න කීයක් ගන්නවාද?
cotton	kah-pu	කපු
country	rah-tah	රට
countryside	gahm-bah-dhah	ගම්බද
cough (n)	kas-sah	කැස්ස
count (v)	gah-nahn kah-rah-nah-vaah	ගණන් කරනවා
cow	e-lah-dhe-nah	එළදෙන
crazy	un-mahth-thah	උන්මත්ත
credit card	kre-dit kaahd e-kah	ක්‍රෙඩිට් කාඩ් එක
Can I pay by credit card?	kre-dit kaahd e-kehn ge-vahn-nah pu-lu-vahn-dhah?	ක්‍රෙඩිට් කාඩ් එකෙන් ගෙවන්න පුළුවන්ද?
cricket	kri-kaht	ක්‍රිකට්
cross (religious)	ku-ru-sah-yah	කුරුසය
cup	kohp-pah-yah	කෝප්පය
cupboard	kah-bahd e-kah • al-maah-ri-yah	කබඩ් එක • අල්මාරිය
customs (traditions)	chaah-rith-rah	චාරිත්‍ර
customs (airport)	reh-gu-wah	රේගුව
cut (v)	kah-pah-nah-vaah	කපනවා
cycle (v)	bai-si-kahl pa-dhee-mah	බයිසිකල් පැදීම
cyclist	bai-si-kahl kah-ru	බයිසිකල් කරු

D

dad	thaahth-thaah • pi-yaah	තාත්තා • පියා
daily	saa-mah-dhaah-mah	සැමදාම
dairy products	ki-ri aah-haah-rah	කිරි ආහාර
dance (v)	nah-tah-nah-vaah	නටනවා
dangerous	ahn-thah-raah-dhaah-yee	අන්තරාදායී
dark	kah-lu-wah-rah	කළුවර
date	dhah-vah-sah • dhi-nah-yah	දවස • දිනය
date (someone, v)	aah-dhah-rah hah-mu-wah	ආදර හමුව
date of birth	u-pahn dhi-nah-yah	උපන් දිනය
daughter	dhu-wah	දුව
dawn	ah-lu-yah-mah	අළුයම
day	dhah-vah-sah	දවස
day after tomorrow	ah-nidh-dhaah	අනිද්දා
day before yesterday	pe-reh-dhaah	පෙරේදා
dead	ma-ri-lah • mi-yah gos	මැරිල • මිය ගොස්
deaf	bi-hi-ri	බිහිරි

death	mah-rah-nah-yah	මරණය
decide (v)	thee-rah-nah-yah kah-rah-nah-vaah	තීරණය කරනවා
deep	gam-bu-ru	ගැඹුරු
deer	mu-waah	මුවා
deforestation	ka-laa vahn-dhah ki-ree-mah	කැලෑ වඳ කිරීම
delay	prah-maah-dhah-yah	ප්‍රමාදය
delicatessen	see-thah kah-lah mahs mahn-shah ah-le-vi hah-lah	සීත කල මස් මාංශ අලෙවි හළ
democracy	prah-jaah-thahn-thrah-vaah-dhah-yah	ප්‍රජාතන්ත්‍රවාදය
demonstration (protest)	pe-lah-paah-li-yah	පෙළපාලිය
dentist	dhahn-thah vai-dhyah-vah-rah-yaah • dhahth dhos-thah-rah	දන්ත වෛද්‍යවරයා • දත් දොස්තර
deny (something, v)	pi-li no-gahn-nah-vaah	පිලි නොගන්නවා
deodorant	di-yod-rahnt e-kah	ඩියොඩ්රන්ට් එක
depart (leave, v)	yah-nah-vaah	යනවා
departure	ba-ha-rah-wah yaa-mah	බැහැරව යෑම
desert	tha-ni-kah-rah yaa-mah	තනිකර යෑම
destination	gah-mah-naahn-thah-yah	ගමනාන්තය
destroy (v)	vi-naah-shah kah-rah-nah-vaah	විනාශ කරනවා
diabetic	dhi-yah-va-di-yaah roh-gee	දියවැඩියා රෝගී
dial tone	dah-yahl tohn e-kah	ඩයල් ටෝන් එක
diaper (nappy)	na-pi-yah	නැපිය
diarrhoea	paah-chah-nah-yah	පාචනය
diary	dhi-nah po-thah	දින පොත
dictionary	shahb-dhah-koh-shah-yah	ශබ්දකෝෂය
die (v)	ma-re-nah-vah	මැරෙනවා
different	ve-nahs	වෙනස්
difficult	ah-maah-ru • ah-pah-hah-su	අමාරු • අපහසු
dining car	aah-pah-nah rah-thah-yah	ආපන රතය
dinner	raa kaa-mah	රෑ කෑම
direct	ke-lin	කෙලින්
dirty	ki-li-ti	කිලිටි
disabled	aah-baah-dhi-thah	ආබාදිත
disadvantage	ah-vaah-si	අවාසි
discount	vaht-tah-mah	වට්ටම
discover (v)	so-yaah gahn-nah-vaah	සොයා ගන්නවා
discrimination	ve-nahs-kahm ki-ree-mah	වෙනස්කම් කිරීම
disease	roh-gah-yah	රෝගය
diving	ki-mi-dhee-mah	කිමිදීම

dizzy	ka-rah-kil-lah	කැරකිල්ල
do (v)	kah-rah-nah-vaah	කරනවා
What are you doing?	o-bah mo-kah-dhah kah-rahn-neh?	ඔබ මොකද කරන්නේ?
I didn't do it.	mah-mah eh-kah ke-ru-weh na-ha	මම ඒක කෙරුවේ නැහැ.
doctor	dhos-thah-rah • vai-dhyah-vah-rah-yek / vai-dhyah-vah-ri-yahk (m/f)	දොස්තර • වෛද්‍යවරයෙක් / වෛද්‍යවරියක්
documentary	vaahr-thaah-mah-yah	වාර්තාමය
dog	bahl-laah	බල්ලා
doll	boh-nik-kaah	බෝනික්කා
door	dho-rah	දොර
dope (drugs)	mahth dhrahv-yah	මත් ද්‍රව්‍ය
double	dhe-kah dhe-kah	දෙක දෙක
double bed	lo-ku / dah-bahl an-dhah	ලොකු / ඩබල් ඇඳ
double room	lo-ku kaah-mah-rah-yah	ලොකු කාමරය
dozen	dhu-si-mah	දුසිම
drama	naaht-tya-yah	නාට්‍යය
dramatic	naaht-tya-yah-kaah-rah	නාට්‍යකාර
dream (v)	si-hi-nah dhah-ki-nah-vaah	සිහින දකිනවා
dress	an-dhu-mah	ඇඳුම
drink	bee-mahk	බීමක්
drink (v)	bo-nah-vaah	බොනවා
drive (v)	pah-dhah-vah-nah-vaah	පදවනවා
driver's licence	ri-yah-dhu-ru bah-lah-pahth-rah-yah • lai-sahn e-kah	රියදුරු බලපත්‍රය • ලයිසන් එක
drugs	mahth-dhrah-vyah	මත්ද්‍රව්‍ය
drums (instrument)	be-rah	බෙර
dummy (baby's)	soop-pu-wah	සූප්පුව

E

each	e-kah-e-kah	එක-එක
ear	kah-nah	කණ
early	veh-laah-sah-nin	වේලාසනින්
earn (v)	u pah-yah-nah-vaah • hahm-bah kah-rah-nah-vaah	උපයනවා • හම්බ කරනවා
earrings	kah-raah-bu	කරාබු
Earth	loh-kah-yah	ලෝකය
earthquake	bhoo-mi kahm-paah-wah	භූමි කම්පාව
east	na-ge-nah-hi-rah	නැගෙනහිර
Easter	paahs-ku	පාස්කු

easy	leh-si • pah-hah-su	ලේසි • පහසු
eat (v)	kah-nah-vaah	කනවා
economy	aahr-thi-kah-yah	ආර්ථිකය
education	ahdh-yaah-pah-nah-yah	අධ්‍යාපනය
elections	ma-thi-vah-rah-nah	මැතිවරණ
electricity	vi-dhu-li-bah-lah-yah	විදුලිබලය
elephant	ah-li-yaah	අලියා
elevator	e-lah-veh-tah e-kah	එලවේට එක
embarrassed	vik-ship-thah vee-mah • lahj-jaah vee-mah (spoken)	වික්ෂිප්ත වීම • ලජ්ජා වීම
embassy	thaah-naah-pah-thi kaar-yaah-lah-yah	තානාපති කාර්යාලය
emergency	hah-dis-si-yahk • hah-di-si ah-vahs-thaah-vah	හදිස්සියක් • හදිසි අවස්ථාව
employee	seh-vah-kah-yaah	සේවකයා
employer	seh-vaah yoh-jah-kah-yaah	සේවා යෝජකයා
empty	his	හිස්
end	ahn-thi-mah • ah-vah-saah-nah-yah	අන්තිම • අවසානය
engagement	raah-jah-kaahr-yaah-yahk (professional / work) • vi-vaah-hah gi-vi-sah ga-nee-mah (romantic)	රාජකාර්යයක් • විවාහ ගිවිස ගැනීම
engine	en-ji-mah	එන්ජිම
engineering	in-ji-neh-ru	ඉන්ජිනේරු
English	in-gree-si	ඉංග්‍රීසි
enjoy (oneself, v)	vi-noh-dhah ve-nah-vaah	විනෝද වෙනවා
enough	a-thi	ඇති
enter (v)	a-thul ve-nah-vaah	ඇතුල්වෙනවා
entertaining	vi-noh-dhah	විනෝද
envelope	li-yum kah-vah-rah-yah	ලියුම් කවරය
environment	pah-ri-sah-rah-yah	පරිසරය
equality	sah-maah-nahth-mah- thaah-vah-yah	සමානාත්මතාවය
euthanasia	ah-naah-yaah-sah mah-rah-nah-yah	අනායාස මරණය
evening	han-dhaa-vah	හැන්දෑව
every day	sa-mah-dhaah-mah	සැමදාම
example	u-dhaah-hah-rah-nah-yah	උදාහරණය
excellent	bo-hoh-mah hon-dhai • vi-shish-tai	බොහොම හොඳයි • විශිෂ්ඨයි
exchange (v)	hu-wah-maah-ru kah-rah-nah-vaah	හුවමාරු කරනවා
exchange rate	vi-dheh-shah vi-ni-mah-yah gaahs-thu	විදේශ විනිමය ගාස්තු
excluded	i-vahth ko-tah	ඉවත් කොට

Excuse me.	mah-tah sah-maah-vahn-nah	මට සමාවන්න.
exhibition	prah-dhar-shah-nah-yah	ප්‍රදර්ශනය
exit	pi-tah-vee-mah	පිටවීම
expensive	va-di mi-lah	වැඩි මිළ
exploitation	soo-rah kaa-mah	සූරා කෑම
express	see-grah-gaah-mi	ශීඝ්‍රගාමී
eye	a-ha	ඇහැ

F

face	mu-hu-nah	මුහුණ
factory	kahm-hah-lah	කම්හල
family	pah-vu-lah	පවුල
famous	prah-sidh-dhah	ප්‍රසිද්ධ
fan (hand-held)	ah-vaah-nah	අවාන
fan (machine)	pah-vahn-kaah-wah • faan e-kah	පවන්කාව • ෆෑන් එක
fan (of a team)	kree-daah loh-lah-yaah	ක්‍රීඩා ලෝලයා
far	dhu-rah	දුර
farm	go-vi-pah-lah	ගොවිපළ
farmer	go-vi-yek/ go-vi kaahn-thaah-vahk (m/f)	ගොවියෙක්/ ගොවි කාන්තාවක්
fast	ik-mah-nin	ඉක්මණින්
fat	mah-hah-thah	මහත
father	thaath-thaah	තාත්තා
father-in-law	maah-maah	මාමා
fault (someone's)	vah-rah-dhah	වරද
fear	bhah-yah • bhi-yah	භය • බිය
feel (v)	dha-ne-nah-vaah	දැනෙනවා
feelings	han-geem	හැඟීම්
fence	va-tah	වැට
festival	uth-sah-vah-yah	උත්සවය
fever	u-nah	උණ
few	sah-mah-hah-rehk	සමහරෙක්
fiance	pem-wah-thaah	පෙම්වතා
fiancee	pem-wah-thi-yah	පෙම්වතිය
fiction	mith-yah kah-thaah-vah	මිත්‍යා කතාව
field (rice paddy)	kum-bu-rah	කුඹුර
fight (v)	rahn-du • kah-lah-hah kah-rah-nah-vaah	රණ්ඩු • කලහ කරනවා
fill (v)	pu-rah-vah-nah-vaah	පුරවනවා
film (cinema)	chith-rah-pah-ti-yah	චිත්‍රපටිය
find (v)	so-yaah gahn-nah-vaah	සොයා ගන්නවා
fine (penalty)	dhah-dah-yah	දඩය
finger	an-gil-lah	ඇඟිල්ල

fire	gin-dhah-rah	ගින්දර
first	pah-lah-mu-wah-nah	පළමුව
first-aid kit	prah-thah-maah-dhaah-rah kaht-tah-lah-yah	ප්‍රථමාධාර කට්ටලය
fish	maah-lu	මාළු
flag	ko-di-yah	කොඩිය
flat (land, etc)	sah-mah-thah-laah	සමතලා
flea	mak-kaah	මැක්කා
flashlight (torch)	flash lait e-kah	ෆ්ලෑෂ් ලයිට් එක
flight	flait e-kah • gu-wahn gah-mah-nah	ෆ්ලයිට් එක • ගුවන් ගමන
floor (ground)	po-lo-wah	පොළව
floor (storey)	mah-hah-lah	මහල
flour	pi-ti	පිටි
flower	mah-lah	මල
fly	mas-saah	මැස්සා
It's foggy.	mee dhum sah-hi-thai	මී දුම් සහිතයි.
follow (v)	anu-gah-mah-nah-yah kah-rah-nah-vaah	අනුගමනය කරනවා
food	kaa-mah • aah-haah-rah	කෑම • ආහාර
foot	kah-ku-lah	කකුළ
football (soccer)	paah-pahn-dhu	පාපන්දු
footpath	ah-di-paah-rah	අඩිපාර
foreign	vi-dheh-shee-yah	විදේශීය
forest	ka-lah-yah	කැලය
forever	sah-dhaah-kaah-li-kah-vah	සදාකාලිකව
forget (v)	ah-mah-thah-kah kah-rah-nah-vah	අමතක කරනවා
I forget.	mah-tah ah-mah-thah-kah ve-nah-vaah	මට අමතක වෙනවා.
Forget about it! (don't worry)	eh-kah ah-mah-thah-kah kah-rah-nah!	ඒක අමතක කරන්න!
forgive (v)	sah-maah-vah dhe-nah-vaah	සමාව දෙනවා
fortnight	dhe-sah-thi-yah-kah-tah vah-rahk • sah-thi dhe-kah-tah vah-rahk	දෙසතියකට වරක් • සති දෙකකට වරක්
free (not bound)	ni-dhah-hahs	නිදහස්
free (of charge)	no-mi-lah-yeh	නොමිළයේ
fresh	ah-luth	අළුත්
Friday	si-ku-raah-dhaah	සිකුරාදා
friend	yah-hah-lu-waah (spoken) • mi-thu-raah	යහළුවා • මිතුරා

frozen foods	shee-thah kah-lah aah-haah-rah	ශීත කළ ආහාර
fruit picking	pah-lah-thu-ru ka-dee-mah	පළතුරු කැඩීම
full	pi-ri-lah	පිරිලා
fun	vi-noh-dhah-yah	විනෝදය
have fun (v)	vi-noh-dhah ve-nah-vaah	විනෝද වෙනවා
funeral	mah-rah-nah-yah	මරණය
future	ah-naah-gah-thah-yah	අනාගතය

G

game	sel-lahm	සෙල්ලම්
game (sport)	kree-daa-vah	ක්‍රීඩාව
garage	gah-raah-jah-yah	ගරාජය
garbage	kah-sah-lah	කසළ
gardening	vah-thu va-dah	වතු වැඩ
garden	(mahl-)vahth-thaah	(මල්)වත්ත
gas cartridge	gaas un-dah-yah	ගෑස් උණ්ඩය
gate	geht-tu-wah	ගේට්ටුව
gay	sah-mah-lin-gi-kah	සමලිංගික
general	saah-maahn-yah	සාමාන්‍ය
Get lost!	pah-lah-yahn yahn-nah!	පලයන් යන්න!
gift	thaag-gah	තෑග්ග
girl	ga-ha-nu lah-mah-yaah	ගැහැණු ළමයා
girlfriend	yah-hah-lu ga-ha-nu lah-mah-yaah • pem-wah-thi-yah	යහළු ගැහැණු ළමයා • පෙම්වතිය
give (v)	dhe-nah-vah	දෙනවා
Could you give me ...?	mah-tah ... dhen-nah pu-lu-vahn-dhah?	මට ... දෙන්න පුළුවන්ද?
glass	vee-dhu-ru-vah	වීදුරුව
go (v)	yah-nah-vah	යනවා
Let's go.	yah-mu	යමු.
goal	dhi-num sthaah-nah-yah • gohl e-kah	දිනුම් ස්ථානය • ගෝල් එක
goat	e-lu-waah	එළුවා
God	dhe-vi-yahn	දෙවියන්
gold	rath-rahn	රත්රන්

Good afternoon.	su-bhah dhah-hah-vah-lahk	සුභ දහවලක්.
Good evening/night.	su-bhah san-dhaa-vahk/ raahth-ri-yahk	සුභ සැන්දෑවක්/ රාත්‍රියක්.
Good luck!	vaah-sah-naah-vahn!	වාසනාවන්!
Good morning.	su-bhah u-dhaa-sah-nahk	සුභ උදෑසනක්.
Goodbye.	aah-yu-boh-vahn	ආයුබෝවන්.

government	rah-jah-yah	රජය
gram (weight)	graam e-kah	ග්‍රෑම් එක
gram (pulse)	kah-dah-lah	කඩල
grandchild	mu-nu-pu-raah (m) • mi-ni-pi-ri-yah (f)	මුනුපුරා • මිනිපිරිය
grandfather	see-yaah	සීයා
grandmother	aahch-chee	ආච්චි
grapes	mi-di	මිදි
grass	thah-nah ko-lah	තණ කොළ
grave	so-ho-nah	සොහොන
great	lo-ku • mah-haah	ලොකු • මහ
greengrocer	sil-lah-rah ve-len-dhaah	සිල්ලර වෙළෙන්දා
grey	ah-lu paah-tah	අළු පාට
guess (v)	hi-thah-lah ki-yah-nah-vaah	හිතල කියනවා
guide (person)	gaid ke-nek	ගයිඩ් කෙනෙක්
guidebook	maahr-goh-pah-dheh-shah po-thah	මාර්ගෝපදේශක පොත
guitar	gi-taah-rah-yah	ගිටාරය
gym (weights)	vyaah-yaahm shaah-laah-wah • jim e-kah	ව්‍යායාම් ශාලාව • ජිම් එක
gymnastics	sah-rahm-bah kree-daah	සරඹ ක්‍රීඩා

H

hair	kon-dah-yah	කොණ්ඩය
hairbrush	kon-daah bu-ru-su-wah	කොණ්ඩා බුරුසුව
half	bhaah-gah-yah	භාගය
ham	ham	හැම්
hammer	mi-ti-yah	මිටිය
hammock	el-le-nah tho-til-lah	එල්ලෙන තොටිල්ල
hand	ah-thah	අත
handbag	ahth baa-gah-yah	අත් බෑගය
handicrafts	ath-kahm	අත්කම්
handmade	ah-thin ni-mah-voo	අතින් නිමවූ
handsome	pi-yah-kah-ru • lahs-sah-nah	පියකරු • ලස්සන
happy	pree-thi-mahth • sahn-thoh-shah	ප්‍රීතිමත් • සන්තෝෂ

Happy birthday!	su-bah u-pahn dhi-nah-yahk!	සුභ උපන් දිනයක්!

harbour	vah-raah-yah	වරාය
hard (solid)	thah-dhah	තද
hard (difficult)	ah-maah-ru	අමාරු
harassment	hi-ri-ha-rah-kahm	හිරිහැරකම්
have (v)	thi-yah-nah-vaah	තියනවා
Do you have ...?	o-bah-tah ... thi-yah-nah-vaah-dhah?	ඔබට ... තියනවාද?
hayfever	pee-nahs roh-gah-yah	පීනස් රෝගය
he	o-hu	ඔහු
head	o-lu-wah	ඔළුව
headache	hi-sah-rah-dhah-yah	හිසරදය
health	sau-khyah	සෞඛ්‍ය
hear (v)	a-he-nah-vaah	ඇහෙනවා
heart	hah-dhah-vah-thah	හදවත
heat	ush-nah-yah	උෂ්ණය
heavy	bah-rah	බර
Hello.	aah-yu-boh-wahn	ආයුබෝවන්.
helmet	hel-maht e-kah	හෙල්මට් එක
help (v)	u-dhav kah-rah-nah-vaah	උදව් කරනවා
Help!	kau-ruth nadh-dhah? (lit: anyone isn't-there?)	කව්රුත් නැද්ද?
herbs	au-shah-dhah pa-lah vahr-gah	ඖෂධ පැල වර්ග
herbalist	au-shah-dhah veh-dhee	ඖෂධ වේදී
here	me-thah-nah	මෙතන
hill	kahn-dhah	කන්ද
hire (v)	ku-li-yah-tah gahn-nah-vaah	කුලියට ගන්නවා
HIV positive	ech-ai-vee sah-hi-thah-voo	එච්.අයි.වී. සහිතවූ
holiday(s)	ni-vaah-du(-vah)	නිවාඩු(ව)
homeless	ah-naah-thah-voo	අනාතවූ
homeopathy	hoh-mi-yoh-pah-thi ve-dhah-kah-ma	හෝමියෝපති වෙදකම
homosexual	sah-mah lin-gi-kah	සම ලිංගික
honey	mee pa-ni	මී පැණි
honeymoon	mah-dhu sah-mah-yah	මදු සමය
horrible	ahn-thi-mai	අන්තිමයි
horse	ahsh-wah-yaah	අශ්වයා

horse riding	ahsh-wah-yaahn pa-dhee-mah	අශ්වයන් පැදීම
hospital	roh-hah-lah • is-pi-ri-thaah-lah-yah	රෝහල • ඉස්පිරිතාලය
hot	ush-nah	උෂ්ණ
It's hot.	rahs-nei	රස්නෙයි.
hot water	u-nu wah-thu-rah	උණු වතුර
house	ge-yah • ge-dhah-rah	ගෙය • ගෙදර
how	ko-ho-mah-dhah	කොහොමද
How do I get to ...?	...-tah mah-mah yahn-neh ko-ho-mah-dhah?	...ට මම යන්නේ කොහොමද?
How do you say ...?	... ki-yahn-neh ko-ho-mah-dhah?	... කියන්නේ කොහොමද?
hug	bah-dhaah ga-nee-mah	බදා ගැනීම
human rights	maah-nah-vah hi-mi-kahm	මානව හිමිකම්
hundred	see-yahk	සීයක්
hungry	bah-dah-gi-ni	බඩගිනි
husband	sa-mi-yaah	සැමියා

I

I	mah-mah	මම
ice	ais	අයිස්
ice cream	ais-kreem	අයිස්ක්‍රීම්
identification	han-dhu-naah ga-nee-mah	හඳුනා ගැනීම
identification card	han-dhu-num pah-thah	හැඳුනුම් පත
idiot	moh dah-yaah	මෝඩයා
ill	ah-sah-nee-pah • le-dah	අසනීප • ලෙඩ
immediately	dhan-mah	දැන්ම
immigration	aah-gah-mah-nah	ආගමන
important	va-dhah-gahth	වැදගත්
It's (not) important.	eh-kah va-dhah-gahth (na-ha)	ඒක වැදගත් (නැහැ).
included	a-thu-lahth	ඇතුළත්
indigestion	ah-jee-rah-nah-yah	අජීරණය
inequality	ah-sah-maah-nahth-vah-yah	අසමානත්වය
injection	be-heth vi-dhee-mah	බෙහෙත් විදීම
injury	thu-vaah-lah-yah	තුවාලය
inside	a-thu-lah • a-thu-lah-thah	ඇතුළ • ඇතුළත
insurance	rahk-shah-nah-yah	රක්ෂණය
interesting	sith a-lum kah-rai	සිත් ඇලුම් කරයි
international	jaah-thyaahn-thah-rah	ජාත්‍යාන්තර

interview	sahm-mu-khah	සම්මුඛ
	pah-reek-shah-nah-yah	පරීක්ෂණය
island	dhoo-pah-thah •	දූපත •
	dhi-vah-yi-nah	දිවයින
itch	ka-sil-lah	කැසිල්ල
itinerary	gah-mahn vis-thah-rah-yah	ගමන් විස්තරය

J

jail	si-rah-ge-yah	සිරගෙය
jar	joh-gu-wah	ජෝගුව
jealous	eer-shyaah-vah	ඊර්ෂ්‍යාව
jeans	kah-li-sah-mah	කලිසම
jeep	jeep e-kah	ජීප් එක
jewellery	aah-bhah-rah-nah	ආභරණ
job	rahk-shaah-wah • ve-dah	රක්ෂාව • වැඩ
jockey	ahsh-vah	අශ්ව රෝහකයා
	roh-hah-kah-yaah	
joke	vi-hi-lu-wah	විහිළුව
joke (v)	vi-hi-lu kah-rah-nah-vaah	විහිළු කරනවා
journalist	leh-khah-kah-yek /	ලේඛකයෙක් /
	leh-khah-kaah-vi-yahk **(m / f)**	ලේඛකාවියක්
journey	gah-mah-nah	ගමන
judge	vi-ni-su-ru •	විනිසුරු •
	vi-nish-chah-yah-kah-ru	විනිශ්චයකරු
juice	yu-shah • is-mah	යුෂ • ඉස්ම
jump (v)	pah-ni-nah-vaah	පනිනවා
jumper	jahm-pah-rah-yah	ජම්පරය
justice	yuk-thi-yah	යුක්තිය

K

key	yah-thu-rah	යතුර
kick	pah-yin gah-hah-nah-vaah	පයින් ගහනවා
kill (v)	mah-rah-nah-vaah	මරණවා
kilogram	ki-loh-graa-mah-yah	කිලෝග්‍රෑමය
kilometre	ki-loh-mee-tah-rah-yah	කිලෝමීටරය
kind	kaah-ru-naah-vahn-thah	කරුණාවන්ත
kindergarten	lah-dah-ru paah-sah-lah	ළදරු පාසල
king	rah-jah	රජ
kiss	kis e-kah	කිස් එක
kitchen	kus-si-yah •	කුස්සිය •
	mu-lu-than ge-yah	මුළුතැන් ගෙය
kitten	bah-lahl pa-ti-yaah	බළල් පැටියා
knapsack	pi-tah mahl-lah	පිට මල්ල
knee	dhah-nah-hi-sah	දණහිස

knife	pi-hi-yah	පිහිය
know (v)	dha-nah gahn-nah-vaah/ dahn-nah-vah	දැන ගන්නවා/ දන්නවා
I (don't) know.	mah-mah dhahn-neh (na-ha)	මම දන්නේ (නැහැ).

L

lace	rehn-dhah-yah	රේන්දය
lake	wa-vah	වැව
land	i-dah-mah	ඉඩම
languages	bhaah-shaah-vahn	භාෂාවන්
large	vi-shaah-lah • lo-ku	විශාල • ලොකු
last	ahn-thi-mah • gi-yah	අන්තිම • ගිය
last month	gi-yah maah-sah-yah	ගිය මාසය
last night	ee-yeh raa	ඊයේ රෑ
last week	gi-yah sah-thi-yah	ගිය සතිය
last year	gi-yah ah-vu-rudh-dhah	ගිය අවුරුද්ද
late	pah-rahk-kuy	පරක්කුයි
laugh (n)	si-nah-hah-wah	සිනහව
launderette	lon-dah-ri-yah	ලොන්ඩරිය
law	nee-thi-yah	නීතිය
lawyer	nee-thee-gnah vah-rah-yek/ vah-ri-yak **(m/f)**	නීතිඥ වරයෙක්/ වරියක්
laxatives	vi-reh-kah-yahn	විරේකයන්
lazy	kahm-ma-li	කම්මැලි
leaded (petrol)	ee-yahm sah-hi-thah	ඊයම් සහිත
learn (v)	i-ge-nah gahn-nah-vaah	ඉගෙන ගන්නවා
leather	hahm	හම්
be left (behind/over, v)	ahth-ha-rah yah-nah-vaah • i-thu-ru ve-nah-vaah	අත්හැර යනවා • ඉතුරු වෙනවා
left (not right)	vah-mah	වම
left luggage	thah-baah gi-yah bah-du	තබා ගිය බඩු
left-wing	vaah-maahn-shah-yah	වාමාංශය
leg	kah-ku-lah	කකුළ
legalisation	nee-thi-gah-thah ki-ree-mah	නීතිගත කිරීම
legislation	vyaah-vahs-thaah-vahn	ව්‍යවස්ථාවන්
lens	kahn-naah-di	කන්නාඩි
(camera/glasses)	vee-dhu-ru-wah	වීදුරුව
lesbian	sah-mah-lin-gi-kah	සමලිංගික
less	ah-du	අඩු
letter	li-pi-yah • li-yu-mah	ලිපිය • ලියුම
liar	bo-ru-kaah-rah-yaah	බොරුකාරයා
library	pus-thah-kaah-lah-yah	පුස්තකාලය

lice	u-ku-nahn • thah-di	උකුණන් • තඩි
lie (v)	bo-ru ki-yah-nah-vaah	බොරු කියනවා
life	jee vi-thah-yah	ජීවිතය
lift (elevator)	lift e-kah	ලිෆ්ට් එක
light (lamp)	lait e-kah	ලයිට් එක
light (not heavy)	sa-hal-lu	සැහැල්ලු
light (daylight)	e-li-yah	එළිය
lightbulb	vi-dhu-li bu-bu-lu-wah	විදුලි බුබුළුව
lighter	lai-tah-rah-yah	ලයිටරය
lighthouse	prah-dee-paah-gaah-rah-yah • lait hous e-kah	ප්‍රදීපාගාරය • ලයිට් හවුස් එක
like (v)	ka-mah-thi ve-nah-vaah	කැමති වෙනවා
line	i-rah • reh-khaah-wah	ඉර • රේඛාව
lips	thol	තොල්
listen (v)	ah-saah si-ti-nah-vaah	අසා සිටිනවා
little (small)	po-di • ku-daah	පොඩි • කුඩා
a little (amount)	ti-kai	ටිකයි
live (v)	jee-vi-thah ve-nah-vaah	ජීවත් වෙනවා
local	pah-laah-theh	පළාතේ
lock	ah-gu-lah • lok e-kah	අගුල • ලොක් එක
lock (v)	yah-thu-ru / ah-gu-lu dhah-mah-nah-vaah	යතුරු / අගුලු දමනවා
long	dhi-gah	දිග
long distance	dhu-rah prah-maah-nah-yah	දුර ප්‍රමාණය
look (v)	bah-lah-nah-vaah	බලනවා
look after (v)	bah-laah gahn-nah-vaah	බලා ගන්නවා
look for (v)	so-yah-nah-vaah	සොයනවා
lose (v)	na-thi kah-rah-nah-vaah	නැති කරනවා
a lot	go-dahk	ගොඩක්
loud	han-dah na-gee-mah	හඬ නැඟීම
love (v)	aah-dhah-rah-yah ki-ree-mah	ආදරය කිරීම
low	pah-hahth • ah-du	පහත් • අඩු
lucky	waah-sah-naah-wahn-thah	වාසනාවත්
luggage	bah-du mah-lu	බඩු මළු
luggage lockers	bah-du sehp-pu	බඩු සේප්පු
lunch	dhah-vahl kaa-mah	දවල් කෑම
luxury	su-koh-pah-boh-gee	සුඛෝපභෝගී

M

machine	yahn-thrah-yah • me-shin e-kah	යන්ත්‍රය • මෙෂින් එක
mad	pis-su • ol-maah-dhah	පිස්සු • ඔල්මාද
magazine	sahn-gah-raah-wah	සඟරාව

mail	tha-pal	තැපැල්
mailbox	li-yum pet-ti-yah	ලියුම් පෙට්ටිය
main road	mah-hah-paah-rah	මහපාර
majority	va-di sahn-kyaah-wah	වැඩි සංඛ්‍යාව
make (v)	saah-dhah-nah-vaah	සාදනවා
make-up	sa-dhum lah-nah • o-pah gan-vee-mah	සැදුම් ලන • ඔප ගැන්වීම
man	mi-ni-saah	මිනිසා
manager	kah-lah-mah-naah-kaah-rah • ma-neh-jahr	කළමනාකාර • මැනේජර්
many	hun-gahk • bo-hoh-mah-yahk	හුඟාක් • බොහොමයක්
map	si-thi-yah-mah	සිතියම
marijuana	mah-ru-vaah-naah • mahth dhrahv-yah	මරුවානා • මත් ද්‍රව්‍ය
market	ve-lahn-dhah-po-lah • maah-kaht e-kah	වෙළඳපොළ • මාකට් එක
marriage	vi-vaah-hah-yah • kah-saah-dhah-yah	විවාහය • කසාදය
marry (v)	vi-vaah-hah ve-nah-vaah • kah-saah-dhah bahn-di-nah-vaah	විවාහ වෙනවා • කසාද බදිනවා
marvellous	aash-chair-yah-mahth	ආශ්චර්යමත්
mass (Catholic)	poo-jaah-wah	පූජාව
massage	mah-saahj e-kah	මසාජ් එක
match (sport)	mach e-kah • thah-rahn-gah-yah	මැච් එක • තරගය
matches	gi-ni-koo-ru	ගිනිකූරු
It doesn't matter.	kah-mahk na-ha	කමක් නැහැ.
What's the matter?	mo-kah-dhah ve-laah thi-yehn-neh?	මොකද වෙලා තියෙන්නේ?
mattress	met-tah-yah	මෙට්ටය
maybe	ven-nah pu-lu-vahn	වෙන්න පුළුවන්
mechanic	yaahn-three-kah • kaahr-mi-kah shil-pi-yek / shil-pi-ni-yahk (m / f)	යාන්ත්‍රික • කාර්මික ශිල්පියෙක්/ශිල්පිනියක්
medicine	be-heth	බෙහෙත්
meet (v)	hah-mu ve-nah-vaah	හමු වෙනවා
member	saah-maah-ji-kah-yaah	සාමාජිකයා
menstruation	o-sahp vee-mah	ඔසප් වීම
menu	kaa-mah waht-toh-ru-wah	කෑම වට්ටෝරුව
message	pah-ni-vu-dah-yah	පණිවුඩය
metal	loh-hah	ලෝහ
metre	mee-tah-rah-yah	මීටරය

midnight	mah-dhyah-mah ra-yah	මධ්‍යම රැය
migraine	i-ru-waah rah-dhah-yah	ඉරුවා රදය
military service	hah-mu-dhaah seh-vah-yah	හමුදා සේවය
milk	ki-ri	කිරි
millimetre	mi-li-mee-tah-rah-yah	මිලිමීටරය
million	mi-li-yah-nah-yah • dhah-shah lahk-shah-yah	මිලියනය • දශ ලක්ෂය
mineral water	bo-nah vah-thu-rah	බොන වතුර
minute (time)	vi-naah-di-yahk	විනාඩියක්
Just a minute.	vi-naah-di-yahk in-nah	විනාඩියක් ඉන්න.
mirror	kahn-naah-di-yah	කන්නාඩිය
miscarriage	gahb-saah-vah	ගබ්සාව
miss (feel absence, v)	paah-lu-wah dha-ne-nah-vaah	පාළුව දැනෙනවා
mistake	ba-ri-vee-mah • va-rah-dhee-mah	බැරිවීම • වැරදීම
mix (v)	mish-rah kah-rah-nah-vaah	මිශ්‍ර කරනවා
mobile phone	moh-bail fohn e-kah	මොබයිල් ෆෝන් එක
modem	moh-dahm e-kah	මෝඩම් එක
moisturising cream	aah-leh-pah-yah • kreem	ආලේපය • ක්‍රීම්
monastery	thaah-pah-saah-raah-mah-yah	තාපසාරාමය
money	sahl-li • mu-dhahl	සල්ලි • මුදල්
monk	bhik-shu-wah	භික්ෂුව
month	maah-sah-yah	මාසය
monument	smaah-rah-kah-yah	ස්මාරකය
more	thah-vahth	තවත්
morning	u-dheh vah-ru-wah	උදේ වරුව
mosque	mus-lim pahl-li-yah	මුස්ලිම් පල්ලිය
mosquito coil	mah-dhu-ru dahn-gah-rah	මදුරු දඟර
mosquito net	mah-dhu-ru da-lah	මදුරු දැල
mother	ahm-maah	අම්මා
mother-in-law	nan-dhahm-maah	නැන්දම්මා
motorboat	moh-toh both-tu-wah	මෝටෝ බෝට්ටුව
motorcycle	moh-toh bai-si-kah-lah-yah	මෝටෝ බයිසිකලය
mountain	kahn-dhah	කන්ද
mountain path	kahn-dhu maah-wah-thah	කඳු මාවත
mouse	mee-yaah	මීයා
mouth	kah-tah	කට
movie	chith-rah-pah-ti-yah	චිත්‍රපටිය
mud	mah-dah	මඩ
mum	ahm-maah	අම්මා
muscle	maahn-shah peh-sheen	මාංශ පේෂීන්

museum	kau-thu-kaah-gaah-rah-yah • kah-tu-ge-yah	කෞතුකාගාරය • කටුගෙය
music	sahn-gee-thah-yah	සංගීතය

N

name	nah-mah	නම
nappy	na-pi-yah	නැපිය
national park	jaah-thi-kah u-dhyaah-nah-yah	ජාතික උද්‍යානය
nationality	jaah-thi-kahth-vah-yah	ජාතිකත්වය
nature	so-baah-dhah-hah-mah	සොබාදහම
naturopath	swaah-bhaa-vi-kah vai-dhyah	ස්වභාවික වෛද්‍ය
nausea	vah-mah-nah-yah gah-thi-yah	වමනය ගතිය
near	lahn-gah • kit-tu-wah	ළඟ • කිට්ටුව
necessary	ah-vah-shyah	අවශ්‍ය
necklace	maah-lah-yah	මාලය
need (v)	ah-vah-shyah ve-nah-vaah	අවශ්‍ය වෙනවා
needle (sewing)	in-dhi-kah-tu-wah	ඉඳිකටුව
needle (syringe)	si-rin-jahr kah-tu-wah	සිරින්ජර් කටුව
neither	hoh	හෝ
net	net e-kah	නෙට් එක
never	kah-vah-dhaah-vahth na-ha	කවදාවත් නැහැ
new	ah-luth	අලුත්
news	prah-vruth-thi • pu-wahth	ප්‍රවෘත්ති • පුවත්
newspaper	pu-wahth-pah-thah	පුවත්පත
New Year's Day	ah-luth ahv-ru-dhu dhi-nah	අලුත් අවුරුදු දින
New Year's Eve	ah-luth ahv-ru-dhu dhi-nah-tah pe-rah dhi-nah	අලුත් අවුරුදු දිනට පෙර දින
next	ee-lahn-gah	ඊළඟ
next month	ee-lahn-gah maah-sah-yah	ඊළඟ මාසය
next week	ee-lahn-gah sah-thi-yah	ඊළඟ සතිය
nice	lahs-sah-nai • hon-dhai	ලස්සණයි • හොඳයි
night	raa • raahth-ri-yah	රෑ • රාත්‍රිය
No.	na-ha	නැහැ.
noisy	shahb-dhah-vahth	ශබ්දවත්
none	ki-si-ve-ku no-veh	කිසිවෙකු නොවේ
noon	dhah-hah-vah-lah	දහවල
north	u-thu-rah	උතුර
nose	nah-hah-yah • naah-sah-yah	නහය • නාසය
notebook	noht po-thah	නෝට් පොත
nothing	ki-si-vahk na-ha	කිසිවක් නැහැ

now	dhan	දැන්
nun	me-he-ni-yah • bhik-shu-ni-yah	මෙහෙණිය • භික්ෂුණිය
nurse	he-dhi-yah • saahth-thu seh-vah-kah-yek/ seh-vi-kaah-vahk **(m/f)**	හෙදිය • සාත්තු සේවකයෙක්/ සේවිකාවක්

O

obvious	pa-ha-di-li	පැහැදිලි
ocean	mu-hu-dhah	මුහුද
offence	vah-rah-dhah	වරද
office	kahn-thoh-ru-wah	කන්තෝරුව
often	ni-thah-rah	නිතර
oil (cooking)	thel	තෙල්
oil (crude)	ah-mu thel	අමු තෙල්
OK	hon-dhai	හොඳයි.
old	pah-rah-nah	පරණ
olive oil	o-liv thel	ඔලිව් තෙල්
olives	ve-rah-lu	වෙරළු
Olympic Games	o-lim-pik kree-daah	ඔලිම්පික් ක්‍රීඩා
on	u-dah • mah-thah	උඩ • මත
on time	ve-laah-vah-tah	වේලාවට
once	e-kah vah-thaah-vahk	එක වතාවක්
one-way (ticket)	ek dhi-saah-vah-kah-tah	එක් දිශාවකට
only	pah-mah-nai • vi-thah-rai	පමණයි • විතරයි
open	vi-vur-thah • a-rah-lah	විවෘත • ඇරල
open (v)	ah-ri-nah-vaah	අරිනවා
opera	sahn-gee-thah naaht-yah	සංගීත නාට්‍ය
opera house	sahn-gee-thah naaht-yah shaah-laah-wah	සංගීත නාට්‍ය ශාලාව
operation	shahl-yah-kahr-mah-yah	ශල්‍යකර්මය
opinion	mah-thah-yah	මතය
opposite (facing)	i-dhi-ri-pi-tah • is-sah-rah-hah	ඉදිරිපිට • ඉස්සරහ
opposite (unlike)	vi-rudh-dhah (unlike)	විරුද්ධ
or	hoh • nath-nahm	හෝ • නැත්නම්
orchestra	thoor-yah vaah-dhah-kah mahn dah-lah-yah	තූර්ය වාදක මණ්ඩලය
order	pi-li-ve-lah	පිළිවෙළ
order (v)	il-lum kah-rah-nah-vaah	ඉල්ලුම් කරනවා
ordinary	saah-maahn-yah	සාමාන්‍ය
organise	sahn-vi-dhaah-nah-yah	සංවිධානය
original	mul	මුල්
other	ve-nahth	වෙනත්

outside	pi-tah-thah	පිටත
over	hah-maah-rai • i-vah-rai	හමාරයි • ඉවරයි
overdose	be-heth prah-maah-nah-yah ik-mah-vee-mah	බෙහෙත් ප්‍රමාණය ඉක්මවීම
owe (v)	nah-yah ga-thi ve-nah vaah	ණය ගැති වෙනවා
owner	ai-thi-kah-ru	අයිතිකරු
oxygen	ok-si-jahn	ඔක්සිජන්
ozone layer	oh-sohn thah-lah-yah	ඕසෝන් තලය

P

pacifier (dummy)	soop-pu-wah	සූප්පුව
package	bah-du mi-ti-yah	බඩු මිටිය
packet	pa-kaht-tu-wah	පැකට්ටුව
padlock	ib-baah	ඉබ්බා
pain	ru-dhah-wah • kak-ku-mah	රුදාව • කැක්කුම
painful	kak-kum-mai	කැක්කුමයි
painkillers	veh-dhah-naah naah-shah-kah	වේදනා නාශක
paint (v)	theen-thah gaah-nah-vaah	තීන්ත ගානවා
painting (art)	chith-rah-kahr-mah-yah	චිත්‍රකර්මය
pair (a couple)	joh-du-wah	ජෝඩුව
palace	maah-li-gah-wah	මාලිගාව
pan	thaahch-chu-wah	තාච්චුව
pap smear	pap smi-yah pi-li-kaah pah-reek-shah-nah-yah	පැප් ස්මිය පිලිකා පරීක්ෂණය
paper	ko-lah	කොළ
paraplegic	ahn-shah-bhaah-gah-yah	අංශභාගය
parcel	paahr-sah-lah-yah	පාර්සලය
parents	dhe-mahv-pi-yahn	දෙමව්පියන්
park	u-dhyaah-nah-yah	උද්‍යානය
park (v)	nah-thah-rah kah-rah thah-bah-nah-vaah	ගතර කර තබනවා
parliament	paahr-li-mehn-thu-wah	පාර්ලිමේන්තුව
party (fiesta)	saah-dhah-yah	සාදය
party (politics)	pahk-shah-yah	පක්ෂය
pass	sah-maahr-thah-yah • pa-su ki-ree-mah	සමාඅර්තය • පසු කිරීම
passenger	mah-gi-yaah	මගියා
passport	gah-mahn bah-lah-pahth-rah-yah • paahs-poht e-kah	ගමන් බලපත්‍රය • පාස්පෝට් එක
passport number	paahs-poht an-kah-yah	පාස්පෝට් අංකය
past	ah-thee-thah-yah	අතීතය
path	ah-di-pah-rah • mah-gah	අඩිපාර • මග
patient (adj)	roh-gi-yaah	රෝගියා
pay (v)	ge-vah-nah-vaah	ගෙවනවා

peace	saah-mah-yah	සාමය
peak	mu-dhu-nah	මුදුන
pedestrian	mah-gi-yaah	මඟියා
pen (ballpoint)	paa-nah	පෑන
pencil	pan-sah-lah	පැන්සල
penis	pu-ru-shah lin-gah-yah	පුරුෂ ලිංගය
penknife	ku-daah pi-hi-yah	කුඩා පිහිය
pensioner	vi-shraah-mi-kah-yaah	විශ්‍රාමිකයා
people	mah-hah-jah-nah-yaah • mi-nis-su	මහජනයා • මිනිස්සු
pepper	gahm-mi-ris	ගම්මිරිස්
percent	prah-thi-shah-thah-yah	ප්‍රතිශතය
performance	rahn-gah dhak-mah	රඟ දැක්ම
period pain	o-sahp ru-dhaah	ඔසප් රුදා
permanent	sthee-rah	ස්ථිර
permission	ah-vah-sah-rah-yah	අවසරය
permit	bah-lah-pahth-rah-yah • ah-vah-sah-rah	බලපත්‍රය • අවසරය
person	pudh-gah-lah-yaah	පුද්ගලයා
petrol	pet-rohl	පෙට්‍රෝල්
pharmacists	au-shah-dah-veh-dhee	ඖෂධවේදී
pharmacy	faah-mah-si-yah	ෆාමසිය
photo	fo-toh e-kah	ෆොටෝ එක
May I take a photo?	mah-mah fo-toh e-kahk gahn-nah-dhah?	මම ෆොටෝ එකක් ගන්නද?
pie	pai e-kah	පයි එක
piece	kaal-lah	කෑල්ල
pig	oo-raah	ඌරා
pill	be-heth peth-thah	බෙහෙත් පෙත්ත
the Pill	pi-li-si-dhee-mah va-lak-vee-meh be-he-thah	පිලිසිඳීම වැළැක්වීමේ බෙහෙත
pillow	kot-tah-yah	කොට්ටය
pillowcase	kot-tah u-rah-yah	කොට්ට උරය
pine	pah-yin gah-sah	පයින් ගස
pink	roh-sah paah-tah	රෝස පාට
pipe	paip-pah-yah	පයිප්පය
place	sthaah-nah-yah	ස්ථානය
plain (not mixed)	ni-kahn	නිකන්
plain (field)	tha-ni-thah-laah-wah	තැනිතලාව
plane	ah-hahs yaah-nah-yah	අහස් යානය
plant	pa-lah-yah	පැලය
plastic	plaahs-tik	ප්ලාස්ටික්
plate	pi-gaah-nah	පිඟාන

plateau	tha-ni-thah-laah-wah	තැනිතලාව
platform	veh-dhi-kaah-wah	වේදිකාව
play (theatre)	naah-dhah-gahm	නාඩගම්
play (a game, v)	sel-lahm kah-rah-nah-vaah	සෙල්ලම් කරනවා
play (music, v)	vaah-dhah-nah-yah kah-rah-nah-vaah	වාදනය කරනවා
player (sport)	kree-dah-kah-yaah	ක්‍රීඩකයා
plug (bath)	a-bah-yah	ඇබය
plug (electricity)	plahg e-kah	ප්ලග් එක
pocket	saahk-ku-wah	සාක්කුව
poetry	kah-vi	කවි
point (v)	an-gil-len pen-vah-nah-vaah	ඇඟිල්ලෙන් පෙන්වනවා
police	po-lee-si-yah	පොලීසිය
politics	dheh-shah-paah-lah-nah-yah	දේශපාලනය
pollen	mahl-reh-nu	මල්රේණු
pollution	dhoo-shah-nah-yah	දූෂණය
poor	dup-path	දුප්පත්
popular	jah-nah-pri-yah	ජනප්‍රිය
port	vah-raah-yah	වරාය
possible	ha-ki	හැකි
It's (not) possible.	(no) ha-ki	(නො) හැකි.
postcard	tha-pal pah-thah	තැපැල් පත
post code	tha-pal sahn-keh-thah	තැපැල් සංකේත
post office	tha-pal kahn-thoh-ru-wah	තැපැල් කන්තෝරුව
pottery	ma-ti kahr-mahn-thah-yah	මැටි කර්මාන්තය
poverty	dhi lin-du bah-vah	දිළිඳු බව
power	bah-lah-yah	බලය
prayer	yaag-gnaah-wah	යාඥාව
prefer (v)	vah-daahth ka-mah-thi ve-nah-vaah	වඩාත් කැමති වෙනවා
pregnant	gab-bah-rah	ගැබ්බර
pre-menstrual tension	o-sahp vee-mah-tah pe-rah a-thi-vah-nah ah-sah-hah-nah thaah-vah-yah	ඔසප් වීමට පෙර ඇතිවන අසහන තාවය
prepare (v)	soo-dhaah-nahm ve-nah-vaah	සූදානම් වෙනවා
present (gift)	thaag-gah	තෑග්ග
president	sah-baah-pah-thi	සභාපති
pressure	pee-dah-nah-yah	පීඩනය
pretty	pi-yah-kah-ru	පියකරු

prevent	va-lak-vee-mah	වැළැක්වීම
price	mi-lah	මිළ
pride	ah-hahn-kaah-rah-yah	අහංකාරය
priest	poo-jah-kah-vah-rah-yaah	පූජකවරයා
prime minister	ah-gah-ma-thi	අගමැති
prison	si-rah ge-yah • bahn-dhah-naah-gaah-rah-yah	සිර ගෙය • බන්ධනාගාරය
private	pudh-gah-li-kah	පුද්ගලික
profession	vruth-thee-yah	වෘත්තීය
profit	laah-bah	ලාභ
programme	va-dah-sah-tah-hah-nah	වැඩසටහන
promise	po-ron-dhu-wah	පොරොන්දුව
protect (v)	aah-rahk-shaah kah-rah-nah-vaah	ආරක්ෂා කරනවා
protest	vi-roh-dhah-yah	විරෝධය
public toilet	po-dhu va-si-ki-li	පොදු වැසිකිලි
pull (v)	ah-dhi-nah-waah	අදිනවා
pump	pom-pah-yah	පොම්පය
puncture	hi-lahk	හිළක්
punish (v)	dhah-du-vahm ki-ree-mah	දඩුවම් කිරීම
pure	pi-ri-si-dhu	පිරිසිදු
purple	dhahm paah-tah	දම් පාට
push (v)	thahl-lu kah-rah-nah-vaah	තල්ලු කරනවා

Q

qualifications	su-dhu-su-kahm	සුදුසුකම්
quality	thahth-vah-yah	තත්වය
quarantine	ni-roh-dhaah-yah-nah-yah	නිරෝධායනය
quarter	kaah-lah	කාල
question	prahsh-nah-yah	ප්‍රශ්නය
queue	poh-li-mah	පෝලිම
quick	ik-mah-nin	ඉක්මණින්
quiet	ni-hahn-dah • nish-shahb-dhah	නිහඬ සේ • නිශ්ශබ්ද
quit (v)	i-vahth ve-nah-vaah	ඉවත් වෙනවා

R

rabbit	haah-waah	හාවා
race (breed)	jaah-thi-yah	ජාතිය
race (sport)	thah-rahn-gah dhi-vee-mah	තරඟ දිවීම
racism	jaah-thi-vaah-dhah-yah	ජාතිවාදය
racquet	dhal pith-thah • ra-kaht e-kah	දැල් පිත්ත • රැකට් එක

railway station	dhum-ri-yah staah-nah-yah	දුම්රිය ස්ථානය
rain	vas-sah	වැස්ස
It's raining.	vah-hi-nah-vaah	වහිනවා.
rape	dhoo-shah-nah-yah	දූෂණය
rare	dhur-lah-bah	දුර්ලභ
rash	kush-tah-yah	කුෂ්ටය
raw	ah-mu	අමු
razor	dha-li pi-hi-yah	දැලි පිහිය
razor blades	blehd thah-lah	බ්ලේඩ් තල
read (v)	ki-yah-vah-nah-vaah	කියවනවා
ready	soo-dhaah-nahm • laas-thi	සූදානම් • ලැස්ති
realise (v)	va-tah-he-nah-vaah	වැටහෙනවා
reason	heh-thu-vah	හේතුව
receipt	bil-pah-thah	බිල් පත
receive (v)	la-be-nah-vaah	ලැබෙනවා
recent(ly)	maa-thah(-kah-dee)	මෑත(කදී)
recognise (v)	hahn-dhu-naah gahn-nah-vaah	හඳුනා ගන්නවා
recommend (v)	nir-dheh-shah kah-rah-nah-vaah	නිර්දේශ කරනවා
recycling	prah-thi-chah-kree-yah-kah-rah-nah-yah	ප්‍රතිචක්‍රියකරණය
referee	vi-ni-su-ru	විනිසුරු
refrigerator	shee-thah-kah-rah-nah-yah	ශීතකරණය
refugee	sah-rah-naah-gah-thah-yaah	සරණාගතයා
refund	aah-pah-su ge-vee-mah	ආපසු ගෙවීම
refuse (v)	prah-thik-sheh-pah kah-rah-nah-vaah	ප්‍රතික්ෂේප කරනවා
registered mail	li-yaah pah-dhin-chi tha-pal	ලියා පදිංචි තැපැල්
relationship	sahm-bahn-dhah-thaah-vah-yah	සම්බන්ධතාවය
relax (v)	vi-veh-kah gahn-nah-vaah	විවේක ගන්නවා
religion	aah-gah-mah	ආගම
remember (v)	si-hi-pahth / mah-thahk kah-rah-nah-vaah	සිහිපත්ශ්‍රීමතක් කරනවා
rent (v)	ku-li-yah-tah dhe-nah-vaah	කුලියට දෙනවා
repair (v)	ah-luth-va-dhi-yaah kah-rah-nah-vaah	අළුත්වැඩියා කරනවා
reservation	ven-kah-rah-nah lah-dhah	වෙන්කරන ලද
reserve (v)	kah-lin ven kah-rah-nah-vaah	කලින් වෙන් කරනවා

rest (relaxation)	vi-veh-kah-yah	විවේකය
rest (what's left)	i-thi-ri-yah	ඉතිරිය
rest (v)	vi-veh-kah gahn-nah-vaah	විවේක ගන්නවා
restaurant	aah-pah-nah shaah-laah-vah	ආපන ශාලාව
resume (CV)	see-vee e-kah	සීවී එක
retired	vi-shraah-mi-kah	විශ්‍රාමික
return (ticket)	yaah-mah-tah eh-mah-tah	යාමට ඒමට
return (v)	aah-pah-su pa-mi-ne-nah-vaah	ආපසු පැමිණෙනවා
rice	bahth	බත්
rich (wealthy)	po-ho-sath	පොහොසත්
right (correct)	ni-va-rah-dhi • hah-ri	නිවැරදි • හරි
You're right.	o-bah hah-ri	ඔබ හරි.
right (not left)	dhah-ku-nah	දකුණ
right-wing	dhah-ku-nu paahr-shah-vah-yah	දකුණු පාර්ශවය
ring (on finger)	mudh-dhah	මුද්ද
ring (of phone)	naah-dhah-ya	නාදය
rip-off	gah-saah ka-mah	ගසා කෑම
risk	u-vah-dhu-rah	උවදුර
river	gahn-gah	ගංගා
road (main)	(mah-hah) paah-rah	(මහ) පාර
road map	maahr-gah si-thi-yah-mah	මාර්ග සිතියම
rock	pahr-vah-thah-yah	පර්වතය
room	kaah-mah-rah-yah	කාමරය
rope	lah-nu-vah	ලණුව
round	rah-vum	රවුම්
(at the) roundabout	vah-tah-rah-vu-mah(dee)	වට රවුම(දී)
rowing	o-ru pa-dhee-mah	ඔරු පැදීම
rubbish	ku-nu	කුණු
rug	paah-pis-sah	පාපිස්ස
ruins	nah-tah-bun	නටබුන්
rules	nee-thi	නීති
run (v)	dhu-wah-nah-vaah	දුවනවා

S

sad	dhu-kah	දුක
safe (n)	sehp-pu-wah	සේප්පුව
safe (adj)	aah-rahk-shaah-vai	ආරක්ෂාවස්
safe sex	aah-rahk-shi-thah lin-gi-kah sahn-sahr-gah-yah	ආරක්ෂිත ලිංගික සංසර්ගය
saint	saahn-thu-vah-rah-yaah	සාන්තුවරයා
salary	va-tu-pah	වැටුප

(on) sale	vi-ki-nee-mah-tah	විකිණීමට
salt	lu-nu	ලුණු
same	eh-kah-mah	එකම
sand	va-li	වැලි
sanitary napkins	paad e-kah	පෑඩ් එක
save (v)	i-thi-ri kah-rah-nah-vaah	ඉතිරි කරනවා
say (v)	ki-yah-nah-vaah	කියනවා
scarf	skaahf e-kah	ස්කාර්ෆ් එක
school	paah-sa-lah •	පාසැල •
	is-koh-leh	ඉස්කොලේ
science	vidh-yaah-vah	විද්‍යාව
scissors	kah-thu-rah	කතුර
score (v)	lah-ku-nu lah-baah	ලකුණු ලබා
	gahn-nah-vaah	ගන්නවා
sculpture	prah-thi-maah	ප්‍රතිමා නිර්මාණය
	nir-maah-nah-yah	
sea	mu-hu-dhah	මුහුද
seasick	mu-hu-dhu yaa-meh-dee	මුහුදු යෑමේදී
	a-thi-vah-nah	ඇතිවන
	vah-mah-nah-yah	වමනය
seat	ah-su-nah • seet e-kah	අසුන • සීට් එක
seatbelt	aah-sah-nah pah-ti	ආසන පටි
second (time)	thahth-pah-rah-yah	තත්පරය
second (not first)	dhe-vah-ni	දෙවනි
see (v)	bah-lah-nah-vaah	බලනවා
We'll see.	bah-lah-mu	බලමු.
I see. (understand)	mah-tah theh-re-nah-vaah	මට තේරෙනව.
See you later.	pahs-seh hah-mu-ve-mu	පස්සේ හමුවෙමු.
self-employed	swah-yahn	ස්වයං රැකියාවේ
	ra-ki yaah-veh ni-yu-thu	නියුතු
selfish	aahth-maar-thah-kaah-mee	ආත්මාර්තකාමී
self-service	swah-yahn seh-vaah	ස්වයං සේවා
sell (v)	vi-ku-nah-nah-vaah	විකුණනවා
send (v)	e-vah-nah-vaah	එවනවා
sensible	budh-dhi-mahth	බුද්දිමත්
sentence (words)	vaahk-yah-yah	වාක්‍යය
sentence (prison)	si-rah dhahn-du-wah-mah	සිර දඬුවම
separate (v)	ven kah-rah-nah-vaah	වෙන් කරනවා
series	kaahn-dah-yah	කාණ්ඩය
serious	bah-lah-vahth • dhah-ru-nu	බලවත් • දරුණු
several	no-yek • vi-vi-dah	නොයෙක් • විවිධ
sex	lin-gah-yah • lin-gi-kah	ලිංගය •
	sahn-sahr-gah-yah	ලිංගික සංසර්ගය

sexism	lin-gi-kahth-vah-yah	ලිංගිකත්වය
shade	se-vah-nah	සෙවන
shampoo	sham-poo	ෂැම්පූ
share (with, v)	be-dhaah gahn-nah-vaah	බෙදා ගන්නවා
shave (v)	ra-vu-lah baah-nah-vaah	රැවුල බානවා
she	a-yah	ඇය
sheep	ba-tah-lu-waah	බැටළුවා
sheet (bed)	a-thi-ril-lah • sheet e-kah	ඇතිරිල්ල • ශීට් එක
sheet (of paper)	ko-lah-yah	කොළය
shell	sip-pi kah-tu	සිප්පි කටු
shelves	thaht-tu	තට්ටු
ship	na-vah	නැව
shirt	kah-mi-sah-yah	කමිසය
shoes	sah-pahth-thu	සපත්තු
shop	kah-dah-yah	කඩය
go shopping (v)	ba-du gahn-nah yah-nah-vaah	බඩු ගන්න යනවා
short (length)	ke-ti	කෙටි
short (height)	ko-tah	කොට
shorts	ko-tah kah-li-sahn	කොට කලිසම්
shoulders	u-rah-his	උරහිස්
shout (v)	kaa gah-sah-nah-vaah	කෑ ගසනවා
show	rahn-gah dhak-mah	රඟ දැක්ම
show (v)	pen-vah-nah-vaah	පෙන්වනවා
Can you show me on the map?	mah-tah si-thi-yah-meh pen-vahn-nah pu-lu-vahn-dhah?	මට සිතියමේ පෙන්වන්න පුළුවන්ද?
shower	wah-thu-rah mah-lah • shah-vahr e-kah	වතුර මල • ෂවර් එක
shrine	poo-jaah sthaah-nah-yah	පූජා ස්ථානය
shut (v)	vah-hah-nah-vaah	වහනවා
sick	ah-sah-nee-pai	අසනීප
sign	sah-lah-ku-nah	සලකුණ
signature	ahth-sah-nah	අත්සන
silk	silk	සිල්ක්
silver	ri-dhee	රිදී
similar	sah-maah-nah	සමාන
since (May)	si-tah / i-dahn (ma-yi)	සිට / ඉඳන් (මැයි)
sing (v)	sin-dhu ki-yah-nah-vaah	සින්දු කියනවා
singer	gaah-yah-kah-yaah	ගායකයා
single (person)	thah-ni	තනි
single (unique)	ah-sah-haah-yah	අසහාය
single room	thah-ni kaah-mah-rah-yah	තනි කාමරය

sister	ahk-kaah (older)	අක්කා
	nahn-gee (younger)	නංගී
	so-hoh-yu-ri-yah (refers to either)	සොහෝයුරිය
sit (v)	in-dhah gahn-nah-vaah	ඉඳ ගන්නවා
size (of anything)	prah-maah-nah-yah • thah-rah-mah	ප්‍රමාණය • තරම
size (clothes • shoes)	sais e-kah	සයිස් එක
skin	hah-mah	හම
sky	ah-hah-sah	අහස
sleep (v)	ni-dhah-nah-vaah	නිදනවා
sleeping bag	slee-pin baag e-kah	ස්ලීපිං බෑග් එක
sleeping car	ni-dhah-nah ma-di-ri-yah	නිදන මැදිරිය
sleeping pills	ni-dhi pe-thi	නිදි පෙති
slide (film)	dhah-lah seh-yaah pah-ti-yah	දළ සේයා පටය
slow	he-min	හෙමින්
slowly	he-min	හෙමින්ම
small	pun-chi • po-di	පුංචි • පොඩි
smell	su-wahn-dhah	සුවඳ
smile (v)	si-naah se-nah-vaah	සිනාසෙනවා
smoke (v)	dhum bo-nah-vaah	දුම් බොනවා
soap	sah-bahn	සබන්
soccer	paah-pahn-dhu	පාපන්දු
social security	sah-maah-jah aah-rahk-shaah-vah	සමාජ ආරක්ෂාව
social welfare	sah-maah-jah ah-bhi-vrudh-dhi-yah	සමාජ අභිවෘද්ධිය
socialist	sah-maah-jah-vaah-dhee	සමාජවාදී
solid	ghah-nah	ඝන
some	a-tham	ඇතැම්
someone	kahv-ru hoh	කව්රු හෝ
something	yah-mahk	යමක්
sometimes	a-tham vi-tah	ඇතැම් විට
son	pu-thaah	පුතා
song	gee-thah-yah • sin-dhu-vah (spoken)	ගීතය • සින්දුව
soon	ik-mah-nin	ඉක්මණින්
I'm sorry.	mah-tah kah-nah-gaah-tuy	මට කණගාටුයි.
south	dhah-ku-nah	දකුණ
souvenir	sa-mah-ru bhaahn-dah-yah • smaah-rah-kah-yah	සැමරු භාණ්ඩය • ස්මාරකය
speak (v)	kah-thaah kah-rah-nah-vaah	කතා කරනවා

Do you speak English?	o-bah in-gree-si kah-thaah kau-rah-nah-vaah-dhah?	ඔබ ඉංග්‍රීසි කතා කරනවාද?
special	vi-sheh-shah	විශේෂ
speed	veh-gah-yah	වේගය
speed limit	veh-gah see-maah-wah	වේග සීමාව
spicy (hot)	ku-lu-bah-du ye-doo •	කුළුබඩු යෙදූ •
	sa-rah-yi	සැරයි
sport	kree-daah	ක්‍රීඩා
sprain	u-luk-ku-wah	උළුක්කුව
spring (season)	wah-sahn-thah kaah-lah-yah	වසන්ත කාලය
square (in town)	chah-thu-rahsh-rah-yah	චතුරශ්‍රය
stadium	kree-daahn-gah-nah-yah	ක්‍රීඩාංගනය
stage	kah-rah-li-yah •	කරලිය •
	veh-dhi-kaah-wah	වේදිකාව
stairway	pah-dhi pe-lah	පඩි පෙළ
stale	pah-rah-nai / nah-rahk ve-laah	පරණයි / නරක් වෙලා
stamp	mudh-dhah-rah-yah	මුද්දරය
standard (usual)	saah-maahn-nyah-yah	සාමාන්‍ය
start (v)	pah-tahn gahn-nah-vaah	පටන් ගන්නවා
station	pola • sthaah-nah-yah	පොළ • ස්ථානය
stationers	li-pi drahv-yah	ලිපි ද්‍රව්‍ය
	saahp-pu-wah	සාප්පුව
statue	pra-thi-maah-wah	ප්‍රතිමාව
stay (remain, v**)**	in-nah-vaah	ඉන්නවා
stay (somewhere, v**)**	nah-vah-thi-nah-vaah	නවතිනවා
steal (v)	so-rah-kahm ki-ree-mah	සොරකම් කිරීම
steep	ah-di-kah baa-vum	අදික බෑවුම්
	sah-hi-thah	සහිත
step	pah-di-yah	පඩිය
stomach	bah-dah	බඩ
stomachache	bah-deh kak-ku-mah	බඩේ කැක්කුම
stone	gah-lah	ගල
stop (v)	nah-vah-thin-nah-vaah	නවතිනවා
Stop!	nah-vah-thin-nu!	නවතිනු!
storm	ku-naah-tu-wah	කුණාටුව
story	kah-thaahn-thah-rah-yah	කතාන්දරය
straight	ke-lin	කෙලින්
strange	pu-dhu-mah sah-hah-gah-thah	පුදුම සහගත
stranger	naahn-dhu-nah-nah ke-nek	නාඳුනන කෙනෙක්
stream	a-lah	ඇල
street	vee-dhi-yah	වීදිය
strike	va-dah	වැඩ
	vahr-jah-nah-yah	වර්ජනය

string	lah-nu-wah	ලණුව
strong	shahk-thi-mahth	ශක්තිමත්
student	shish-yah-yek / shish-yaah-wahk (m/f)	ශිෂ්‍යයෙක් / ශිෂ්‍යාවක්
stupid	mot-tah • ah-mah-nah	මොට්ට • අමන
subtitles	u-pah sheer-shah	උප ශීර්ෂ
suburb	pah-laah-thah	පළාත
success	saahr-thah-kah	සාර්ථක
suffer (v)	dhuk vin-dhi-nah-vaah	දුක් විඳිනවා
sugar	see-ni	සීනි
suitcase	soot-kehs e-kah	සූට්කේස් එක
summer	ush-nah kaah-lah-yah	උෂ්ණ කාලය
sun	i-rah • hi-ru	ඉර • හිරු
sunburn	ahv rahsh-nah-yah-tah pich-chee-mah	අව් රශ්නයට පිච්චීම
sunglasses	ahv-kahn-naah-di	අව්කන්නාඩි
sunny	ahv-vai	අව්වයි
sunrise	hi-ru u-dhaah-vah	හිරු උදාව
sunset	hi-ru bas-mah	හිරු බැස්ම
surface mail	saah-maahn-yah tha-pal	සාමාන්‍ය තැපැල්
surname	vaah-sah-gah-mah	වාසගම
surprise	bah-laah-po-roth-thu no-voo • pu-dhu-mah-yah	බලාපොරොත්තු නොවූ • පුදුමය
survive (v)	no-ma-ree jee-vahth ve-nah-vaah	නොමැරී ජීවත් වෙනවා
sweet	pa-ni rah-sah	පැණි රස
swim (v)	pi-hi-nah-nah-vaah	පිහිනනවා
swimming pool	pool e-kah • pi-hi-num thah-taah-kah-yah	පූල් එක • පිහිනුම් තටාකය
swimsuit	pi-hi-num an-dhum kaht-tah-lah-yah	පිහිනුම් ඇඳුම් කට්ටලය
sympathetic	saah-nu-kahm-pi-thah	සානුකම්පිත
synagogue	yu-dhev poo-jahs-sthaah-nah-yah	යුදෙව් පූජාස්ථානය
synthetic	kru-thri-mah	කෘත්‍රිම
syringe	si-rin-jah-rah-yah	සිරින්ජරය

T

table	meh-sah-yah	මේසය
table tennis	teh-bahl te-nis kree-daah-vah	ටේබල් ටෙනිස් ක්‍රීඩාව
tail	vah-li-gah-yah	වලිගය
take (away, v)	pah-se-kah-tah gahn-nah-vaah	පසෙකට ගන්නවා

take (food, v)	gahn-nah-vaah	ගන්නවා
take (train, v)	yah-nah-vaah	යනවා
take photographs (v)	fo-toh gahn-nah-vaah	ෆොටෝ ගන්නවා
talk (v)	kah-thaah kah-rah-nah-vaah	කතා කරනවා
tall	u-sah	උස
tampons	tam-pahn e-kah	ටැම්පන් එක
tasty	rah-sah	රස
tax	bah-dhu	බදු
taxi stand	ku-lee rah-thah gaah-lah	කුලී රථ ගාල
team	kahn-daah-yah-mah	කණ්ඩායම
tear (crying)	kahn-dhu-lah	කඳුල
teeth	dhahth	දත්
telephone	dhu-rah-kah-thah-nah-yah • fohn e-kah	දුරකතනය • ෆෝන් එක
telephone (v)	te-li-fohn kah-rah-nah-vaah	ටෙලිෆෝන් කරනවා
television	roo-pah-vaah-hi-ni-yah • tee-vee e-kah	රූපවාහිනිය • ටීවී එක
tell (v)	ki-yah-nah-vaah	කියනවා
temperature (fever)	u-nah	උණ
temperature (weather)	ush-nahth-vah-yah	උෂ්ණත්වය
temple	pahn-sah-lah	පන්සල
tennis	te-nis kree-daah-wah	ටෙනිස් ක්‍රීඩාව
tent	koo-dhaah-rah-mah	කූඩාරම
tent pegs	koo-daah-rahm a-bah	කූඩාරම් ඇබ
terrible	bhah-yaah-nah-kai	භයානකයි
test	pah-reek-shah-nah-yah	පරීක්ෂණය
thank (v)	sthoo-thi kah-rah-nah-vaah	ස්තූති කරනවා
Thank you.	sthoo-thiy	ස්තූතියි.
theatre	nru-thyah shaah-laah-wah	නෘත්‍ය ශාලාව
they	o-vun	ඔවුන්
thick	ghah-nah	ඝන
thief	ho-raah	හොරා
thin	thu-nee	තුනී
think (v)	hi-thah-nah-vaah	හිතනවා
third	thun-ve-ni	තුන්වෙනි
thirsty	pi-paah-sah-yah • thi-bah-hah (spoken)	පිපාසය • තිබහ
this (one)	meh-kah	මේක
thought	si-thu-vi-li	සිතුවිලි
throat	u-gu-rah	උගුර
ticket	ti-kaht e-kah	ටිකට් එක
ticket collector	ti-kaht e-kah-thu kah-rahn-naah	ටිකට් එකතු කරන්නා

ticket machine	ti-kaht ma-shi-mah	ටිකට් මැෂිම
ticket office	ti-kaht kahn-thoh-ru-wah	ටිකට් කන්තෝරුව
time	veh-laah-vah	වේලාව
timetable	kaah-lah-sah-tah-hah-nah	කාලසටහන
tin (can)	tin e-kah	ටින් එක
tin opener	tin ah-ri-nah e-kah	ටින් අරින එක
tip (gratuity)	tip e-kahk	ටිප් එකක්
tired	mah-hahn-siy	මහන්සියි
tissue (paper)	ti-shoo kah-dah-dhaah-si	ටිෂූ කඩදාසි
tobacco	dhum-ko-lah	දුම්කොළ
tobacco kiosk	dhum-ko-lah kah-deh	දුම්කොළ කඩේ
today	ah-dhah	අද
together	e-kah-tah ek-vah	එකට එක්ව
toilet paper	toi-laht peh-pahr	ටොයිලට් පේපර්
toilets	va-si-ki-li	වැසිකිළි
tomorrow	he-tah	හෙට
tonight	ah-dhah raa	අද රෑ
too (as well)	...-th	...ත්
too expensive	mi-lah va-diy	මිළ වැඩි
too much / many	va-di • hun-gaahk	වැඩි • හුඟාක්
tooth	dhah-thah	දත
toothbrush	dhahth bu-ru-su-wah	දත් බුරුසුව
toothpaste	dhahth be-heth	දත් බෙහෙත්
toothpick	dhahth kah-tu-wah	දත් කටුව
torch (flashlight)	tohch e-kah	ටෝච් එක
touch (v)	ahl-lah-nah-vaah	අල්ලනවා
tour	sahn-chaah-rah-yah	සංචාරය
tourist	sahn-chaah-rah-kah-yaah	සංචාරකයා
tourist information office	sahn-chaah-rah-kah tho-rah-thu-ru kaahr-yaah-lah-yah	සංචාරක තොරතුරු කාර්යාලය
towards	ve-thah-tah	වෙතට
towel	thu-waah-yah	තුවාය
track (path)	ah-di-paah-rah	අඩිපාර
trade union	vruth-thee-yah sahn-gah-mah-yah	වෘත්තීය සංගමය
traffic	rah-thah-vaah-hah-nah gah-mah-naah-gah-mah-nah-yah	රථවාහන ගමනාගමනය
traffic lights	tra-fik lait	ට්‍රැෆික් ලයිට්
trail (route)	paah-rah • maahr-gah-yah	පාර • මාර්ගය
train	dhum-ri-yah	දුම්රිය
train station	dhum-ri-yah sthaah-nah-yah	දුම්රිය ස්ථානය

translate (v)	pah-ri-vahr-thah-nah-yah kah-rah-nah-vaah	පරිවර්තනය කරනවා
travel (v)	sahn-chaah-rah-yah kah-rah-nah-vaah	සංචාරය කරනවා
travel agency	sahn-chaah-rah-kah eh-jahn-si-yah	සංචාරක ඒජන්සිය
travel sickness	gah-mahn ki-ree-meh-dee a-thi-vah-nah vah-mah-nah-yah	ගමන් කිරීමේදි ඇතිවන වමනය
tree	gah-hah	ගහ
trek	trek	දුර ගමනක්
trip	gah-mah-nahk	ගමනක්
trousers	kah-li-sah-mah	කලිසම
It's true.	eh-kah ath-thah	ඒක ඇත්ත.
trust (v)	vish-waah-sah kah-rah-nah-vaah	විශ්වාස කරනවා
truth	ath-thah	ඇත්ත
try (v)	uth-sah-hah kah-rah-nah-vaah	උත්සාහ කරනවා
T-shirt	tee-shaht e-kah	ටී-ෂර්ට් එක
Turn left.	vah-mah-tah ha-ren-nah	වමට හැරෙන්න.
Turn right.	dhah-ku-nah-tah ha-ren-nah	දකුණට හැරෙන්න.
twice	dhe-sah-rah-yahk	දෙසරයක්
twin beds	an-dhahn dhe-kah-dhe-kah	ඇඳන් දෙක-දෙක
typical	ni-yah-mai	නියමයි
tyres	tah-yahr	ටයර්

U

umbrella	ku-dah-yah	කුඩය
understand (v)	theh-rum gahn-nah-vaah	තේරුම් ගන්නවා
I (don't) understand.	mah-tah theh-ren-neh (na-ha)	මට තේරෙන්නේ (නැහැ).
unemployed	ra-ki-yaah vi-rah-hi-thah	රැකියා විරහිත
unemployment	ra-ki-yaah vi-rah-hi-thah bhaa-vah-yah	රැකියා විරහිත භාවය
university	vish-vah vidh-yaah-lah-yah	විශ්ව විද්‍යාලය
unleaded	ee-yahm rah-hi-thah	ඊයම් රහිත
unsafe	ah-naah-rahk-shi-thah	අනාරක්ෂිත
until (June)	thek (joo-ni)	තෙක් (ජූනි)
unusual	ah-saah-maahn-yah	අසාමාන්‍ය
up	u-dah	උඩ
uphill (during a journey)	i-hah-lah-tah	ඉහළට
urgent	hah-dhi-si	හදිසි
useful	prah-yoh-jah-nah-vahth	ප්‍රයෝජනවත්

V

vacant	his	හිස්
vacation	ni-vaah-du-wah	නිවාඩුව
vaccination	en-nah-thah	එන්නත
valley	mi-ti-yaah-wah-thah	මිටියාවත
valuable	wah-ti-naah	වටිනා
value (price)	ah-gah-yah	අගය
vegetable	e-lah-vah-lu	එළවළු
vegetarian	e-lah-vah-lu pah-mah-nahk kah-nah	එළවළු පමණක් කන්නා
I'm vegetarian.	mah-mah e-lah-vah-lu pah-mah-nai kahn-neh	මම එළවළු පමණයි කන්නේ.
vegetation	gahs ko-lahn	ගස් කොළං
venue	sthaah-nah-yah	ස්ථානය
very	bo-hoh	බොහෝ
view	dhahr-shah-nah-yah	දර්ශනය
village	gah-mah	ගම
vineyard	mi-dhi wahth-thah	මිදි වත්ත
virus	vai-rah-sah-yah	වෛරසය
visa	vee-saah e-kah • aah-gah-mah-nah ah-vah-sah-rah-yah	වීසා එක • ආගමන අවසරය
visit (v)	ba-ha dhah-ki-nah-vaah	බැහැ දකිනවා
vitamins	vi-tah-min	විටමින්
vote (v)	chahn-dhah-yah dhah-mah-nah-vaah	ඡන්දය දැමීම

W

Wait!	In-nah!	ඉන්න!
waiter	weh-tahr • u-pah-tan vah-rah-yek / vah-ri-yahk (m / f)	වේටර් • උපටැන් වරයෙක් / වරියක්
waiting room	weh-tin room e-kah	වේටින් රූම් එක
walk (v)	a-vi-dhi-nah-vaah	ඇවිදිනවා
wall (inside)	a-thu-lah-thah bith-thi-yah	ඇතුළත බිත්තිය
wall (outside)	pi-tah-thah bith-thi-yah	පිටත බිත්තිය
want (v)	oh-neh ve-nah-vaah	ඕනේ වෙනවා
war	yudh-dhah-yah	යුද්ධය
wardrobe	ahl-maah-ri-yah	අල්මාරිය
warm	u-nu-sum	උණුසුම්
wash (v)	soh-dhah-nah-vaah	සෝදනවා

washing machine	re-dhi soh-dhah-nah me-shin e-kah	රෙදි සෝදන මැෂින් එක
watch (timepiece)	o-rah-loh-su-vah	ඔරලෝසුව
watch (v)	bah-lah-nah-vaah •	බලනවා •
	bah-laah in-nah-vaah	බලා ඉන්නවා
water	wah-thu-rah	වතුර
mineral water	bim jah-lah-yah	බිම් ජලය
waterfall	dhi-yah al-lah	දිය ඇල්ල
wave (sea)	rah-lah	රළ
way	mah-gah	මඟ
Please tell me the way to ...	kah-ru-naah-kah-rah mah-tah	කරුණාකරල මට
	... mah-gah pen-vahn-nah	... මඟ පෙන්වන්න.
	...paah-rah pen-vahn-nah (spoken)	... පාර පෙන්වන්න
Which way?	koi path-then-dhah?	කොයි පැත්තෙන්ද?
we	ah-pi	අපි
weak	dhur-wah-lah	දුර්වල
wealthy	po-ho-sahth	පොහොසත්
wear (v)	ahn-dhi-nah-vaah	අඳිනවා
weather	kaah-lah-gu-nah-yah	කාලගුණය
wedding	vi-vaah-hah mahn-gahl-yah	විවාහ මංගල්‍යය
week	sah-thi-yah	සතිය
weekend	sah-thi ahn-thah-yah	සති අන්තය
weigh (v)	ki-rah-nah-vaah	කිරනවා
welcome	saah-dhah-rah-yen pi-li-gah-ni-mu	සාදරයෙන් පිලිගනිමු
well	sah-nee-pah-yah	සනීපය
west	bah-tah-hi-rah	බටහිර
wet	the-thah	තෙත
what	ku-mahk-dhah?/ mo-kahk-dhah	කුමක්ද?/ මොකක්ද
What happened?	ku-mahk-dhah vu-neh?	කුමක්ද වුණේ?
wheelchair	roh-dhah pu-tu-wah	රෝද පුටුව
when	kah-vah-dhaah-dhah	කවදාද
When does it leave?	e-kah pi-tahth ven-neh kah-vah-dhaah-dhah? (date) •	ඒක පිටත් වෙන්නේ කවදාද? •
	koi veh-laah-veh-dhah? (time)	කොයි වේලාවේද?
where	ko-heh-dhah	කොහේද
Where's the bank?	ban-ku-wah thi-yen-neh ko-heh-dhah?	බැංකුව තියෙන්නේ කොහේද?

which	koi e-kah-dhah	කොයි එකද
who	kau-dhah	කව්ද
Who is it?	eh kau-dhah?	ඒ කව්ද?
whole	sahm-poor-na	සම්පූර්ණ
why	a-yi	ඇයි
wide	pah-lahl	පළල්
wife	bi-rin-dhah	බිරිඳ
win (v)	dhi-nah-nah-vaah	දිනනවා
wind	su-lahn-gah	සුළඟ
window	jah-neh-lah-yah	ජනේලය
window-shopping (v)	saahp-pu-wah-lah bah-du bah-lah-min a-vi-di-nah-vaah	සාප්පුවල බ බලමින් ඇවිදිනවා
windscreen / windshield	vin skreen	වින් ස්ක්‍රීන්
wine	wain	වයින්
winner	jah-yah-grah-hah-kah-yaah	ජයග්‍රාහකයා
winter	see-thah kaah-lah-yah	ශීත කාලය
wish (v)	pah-thah-nah-vah	පතනවා
with	sah-mah-gah	සමඟ
within	a-thu-lah-thah	ඇතුළත
within an hour	pa-yahk a-thu-lah-thah	පැයක් ඇතුළත
without	na-thi-vah	නැතිව

Y

yet	thah-vah-mah	තවම
not yet	thah-vah-mah na-ha	තවම නැහැ
you	o-bah	ඔබ
young	thah-ru-nah	තරුණ
youth hostel	thah-ru-nah nah-vaah-tha-nah	තරුණ නවාතැන

Z

zebra	see-braah	සීබ්‍රා
zodiac	grah-hah raah-shee chahk-rah-yah	ග්‍රහ රාශි චක්‍රය
zoo	sahth-vah ud-dhyaah-nah-yah	සත්ව උද්‍යානය

TAMIL

Introduction

Ever wondered who made the first curry? While experts may dispute the origins of the dish, it's almost certain that the Tamil word *ka*·ri கறி gave us its English name. With records of the language's existence going back more than 2000 years, it's not surprising that many Tamil words have been shared around. Tamil belongs to the Tamil-Kannada group from the southern branch of the Dravidian language family. The Tamil script is aptly named vat·*te*·lut·tu வட்டெழுத்து (meaning 'rounded writing') – so styled because curved lines were gentler on palm leaves, the traditional material for writing.

The global distribution of the Tamil language began during the years of European colonialism, when many South Indian Tamil people migrated across the world as both indentured labourers and traders for business. This took Tamil people to former British colonies like Singapore, Myanmar, Malaysia, Fiji, the West Indian islands of Trinidad and Tobago, Mauritius, Seychelles and South Africa, among others, where Tamil is still spoken today.

In Sri Lanka, Tamil people are subdivided into two main groups: (i) Sri Lankan Tamils – the descendants of people who migrated from South India many centuries ago (some as far back as the 2nd century BCE) – and (ii) 'Up Country Tamils' (or 'estate' Tamils) – descendants of comparatively recent work migrants brought from southern India into the island by British colonisers. Both subgroups are predominantly Hindu and speak Tamil as a first language, the umbrella term for which is Sri Lankan Tamil (SLT).

SLT dialects are more linguistically conservative compared to the dialects spoken in India. Because of how the dialects evolved compared to their Indian counterparts, they preserve features of Old and Medieval Tamil. Meanwhile, Indian Tamil (particularly in Tamil Nadu) has undergone more noticeable change and variation. Despite this, Indian Tamil and Sri Lankan Tamil are mutually intelligible.

This book largely focuses on spoken SLT (which is different from its literary and written counterpart).

Alphabet

Vowels					
அ a	ஆ aa	இ i	ஈ ee	உ u	ஊ oo
எ e	ஏ ey	ஐ ai	ஒ o	ஓ ow	ஔ aw

Consonants					
க ka	ங nga	ச cha	ஞ nya	ட ţa	ண ṇa
த ta	ந na	ப pa	ம ma	ய ya	ர ra
ல la	வ va	ழ źa	ள ļa	ற ra	ன na
ஜ ja	ஷ sha	ஹ ha	ஸ sa	பா ba	து da
ஷ şa	சை zai				

Pronunciation

Vowels	
Symbol	**English sound**
a	run
aa	father
ai	aisle
aw	law
e	bet
ee	see
ey	as in 'late'
i	hit
o	pot
oo	zoo
u	put

In this chapter, the Tamil pronunciation is given in yellow after each phrase.

Unlike most other Indian languages, Tamil has no 'aspirated' sounds (pronounced with a puff of air). Some consonants can be 'retroflex' (pronounced with the tip of the tongue bent backwards).

Each syllable is separated by a dot, and the syllable stressed in each word is italicised. For example:

மன்னிக்கவும். *man*·nik·ka·vum

Consonants	
Symbol	**English sound**
b	bed
ch	cheat
d	dog
h	hat
j	jar
k	kit
l	lot
ḷ	retroflex l
m	man
n	not
ṇ	retroflex n
ng	sing
ny	canyon
p	pet
r	red
s	sun
ş	retroflex s
sh	shoot
t	top
ṭ	retroflex t
th	voiceless dental /th/
v	very
y	yes
z	zero
ż	retroflex z

Travel Phrases

LANGUAGE DIFFICULTIES

Do you speak English?
நீங்கள் ஆங்கிலம் கதைப்பீங்களா? — *neeng*·kaḷ *aang*·ki·lam ka·*thai*·peeng·ga·*laa*

Do you understand?
உங்களுக்கு விளங்குதா? — ung·ka·ḷuk·*ku* vi·*lang*·gu·*thaa*

I understand.
எனக்கு விளங்குது. — e·*nak*·ku *vi*·lang·ku·thu

I don't understand.
எனக்கு விளங்கேல்லை. — e·*nak*·ku *vi*·lang·kel·lai

Could you please ...?	நீங்கள் தயவு செய்து ...?	*neeng*·kaḷ tha·ya·*vu* *sei*·thu ...
repeat that	அதை திருப்பி சொல்லுறீங்களா	a·thai thi·rup·pi *sol*·lu·reeng·ga·*laa*
speak more slowly	இன்னும் மெதுவாகப் கதைக்கிறீங்களா	*in*·num me·thu·vaa ka·*thaik*·ki·reeng·ga·*laa*

NUMBERS

0	சைவர்	sai·var	**20**	இருபது	i·ru·pa·thu
1	ஒன்று	oṇ·ṭu	**30**	முப்பது	mup·pa·thu
2	இரண்டு	i·*raṇ*·ṭu	**40**	நாப்பது	naap·pa·thu
3	மூன்று	*moon*·dru	**50**	ஐம்பது	aim·pa·thu
4	நாலு	naa·lu	**60**	அறுபது	a·ru·pa·thu
5	ஐஞ்சு	ain·*ju*	**70**	எழுபது	*e·ḻu*·pa·*thu*
6	ஆறு	aa·ru	**80**	எண்பது	eṇ·pa·*thu*
7	ஏழு	*ey*·ḻu	**90**	தொண்ணூறு	thoṇ·ṇoo·ru
8	எட்டு	eṭ·*ṭu*	**100**	நூறு	noo·*ru*
9	ஒன்பது	on·pa·*thu*	**1000**	ஆயிரம்	aa·yi·ram
10	பத்து	path·*thu*	**1,000,000**	பத்து லட்சம்	*path*·thu lach·*cham*

TIME & DATES

What time is it?	மணி என்ன?	ma·*ṇi* *en*·na
It's (two) o'clock.	(இரண்டு) மணி	ma·*ṇi* (i·*raṇ*·ţu)
Quarter past (two).	(இரண்டே) கால்.	(i·*raṇ*·ţey) kaal
Half past (two).	(இரண்டு) முப்பது.	(i·*raṇ*·ţu) mup·pa·*tu*
Quarter to (three).	(மூன்றே) முக்கால்.	(*moon*·drey) muk·*kaal*
At what time ...?	எத்தனை மணிக்கு ...?	*eth*·tha·nai ma·*ṇik*·ku ...
At ...	... மணிக்கு.	... ma·*ṇik*·ku
It's (15 December).	(டிசம்பர் பதினஞ்சாம்) திகதி.	(di·sam·bar pa·thi·nan·jaam) thi·ha·thi

yesterday	நேற்று	*neyt*·tru
today	இண்டைக்கு	iṇ·*daik*·ku
tomorrow	நாளைக்கு	*naa*·ļaik·ku

Monday	திங்கள்	*thing*·gaļ
Tuesday	செவ்வாய்	sev·*vaai*
Wednesday	புதன்	pu·*than*
Thursday	வியாழன்	vi·*yaa*·żan
Friday	வெள்ளி	veļ·*ļi*
Saturday	சனி	sa·*ni*
Sunday	ஞாயிறு	*nyaa*·yi·ru

BORDER CROSSING

I'm here ...	நான் இங்கே இருக்கிறேன் ...	naan *ing*·key i·*ruk*·ki·reyn ...
in transit	பயணத்தில்	*pa*·ya·ṇat·til
on business	வேலையாக	*vey*·lai·yaa·ka
on holiday	வீடுமுறையில்	*vi*·ţu·mu·rai·*yil*

I'm here for ...	நான் இங்கே இருப்பது ...	naan *ing*·key i·*rup*·pa·tu ...
(10) days	(பத்து) நாட்களுக்கு	(pat·*tu*) *naaţ*·ka·ļuk·ku
(three) weeks	(மூன்று) கிழமைக்கு	(*moon*·dru) ki·ża·maik·ku
(two) months	(இரண்டு) மாதங்களுக்கு	(i·*raṇ*·ţu) *maa*·tang·ka·ļuk·ku

I'm going to (Chennai).

நான் (சென்னைக்குப்) போறேன்.	naan (*chen*·naik·kup) *paw*·reyn

I'm staying at the (Taj Hotel).

நான் (தாஜ் ஹொடெல்ல) தங்கியிருக்கிறேன்.	naan (taaj *hoṭ*·ṭel·la) tang·ki·yi·*ruk*·ki·reyn

I have nothing to declare.

அறிவிக்க என்னட்டை ஒண்டும் இல்லை.	a·ri·vik·ka *en*·nat·tai *oṇ*·dum il·lai

TICKETS & LUGGAGE

Where can I buy a ticket?

ரிக்கெட் எங்க வாங்கலாம்?	tik·ket *eng*·ga *vaang*·ga·laam

Do I need to book a seat?

சீட் முன்பதிவு செய்ய வேணுமா?	seet *mun*·pa·thi·vu sey·ya *ve*·*ṇu*·*maa*

One ... ticket (to Madurai), please.	தயவு செய்து (மதுரைக்கு) ஒரு டிக்கெட்	*tha*·ya·vu·*sei*·thu (ma·thu·raik·ku) o·*ru* tik·ket
one-way	ஒரு வழிப்பயண	o·*ru* va·*źip*·pa·ya·ṇa
return	இரு வழிப்பயண	i·*ru* va·*źip*·pa·ya·ṇa

I'd like to ... my ticket, please.	எண்ட டிக்கெடை ...வேணும்.	*en*·ta tik·ket·ai ... *ve*·ṇum
cancel	ரத்து செய்ய	*rat*·tu *sei*·ya
change	மாற்ற	*maat*·tra

Is there a toilet?

கழிவறை இருக்கா	ka·*źi*·va·rai i·ruk·*kaa*

How long does the trip take?

பயணம் எவ்வளவு நேரம் எடுக்கும்?	pa·ya·*ṇam* ev·*va*·ḷa·vu ney *ram* e·*ṭuk*·kum

Is it a direct route?

இது நேரடியான பாதையா?	i·*tu* ney·ra·ṭi·*yaa*·na *paa*·tai·yaa

My luggage has been ...	என்ட பாக் ... போய்ற்று.	*en·ta baag* ... *pawi*·tu
lost	காணாமல்	*kaa*·ṇaa·mal
stolen	களவு	*ka*·ḷa·vu

TRANSPORT

Where does flight (IC 975) arrive/depart?

(IC 975) விமானம்	(ai see on·pa·*tu ey*·*żu* ain·*tu*) vi·*maa*·nam
எங்கே வந்தடையும்/புறப்படும்?	*eng*·key *van*·tha·ṭa·yum/ pu·*rap*·pa·ṭum

Is this the ... to (New Delhi)?	இது தானா (புதுடில்லிக்குப்) புறப்படும் ...?	*i*·thu *thaa*·naa (pu·*tu* ṭil·lik·*kup*) pu·*rap*·pa·ṭum...
bus	பஸ்	bas
plane	விமானம்	vi·*maa*·nam
train	இரயில்	i·ra·*yil*

What time's the first/last bus?

எத்தனை மணிக்கு முதல்/இறுதி பஸ் வரும்?	*et*·ta·nai ma·*ṇik*·ku mu·*tal*/i·ru·*ti* pas va·*rum*

How long will it be delayed?

எவ்வளவு நேரம் அது பிந்தும்	*ev*·va·ḷa·vu *ney*·ram a·*tu* *pin*·thum

Please tell me when we get to (Ooti).

(ஊட்டிக்குப்) போன உடன தயவு செய்து எனக்குக் சொல்லுங்க	(ooṭ·ṭik·*kup*) *paw*·na·*u*·da·na ta·ya·*vu* chey·*tu* e·*nak*·kuk *sol*·lun·ga

That's my seat.

அது என்ட இருக்கை.	a·thu *en*·da i·*ruk*·kai

I'd like a taxi ...	எனக்கு ஒரு டக்சி ...வேணும்	e·*nak*·ku o·*ru* *tak*·si ... *ve*·ṇum
at (9am)	(காலை ஒன்பது) மணிக்கு	(*kaa*·lai on·pa·*tu*) ma·*ṇik*·ku
now	இப்ப	*ip*·pa

How much is it to (Maamallapuram)?

(மாமல்லபுரத்துக்கு) எவ்வளவு	(maa·mal·*la*·pu·rat·*tuk*·ku) *ev*·va·ḷa·*vu*

Please put the meter on.

தயவு செய்து மீட்டரைப் போடுங்க	ta·ya·*vu sey*·thu *meeṭ*·ṭa·raip *paw*·ṭung·ga

Please take me to (this address).

தயவு செய்து என்னை இந்த (விலாசத்துக்குக்) கூட்டிக்கொண்டு போங்க	ta·ya·*vu* chey·*tu en*·nai *in*·ta (vi·*laa*·chat·tuk·kuk) *koot*·ti·koṇ·ṭu *pawng*·ga

Please stop/wait here.

தயவு செய்து இங்கே நிப்பாட்டுங்க/நில்லுங்க.	ta·ya·*vu sey*·thu *ing*·key *nip*·paat·tung·ga/*i*·rung·ga

I'd like to hire a car (with a driver).

எனக்கு ஒரு மோட்டர்சயிக்கில் (டிரைவரோட) வாடகைக்கு எடுக்க வேணும்.	naan o·*ru mawṭ*·tar *saik*·kil (*drai*·va·*raw*·da) vaa·ṭa·*haik*·ku e·*ṭuk*·ka *ve*·ṇum

I'd like to hire a 4WD (with a driver).

எனக்கு ஒரு 4WD (டிரைவரோட) வாடகைக்கு எடுக்க வேணும்.	naan o·*ru* for weel draiv (*drai*·va·*raw*·da) vaa·ṭa·*haik*·ku e·*ṭuk*·ka *ve*·ṇum

How much for daily/weekly hire?

நாள்/கிழமை வாடகை எவ்வளவு?	naaḷ/*ki*·ḷa·mai vaa·ṭa·*hai* e·va·ḷa·*vu*

DIRECTIONS

Where's the ...?	... எங்க இருக்கு	... *eng*·key *i*·ruk·*ku*
bank	வங்கி	*vang*·ki
foreign currency exchange	நாணய மாற்றுச் சந்தை	*naa*·ṇa·ya *maat*·truch *chan*·thai
post office	தபால் நிலையம்	ta·*paal* ni·*lai*·yam

Is this the road to (Maamallapuram)?

இது தான் (மாமல்லபுரத்துக்கு) செல்லும் வீதியா?	i·*tu* taan (maa·mal·*la*·pu·rat·*tuk*·ku) *chel*·lum *vee*·thi·*yaa*

Can you show me (on the map)?

எனக்கு (வரைபடத்தில்) காட்ட முடியுமா?	e·*nak*·ku (va·*rai*·pa·*ṭat*·til) *kaaṭ*·ṭa mu·ṭi·yu·*maa*

What's the address?

விலாசம் என்ன?	vi·*laa*·sam *en*·na

How far is it?

எவ்வளவு தூரம்?	*ev*·va·ḷa·vu *thoo*·ram

How do I get there?

நான் அங்கே எப்பிடி போறது? naan *ang*·key *ep*·pi·di *paw*·ra·thu

Turn left/right.

இடது/வலது புறத்தில் திரும்புக. i·ṭa·*tu*/va·la·*tu* pu·*rat*·til *ti*·rum·pu·ka

It's ...	அது ... இருக்குது	a·*tu* ... *i*·ruk·ku·thu
behind ...	... க்குப் பின்னால்	... kup *pin*·naal
in front of ...	... க்கு முன்னால்	... ku *mun*·naal
near (to ...)	(... க்கு) கிட்ட	(... ku) *kiṭ*·ṭa
on the corner	திருப்பத்தில	*thi*·rup·pa·thi·la
there	அங்கே	*ang*·key

ACCOMMODATION

Where's a guesthouse nearby?

அருகே ஒரு சுற்றுலா இல்லம் எங்கே இருக்கு?	a·ru·*ke* o·*ru* *sut*·tru·laa *il*·lam *eng*·ke *i*·ruk·*ku*

Where's a hotel nearby?

கிட்ட ஒரு ஹோட்டல் எங்கே இருக்கு?	*kiṭ*.ṭa o·*ru* *hoṭ*·ṭal *eng*·ke *i*·ruk·*ku*

Can you recommend somewhere cheap/good?

எங்கேனும் மலிவா/ நல்லதா இருக்குமா	*eng*·key·num *ma*·li·*vaa*/ *nal*·la·thaa *i*·ruk·ku·*maa*

I'd like to book a room, please.

எனக்கு ஒரு அறை முன்னெற்பாடு செய்ய வேணும்.	e·nak·ku o·ru a·rai *mun*·eyt·paa·du *sey*·ya *vey*·ṇum

I have a reservation.

நான் ஒரு அறை முன்னேற்பாடு செய்திருக்கிறேன்.	naan o·ro a·*rai* *mun*·neyr·paa·ṭu *sey*·thi·ruk·ki·ran

Do you have a ... room?	ஒரு ... அறை இருக்கா?	*o*·ru ... a·*rai* *i*·ruk·*kaa*
single	தனி	tha·ni
double	இரட்டை	i·raṭ·*ṭai*
twin	இரண்டு கட்டில் இருக்கிற	*ren*·du *kat*·til i·ruk·ki·ra

How much is it per night/person?
ஒரு இரவுக்கு/ஒராளுக்கு எவ்வளவு? — o·ru i·ra·vuk·ku/o·ru aa·*ḷuk*·ku e·va.ḷa·*vu*

I'd like to stay for (two) nights.
நான் (இரண்டு) இரவுகள் தங்க விரும்புகிறேன். — naan (i·*raṇ*·ţu) i·*ra*·vu·kaḷ *tang*·ka vi·*rum*·pu·ki·reyn

Can I have my key, please?
எனது சாவியை தயவு செய்து கொடுக்க முடியுமா? — e·*na*·tu *chaa*·vi·yai ta·ya·*vu* chey·*tu* ko·*ţuk*·ka mu·*ţi*·yu·maa

Can I get another (blanket)?
எனக்கு இன்னும் ஒரு (போர்வை) கிடைக்குமா? — e·*nak*·ku *in*·num o·*ru* (*pawr*·vai) ki·*ţaik*·ku·maa

The (air conditioning) doesn't work.
(குளிர்சாதனம்) வேலை செய்யவில்லை. — (ku·*ḷir*·saa·tha·nam) vey·*lai* sey·ya·*vil*·lai

Is there a lift/elevator?
லிப்ட் இருக்கா? — lipt *i*·ruk·*kaa*

Is there a safe?
பாதுகாப்புப் பெட்டி இருக்கா? — paa·tu·kaap·*pup* peţ·*ţi i*·ruk·*kaa*

What time is checkout?
எத்தனை மணிக்கு வெளியேற வேணும்? — *eth*·tha·nai ma·*ṇik*·ku ve·*ḷi*·yey·ra vey·ṇum

Can I have my (passport), please?
தயவு செய்து என்ட (பாஸ்போர்ட்) தாறீங்களா? — *tha*·ya·vu *sey*·thu en·da (*paas*·pawrt) *thaa*·reeng·ga·*ḷaa*

BANKING & COMMUNICATIONS

Where's an ATM?
ATM எங்க இருக்கு? — *ey*·*ti*·*em eng*·ga i·ruk·*ku*

I'd like to ...	எனக்கு ... வேணும்.	e·nak·ku *vey*·ṇum
arrange a transfer	பணம் அனுப்ப	pa·*ṇam* a·*nup*·pa
change money	பணத்தை மாற்ற	pa·*ṇat*·tai *maat*·tra
withdraw money	பணத்தை எடுக்க	pa·*ṇat*·tai e·*ţuk*·ka

What's the ...?	... கட்டணம் என்ன?	... kaţ·ţa·*ṇam en*·na
charge for that	அதற்குரிய	a·*tar*·ku·ri·ya
exchange rate	பங்கு மாற்று	*pang*·ku *maat*·tru
I'd like to ...	எனக்கு ... பாவிக்க வேணும்.	e·nak·ku ... *paa*·vik·ka *vey*·ṇum
use a printer/ scanner	பிரிண்டர்/ ஸ்கானர்	*prin*·tar/ *skaan*·er
I'd like a ...	எனக்கு ... வேணும்.	e·nak·ku ... *vey*·ṇum
mobile/cell phone for hire	வாடகைக்கு கைத்தொலைபேசி	vaa·ţa·*kaik*·ku *kait*·to·lai·pey·*chi*
SIM card for your network	உங்கள் தொடர்புக்கு அட்டை	*ung*·kal to·ţar·*puk*·ku sim·aţ·ţai

What are the rates?
கட்டணங்கள் என்ன? — kaţ·ţa·*ṇang*·kaḷ *en*·na

The number is ...
இலக்கம் ... — i·*lak*·kam ...

I want to ...	எனக்கு ... வேணும்.	e·nak·ku ... *vey*·ṇum
call (Canada)	(கனடா) வுக்கு அழைக்க	(ka·na·*ţaa*) vuk·*ku* a·źaik·*ka*

I want to buy a stamp.
எனக்கு ஒரு அஞ்சல் தலை வாங்க வேணும். — e·nak·ku o·ru *an*·chal tha·lai *vaang*·*ga vey*·um

I want to buy an envelope.
எனக்கு ஒரு தபால் உறை வாங்க வேணும். — e·nak·ku o·ru *tha*·baal u·rai *vaang*·*ga vey*·um

Please send it (to Australia).
தயவு செய்து இதை (ஆஸ்திரேலியாவுக்கு) அனுப்பவும். — *tha*·ya·vu *sey*·thu i·thai (*aas*·ti·*rey*·li·yaa·vuk·ku) a·*nup*·pa·vum

SIGHTSEEING

What time does it open/close?

அது எத்தனை மணிக்கு திறக்கும்/மூடும்?	a·thu *eth*·tha·nai *ma*·ṇik·ku *thi*·rak·kum/*moo*·ţum

What's the admission charge?

நுழைவு கட்டணம் எவ்வளவு?	nu·*źai*·vu *kaţ*·ţa·nam *ev*·va·ḷa·*vu*

Is there a discount for students/children?

மாணவர்களுக்கு/ சிறுவர்களுக்கு கழிவு இருக்கா?	maa·ṇa·*var*·ka·*ḷuk*·ku/ chi·ru·*var*·ka·*ḷuk*·ku ka·*źi*·vu *i*·ruk·*kaa*

I'd like to hire a guide.

நான் ஒரு வழிகாட்டியை வாடகைக்கு பிடிக்க வேணும்	naan o·*ru* va·*źi*·kaaţ·*ţi*·yai vaa·ţa·*kaik*·ku *pi*·ţik·ka *vey*·ṇum

I'd like a catalogue/map.

எனக்கு ஒரு பொருள்பட்டியல்/ வரைபடம் வேணும்	e·*nak*·ku o·*ru* po·*ruḷ*·paţ·*ţi*·yal/ va·*rai*·pa·ţam *vey*·ṇum

I'd like to see ...

நான் ஒரு ... பார்க்க விரும்புகிறேன்.	naan o·*ru* ... *paark*·ka vi·rum·*pu*·ki·reyn

Can I take a photo?

நான் ஒரு புகைப்படம் எடுக்கலாமா?	naan o·*ru* pu·*kaip*·pa·ţam e·*ţuk*·ka·*laa*·maa

I'd like to go somewhere off the beaten track.

வழக்கமாக இல்லாத பகுதிக்கு நான் செல்ல விரும்புகிறேன்.	va·*źak*·ka·maa·ha *il*·laa·ta pa·ku·*tik*·ku naan *chel*·la vi·*rum*·pu·ki·reyn

When's the next tour?

அடுத்த சுற்றுப்பயணம் எப்ப?	a·*ţuth*·tha *sut*·trup·pa·ya·ṇam *ep*·pa

How long is the tour?

அந்த சுற்றுப்பயணம் எவ்வளவு தூரம்?	*an*·tha *sut*·trup·pa·ya·ṇam *ev*·va·ḷa·vu *thoo*·ram

Is ... included?	... சேர்க்கப்பட்டுள்ளதா?	... cheyr·*kap*·paţ·*ţuḷ*·ḷa·thaa
accommodation	தங்குமிடம்	*thang*·ku·mi·ţam
food	உணவு	u·*ṇa*·vu
transport	போக்குவரத்து	*powk*·ku·va·rath·*thu*

SIGHTSEEING

fort	கோட்டை	*kawṭ*·ṭai
mosque	பள்ளி வாசல்	*paḷ*·ḷi *vaa*·sal
palace	அரண்மனை	a·*raṇ*·ma·nai
ruins	பாழடைந்த இடம்	paa·*ẓa*·*ṭain*·ta i·*ṭam*
temple	கோவில்	*kaw*·vil

SHOPPING

Where's a ... ?	எங்கே ... இருக்கு?	*eng*·key ... *i*·ruk·*ku*
camera shop	கமரா கடை	*ka*·ma·raa ka·*ṭai*
market	சந்தை	*chan*·tai
souvenir shop	நினைவுச் சின்ன கடை	ni·nai·*vu chin*·na ka·*ṭai*

I'm looking for ...
நான் தேடிக்கொண்டிருப்பது ... — naan tey·ṭik·koṇ·ṭi·*rup*·pa·tu ...

Can I look at it?
நான் இதைப் பார்க்கலாமா? — naan i·*thaip paark*·ka·laa·maa

Can I have it sent overseas?
நான் இதை வெளிநாட்டுக்கு அனுப்பலாமா? — naan i·*thai* ve·ḷi·*naad*·duk·ku a·*nup*·pa·laa·maa

Can I have my (camera) repaired?
என்ட (கமராவை) திருத்த முடியுமா? — en·da (*ka*·ma·*raa*·val) *thi*·ruth·tha mu·di·yu·*maa*

It's faulty.
இது பழுதாப்ப்போச்சு — i·*tu pa*·ḷu·thaap·*pawch*·chu

How much is it?
இது என்ன விலை? — i·*tu en*·na vi·*lai*

That's too expensive.
அது விலை கூட — a·thu *vi*·lai *koo*·da

I'll give you (300 rupees).
நான் உங்களுக்கு (300 ரூபா) தாறேன். — naan *ung*·ka·*ḷuk*·ku (*moon*·noo·ru roo·*paai*) *thaa*·ren

There's a mistake in the bill.	இந்த விலைச்சீட்டில் ஒரு ஒரு பிழை இருக்கு	*in*·ta vi·*laich*·cheeṭ·ṭil o·ru *pi*·ḷai i·*ruk*·ku
Do you accept ...?	நீங்கள் ... எடுப்பீங்களா?	*neeng*·gaḷ ... e·dup·peeng·ga·*ḷaa*
credit cards	கிரேடிட் அட்டைகள்	ki·rey·*ṭit* aṭ·ṭai·kaḷ
I'd like (a) ..., please.	தயவு செய்து எனக்கு ... வேணும்.	ta·ya·*vu sey*·thu e·*nak*·ku ... *vey*·ṇum
receipt	ஒரு ரசீது	o·*ru* ra·*chee*·tu
refund	என் பணம் திரும்ப	en pa·*ṇam* ti·*rum*·pa
Less./More.	குறைவு./அதிகம்.	ku·rai·*vu*/a·*ti*·kam
Enough.	போதும்.	*pow*·tum

☑ ESSENTIAL PHRASES

Yes./No.	ஓம்./இல்லை.	awm / *il*·lai
Please./ Thank you.	தயவு செய்து./நன்றி.	ta·ya·*vu* chey·*tu*/ *nan*·dri
Excuse me.	தயவு செய்து.	ta·ya·*vu* sei·*du*
Sorry.	மன்னிக்கவும்.	*man*·nik·ka·vum

MAKING CONVERSATION

Hello.	வணக்கம்.	va·*ṇak*·kam
Good night.	இரவு வணக்கம்.	i·ra·*vu* va·*ṇak*·kam
Goodbye.	போய்ற்று வாறன்.	*pawit*·tru *vaa*·ren
Mr/Mrs	திரு/திருமதி	ti·ru/ti·ru·ma·*ti*
Miss/Ms	செல்வி/திருவாட்டி	*sel*·vi/ti·ru·*vaṭ*·ṭi
How are you?	எப்பிடி சுகம்?	*ep*·pi·di *su*·ham
Fine, thanks.	நல்ல சுகம், நன்றி.	*nal*·la *su*·ham *nan*·dri
And you?	நீங்கள்?	*neeng*·kaḷ

What's your name?	உங்கட பெயர் என்ன?	*ung*·ga·da pe·*yar en*·na
My name is ...	என்ட பெயர் ...	*en*·ţa pe·*yar* ...
I'm pleased to meet you.	உங்களைச் சந்திச்சது சந்தோஷம்.	*ung*·ka·ļaich *chan*·thich·cha·thu *san*·tho·sham
This is my ...	இவர் என்ட ...	i·*var en*·da ...
brother	தம்பி	*tham*·bi
daughter	மகள்	ma·*kaļ*
friend	நண்பன்	*naņ*·pan
sister	தங்கை	*tang*·kai
son	மகன்	ma·*kan*

Here's my (address).
இந்தாங்கோ என்ட (விலாசம்). — *in*·thaang·go *en*·da (vi·*laa*·sam)

What's your (email)?
உங்கட (மின்னஞ்சல் முகவரி) என்ன? — *ung*·ga·da (min·nan·*chal* mu·ka·va·*ri*) *en*·na

Where are you from?
நீங்கள் எங்கிருந்து வாறீங்கள்? — *neeng*·kaļ *eng*·ki·run·tu *vaa*·reeng·*gaļ*

I'm from (New Zealand).
நான் இங்கிருந்து வாறேன் (நியுசிலாந்து). — naan *ing*·ki·run·tu *vaa*·reyn (ni·yoo·chi·*laan*·tu)

What's your occupation?
உங்கட வேலை என்ன? — *ung*·ga·da vey·*lai en*·na

I'm a/an ...	நான் ஒரு ...	naan o·*ru* ...
businessperson	வியாபாரி	vi·yaa·paa·*ri*
office worker	அலுவலக ஊழியர்	a·*lu*·va·la·ka *oo*·źi·yar
tradesperson	தொழிற்துறையாளர்	to·*źir*·tu·rai·yaa·ļar
Do you like ...?	உங்களுக்கு ... பிடிக்குமா?	*ung*·ka·*ļuk*·ku ... pi·*ţik*·ku·maa
I like ...	எனக்கு ... பிடிக்கும்.	e·*nak*·ku ... pi·*ţik*·kum
I don't like ...	எனக்கு ... பிடிக்காது.	e·*nak*·ku ... pi·*ţik*·kaa·thu
art	கலை	*ka*·lai
sport	விளையாட்டு	vi·ļai·*yaaţ*·ţu

EATING OUT

Can you recommend a ...?	நீங்கள் ஒரு ... பரிந்துரைக்க முடியுமா?	*neeng*·kaḷ o·*ru* ... pa·rin·tu·*raik*·ka mu·ṭi·*yu*·maa
bar	பார்	baar
place to eat	உணவகம்	u·ṇa·va·*ham*
I'd like (a/the) ..., please.	எனக்கு தயவு செய்து ... தாங்க	e·*nak*·ku ta·ya·*vu* chey·*tu* ... *thaang*·ga
bill	விலைச்சீட்டு	vi·*laich*·cheeṭ·ṭu
menu	உணவுப்பட்டியல்	u·ṇa·*vup*·paṭ·ṭi·yal
table for (four)	(நான்கு) பேருக்குரிய ஒரு மேசை	(naan·*ku*) pey·*ruk*·ku·ri·ya o·*ru* mey·*sai*
that dish	அந்த சாப்பாடு	*an*·ta *saap*·paa·ṭu
breakfast	காலை சாப்பாடு	kaa·*lai saap*·paa·ṭu
lunch	மதிய சாப்பாடு	ma·*ti*·ya *saap*·paa·ṭu
dinner	இரவு சாப்பாடு	i·ra·*vu saap*·paa·ṭu

I'll have boiled/mineral water.

எனக்கு கொதிக்க வைச்ச/ மினரல் தண்ணீர் வேணும் — e·*nak*·ku ko·*thik*·ka *vaich*·cha/ mi·na·*ral taṇ*·ṇeyr *vey*·ṇum

What would you like?

உங்களுக்கு எது வேணும்? — *ung*·ka·ḷuk·ku e·*thu vey*·ṇum

(cup of) coffee/ tea ...	(கப்) கோப்பி/ ... தேத்தண்ணி	(kap) *kawp*·pi/ *they*·thaṇ·ṇi ...
with milk	பாலுடன்	paa·lu·*ṭan*
without sugar	சீனிஇல்லாமல	*see*·ni·*il*·laa·mal
(orange) juice	(ஆரஞ்சு) சாறு	(aa·ra·*nyu*) chaa·*ru*
lassi	லாசி	*la*·si
soft drink	குளிர் பானம்	ku·*ḷir* paa·*nam*
a bottle/glass of beer	ஒரு போத்தல்/கிளாஸ் பியர்	o·*ru pawth*·thal/glaas *bi*·yar
a bottle/glass of ...wine	ஒரு போத்தல்/ கிளாஸ் ... வைன்	o·*ru paaṭ*·ṭil/ glaas ... vain
red	சிவப்பு	si·*vap*·pu
white	வெள்ளை	*veḷ*·ḷai

SPECIAL DIETS & ALLERGIES

Do you have vegetarian food?

உங்களிட்ட சைவ சாப்பாடு இருக்கா? — ung·ga·ḷit·tai *sai*·va *saap*·paa·du *i*·ruk·*kaa*

I'm allergic to ...	எனக்கு ... ஒத்துக்கொள்ளாது	e·*nak*·ku ... *oth*·thuk·koḷ·ḷaa·*thu*
dairy products	பால் சார்ந்த	paal *saarn*·tha
eggs	முட்டை	*muṭ*·ṭai
meat stock	இறைச்சி வகை	i·*raich*·chi va·*kai*
nuts	பருப்பு வகை	pa·*rup*·pu va·*kai*
seafood	கடல் சார்ந்த	ka·*ṭal saarn*·tha

EMERGENCIES

Help!	உதவி!	u·tha·*vi*
Stop!	நிறுத்து!	ni·*rut*·thu
Go away!	போய் விடு!	*pow*·i *vi*·ṭu
Thief!	திருடன்!	*ti*·ru·ṭan
Fire!	நெருப்பு!	ne·*rup*·pu
Watch out!	கவனம்!	*ka*·va·nam

Call ...!	ஐ அழைக்கவும் ...!	i a·*źai*·ka·vum ...
an ambulance	ஒரு ஆம்புலன்ஸ்	o·*ru aam*·pu·lans
a doctor	ஒரு மருத்துவர்	o·*ru ma*·ruth·thu·var
the police	பொலிஸ்	*po*·lis

Could you help me, please?

நீங்கள் எனக்கு தயவு செய்து உதவி செய்ய முடியுமா? — *neeng*·kaḷ e·*nak*·ku *tha*·ya·vu *sei*·thu *chey*·ya mu·*ṭi*·yu·maa

I have to use the phone.

நான் தொலைபேசியை பாவிக்க வேணும் — naan *to*·lai·pey·si·yai *paa*·vik·ka *vey*·ṇum

I'm lost.

நான் வழி தவறி போய்விட்டேன். — naan va·*źi tha*·va·*ri* paw·i·*viṭ*·ṭeyn

Where are the toilets?

கழிவறைகள் எங்கே? — ka·*źi*·va·rai·kaḷ *eng*·key

Where's the police station?

காவல் நிலையம் எங்கே இருக்கு? kaa·*val* ni·*lai*·yam *eng*·key *i*·ruk·*ku*

I have insurance.

என்னிடம் காப்புறுதி இருக்கு *en*·ni·ţam *kaap*·pu.ru.thi *i*·ruk·*ku*

I want to contact my embassy.

நான் என்ட தூதரகத்துடன் தொடர்பு கொள்ள விரும்புகிறேன். naan *en*·da *thoo*·tha·ra·hath·thu·dan tho·*ţar*·pu *koḷ*·ḷa vi·*rum*·pu·ki·ren

I've been raped.

நான் கற்பழிக்கப்பட்டுள்ளேன். naan kar·pa·*źik*·kap·paţ·*ţuḷ*·ḷeyn

I've been robbed.

நான் கொள்ளையிடப்பட்டுள்ளேன். naan koḷ·ḷai·yi·*ţap*·paţ·*ţuḷ*·ḷeyn

I've lost my bag/money.

நான் என்ட பை/பணம் துலைச்சிட்டன் naan en·da pai/pa·*ṇam* thu·*laich*·chiţ·ţan

HEALTH

Where's the nearest ...?	கிட்ட இருக்கிற ... எங்கே?	*kiţ*·ţa *i*·ruk·ki·ra ... *eng*·key
dentist	பல் மருத்துவர்	pal ma·*ruth*·thu·var
doctor	மருத்துவர்	ma·*ruth*·thu·var
hospital	மருத்துவமனை	ma·*ruth*·thu·va·ma·nai
pharmacist	மருந்தகம்	ma·*run*·tha·ham

I need a doctor (who speaks English).

(ஆங்கிலம் பேசக்கூடிய) ஒரு மருத்துவர் எனக்கு தேவை. (*aang*·ki·lam pey·chak·*koo*·ţi·ya) o·*ru* ma·*ruth*·thu·var e·*nak*·ku *tey*·vai

Could I see a female doctor?

நான் ஒரு பெண் மருத்துவரை பார்க்க முடியுமா? naan o·*ru* peṇ ma·*ruth*·thu·va·*rai* paark·*ka* mu·ţi·*yu*·maa

I've run out of my medication.

என்ட மருந்துகள் முடிந்து விட்டன. *en* da ma·*run*·thu·kaḷ mu·*ţin*·thu *viţ*·ţa·na

I have (a) ...	எனக்கு ... உள்ளது.	e·*nak*·ku ... *uḷ*·ḷa·*thu*
constipation	மலச்சிக்கல்	ma·*lach*·chik·kal
diarrhoea	வயிற்றுப்போக்கு	va·yit·*trup*·pawk·ku
fever	காய்ச்சல்	*kaich*·chal
heart condition	இருதய நோய்	*i*·ru·tha·ya·*naw*·i
nausea	குமட்டல்	ku·*maṭ*·ṭal
I'm allergic to ...	எனக்கு ... ஒத்துக்கொள்ளாது.	e·*nak*·ku ... *oth*·thuk·*koḷ*·ḷaa·thu
anti-inflammatories	அழற்சிக்கான மருந்து	a·*źar*·*chik*·kaa·na ma·*run*·thu
bees	தேனிக்கள்	*they*·ni·kaḷ
codeine	கொடெய்ன் மருந்து வகை	ko·*ṭeyn* ma·*run*·thu va·*kai*

RESPONSIBLE TRAVEL

I'd like to learn some Tamil.
நான் தமிழ் படிக்க விரும்புகிறேன். naan tha·mil *pa*·ṭik·ka vi·*rum*·pu·ki·reyn

Would you like me to teach you some English?
உங்களுக்கு நான் கொஞ்சம் ஆங்கிலம் சொல்லி தரட்டுமா?
ung·ka·*ḷuk*·ku naan *kon*·jam *aang*·ki·lam *sol*·li ta·*raṭ*·ṭu·maa

I didn't mean to do anything wrong.
நான் தவறாக எதையும் செய்ய நினைக்கவில்லை.
naan ta·va·raa·*ka* e·*tai*·yum sei·ya ni·*naik*·ka·*vil*·lai

Is this a local or national custom?
இது ஒரு உள்ளூர் வழக்கமா நாட்டு வழக்கமா?
i·thu o·ru *uḷ*·ḷoor va·*źak*·ka·maa *naaṭ*·ṭu va·*źak*·ka·maa

I'd like to stay at a locally run hotel.
நான் உள்ளூரில் நடத்தப்படும் ஒரு ஹோட்டலில் தங்க விரும்புகிறேன்.
naan *uḷ*·ḷoo·ril na·*ṭat*·tap·pa·ṭum o·*ru hoṭ*·ṭa·lil *thang*·ka vi·*rum*·pu·ki·reyn

Where can I buy locally produced goods?
உள்ளூரில் செய்த பொருட்கள் நான் எங்கே வாங்க முடியும்?
uḷ·ḷoo·ril *sei*·tha po·*ruṭ*·kaḷ naan *eng*·key *vang*·ka mu·ṭi·*yum*

I'd like to do some volunteer work.
நான் சில பொதுநலத் தொண்டு செய்ய விரும்புகிறேன்.
naan si·la po·*thu*·na·*lat* *toṇ*·ṭu *chey*·ya vi·*rum*·pu·ki·reyn

Dictionary

ENGLISH–TAMIL

Words in this dictionary are marked as n (noun), a (adjective), v (verb), m (masculine), f (feminine), sg (singular), pl (plural), inf (informal) and pol (polite) where necessary.

A

accident	விபத்து	vi.path.thu
accommodation	தங்குமிடம்	*tang*·ku·mi·ţam
adaptor	பொருத்துங்கருவி	po·*rut*·tung·ka·ru·vi
address n	விலாசம்	vi·*laa*·sam
after	பிறகு	pi·ra·*ku*
air-conditioned	குளிர்சாதன வசதியுடையது	ku·*ļir*·chaa·ta·na va·*cha*·ti·yu·*ţai*·ya·tu
airplane	விமானம்	vi·*maa*·nam
airport	விமான நிலையம்	*vi*·maa·na *ni*·lai·yam
alcohol	சாராயம்	saa·raa·yam
all	எல்லாம்	*el*·laam
allergy	ஒவ்வாமை	*ov*·vaa·mai
ambulance	ஆம்புலன்ஸ்	*aam*·pu·lans
and	மற்றும்	*mat*·trum
ankle	கணுக்கால்	ka·*ņuk*·kaal
antibiotics	அன்டிபயோட்டிக்	*an*·ti·ba·yaw·*tik*
arm	கை	kai
ATM	ATM	ey ti em

B

baby	குழந்தை	ku·*źan*·thai
back (of body)	முதுகு	mu·*thu*·hu
backpack	முதுகுப்பை	mu·thu·*kup*·pai
bad	கெட்ட	*keţ*·ţa
bag	பை	pai
baggage claim	பயணப்பெட்டி பெறுமிடம்	pa·ya·ņap·*peţ*·ţi pe·*ru*·mi·ţam
bank	வங்கி	*vang*·ki
bar	பார்	baar
bathroom	குளியலறை	ku·ļi·*ya*·la·rai
battery	பட்டரி	*bat*·ta·ri
beautiful	அழகு	a·*źa*·hu
bed	படுக்கை	pa·*ţuk*·kai
before	முன்	mun
behind	பின்புறம்	*pin*·pu·ram
bicycle	சைக்கிள்	*saik*·kiļ
big	பெரிய	pe·*ri*·ya
bill	விலைச்சீட்டு	vi·*laich*·cheeţ·ţu
blanket	போர்வை	*pawr*·vai
blood group	இரத்தப் பிரிவு	i·*rat*·tap pi·*ri*·vu
boat	படகு	pa·ţa·*ku*
book (reserve) v	புத்தகம்	*put*·ta·kam
bottle	போத்தல்	*pawth*·thal

boy	பையன்	*pai*·yan
brakes (car)	வேகத்தடைகள்	vey·kath·tha·ṭai·kaḷ
breakfast	காலை உணவு	kaa·*lai* u·ṇa·*vu*
broken (faulty)	உடைந்தது	u·*ṭain*·ta·tu
bus	பஸ்	bas
business	வியாபாரம்	*vi*·yaa·paa·ram
buy v	வாங்குதல்	*vaang*·ku·tal

C

camera	கமரா	ka·ma·*raa*
cancel	தடைசெய்தல்	*ta*·ṭai·*chey*·tal
car	மோட்டார் வண்டி	*mowṭ*·ṭaar *vaṇ*·ṭi
cash n	காசு	*kaa*·su
cash (a cheque) v	பணம் பெறுதல்	pa·*ṇam* pe·*ru*·tal
cell phone	கைத்தொலைபேசி	*kait*·to·lai·pey·*chi*
centre n	மையம்	*mai*·yam
change (money) v	மாற்றுதல்	*maat*·tru·thal
cheap	மலிவு	ma·*li*·vu
check (bill)	விலைச்சீட்டு	vi·*laich*·cheeṭ·ṭu
check-in n	பதிவிடம்	pa·ti·*vi*·ṭam
chest (body)	நெஞ்சு	*nen*·ju
child	சிறுவன் / சிறுமி	chi·*ru*·van / chi·*ru*·mi m/f
cigarette	சிகரெட்	*si*·ga·rat
city	நகரம்	na·ha·*ram*
clean a	சுத்தம்	*suth*·tham
closed	மூடப்பட்டுள்ளது	moo·ṭap·*paṭ*·ṭuḷ·ḷa·*thu*
cold a	குளிர்	ku·*ḷir*
collect call	கலெக்ட் அழைப்பு	ka·*lekt* a·*źaip*·pu
come	வா	vaa
computer	கணினி	ka·*ṇi*·ni
condom	ஆணுறை	*aa*·ṇu·rai
contact lenses	உள் கண்ணாடி வில்லை	uḷ *kaṇ*·ṇaa·ṭi *vil*·lai
cook v	சமையல்காரர்	*sa*·mai·*yal*·kaa·rar
cost n	விலை	vi·*lai*
credit card	கிரேடிட் அட்டை	ki·rey·*ṭiṭ* *aṭ*·ṭai
currency exchange	நாணய மாற்றம்	*naa*·ṇa·ya *maat*·tram
customs (immigration)	சுங்கத்துறை	*sung*·gath·thu·rai

D

dangerous	அபாயம்	a·*paa*·yam
date (time)	தேதி	*tey*·thi
day	நாள்	naaḷ
delay n	தாமதம்	*thaa*·ma·tham
dentist	பல் மருத்துவர்	pal ma·*ruth*·thu·var
depart	புறப்பாடு	pu·*rap*·paa·ṭu
diaper	குழந்தை அணையாடைத் துணி	ku·*źan*·thai a·ṇai·yaa·*ṭait* tu·*ṇi*
dinner	இரவு உணவு	i·ra·*vu* u·ṇa·*vu*
direct a	நேரடி	ney·ra·*ṭi*
dirty	அழுக்கு	a·*źuk*·ku
disabled	முடக்கிவிடுதல்	mu·*ṭak*·ki·vi·ṭu·thal
discount n	கழிவு	ka·*źi*·vu
doctor	மருத்துவர்	ma·*ruth*·thu·var
double bed	இரட்டைப்படுக்கை	i·*raṭ*·ṭaip·pa·*ṭuk*·kai
double room	இரட்டையறை	i·*raṭ*·ṭai·ya·rai
drink n	பானம்	paa·*nam*

drive v	ஓட்டுதல்	*owṭ*·ṭu·thal
drivers licence	வாகனமோட்டும் லைசன்ஸ்	vaa·ka·na·*mowṭ*·ṭum lai·*sans*
drug (illicit)	போதைப்பொருள்	paw·*thaip*·po·ruḷ

E

ear	காது	kaa·thu
east	கிழக்கு	ki·*źak*·ku
eat	சாப்பிடு	*saap*·pi·ṭu
economy class	சிக்கன வகுப்பு	*chik*·ka·na va·*kup*·pu
electricity	மின்சாரம்	min·saa·ram
elevator	லிப்ட்	lipt
email	மின்னஞ்சல்	min·nan·*chal*
embassy	தூதரகம்	*thoo*·tha·ra·ham
emergency	நெருக்கடி	ne·ruk·ka·*ṭi*
English (language)	ஆங்கிலம்	*aang*·ki·lam
entrance	நுழைவாயில்	nu·zai·vaa·*yil*
evening	மாலை	maa·*lai*
exit n	வெளியேறுமிடம்	ve·ḷi·yey·*ru*·mi·ṭam
expensive	விலையுயர்ந்தது	vi·*lai*·yu·yarn·tha·thu
eye	கண்	kaṇ

F

far	தூரம்	*thoo*·ram
fast	வேகம்	*vey*·ham
father	அப்பா	*ap*·paa
film (camera)	படச்சுருள்	pa·*ṭach*·chu·ruḷ
finger	விரல்	*vi*·ral
first-aid kit	முதலுதவிப்பெட்டி	mu·tha·lu·tha·*vip peṭ*·ṭi
first class	முதல் வகுப்பு	mu·*thal* va·*kup*·pu
fish n	மீன்	meen
food	சாப்பாடு	*saap*·paa·du
foot	கால்	kaal
free (of charge)	இலவசம்	i·la·va·*sam*
friend	நண்பன்	*naṇ*·pan
fruit	பழம்	pa·*źam*
full	நிறைய	ni·*rai*·ya

G

gift	பரிசு	pa·ri·*su*
girl	சிறுமி	*si*·ru·mi
glass (drinking)	கிளாஸ்	gḷaas
glasses	மூக்குக் கண்ணாடி	mook·*kuk kaṇ*·ṇaa·ṭi
go	போவது	*paw*·va·thu
good	நல்லது	*nal*·la·thu
guide n	வழிகாட்டி v	a·*źi*·kaaṭ·ṭi

H

half n	பாதி	paa·*thi*
hand	கை	kai
happy	மகிழ்ச்சி	ma·*kiźch*·chi
have	இருத்தல்	i·*ruth*·thal
he	அவன்	a·*van*
head n	தலை	tha·*lai*
heart	இருதயம்	i·*ru*·tha·yam

247

heavy	பாரம்	paa·*ram*
help v	உதவி	u·tha·*vi*
here	இங்கே	*ing*·key
high	உயரம்	u·ya·*ram*
highway	நெடுஞ்சாலை	ne·*ṭuny*·chaa·lai
hike v	நடைப்பயணம்	na·*ṭaip*·pa·ya·ṇam
holiday	விடுமுறை	vi·ṭu·*mu*·rai
hospital	மருத்துவமனை	ma·ruth·thu·va·ma·*nai*
hot	சூடு	*soo*·ṭu
hotel	ஹோட்டல்	*hoṭ*·ṭal
hungry	பசி	pa·*si*
husband	கணவன்	ka·ṇa·*van*

I

I	நான்	naan
identification (card)	அடையாள அட்டை	a·*ṭai*·yaa·ḷa *aṭ*·ṭai
ill	உடல்நலக்குறைவு	u·ṭal·na·*lak*·ku·rai·vu
important	முக்கியம்	*muk*·ki·yam
injury	காயம்	kaa·*yam*
insurance	காப்பீடு	*kaap*·pee·ṭu
internet	இணையம்	i·ṇai·*yam*
interpreter	மொழிபெயர்ப்பாளர்	mo·li·pe·yarp·paa·lar

J

jewellery	நகை	na·*kai*
job	வேலை	*vey*·lai

K

key	சாவி	*chaa*·vi
kilogram	கிலோகிராம்	ki·*low*·ki·raam
kitchen	சமையலறை	cha·mai·ya·*la*·rai
knife	கத்தி	*kath*·thi

L

laundry (place)	துணி துவைக்குமிடம்	*tu*·ṇi tu·*vaik*·ku·mi·ṭam
lawyer	வழக்கறிஞர்	va·*żak*·ka·ri·nyar
left (direction)	இடது	i·ṭa·*thu*
leg (body)	கால்	kaal
less	குறைவு	ku·rai·*vu*
letter (mail)	கடிதம்	ka·ṭi·*tam*
lift	லிப்ட்	lipt
light n	ஒளி	o·*ḷi*
like v	பிடித்தல்	pi·*ṭit*·tal
lock n	பூட்டு	*pooṭ*·ṭu
long	நீண்டது	*neeṇ*·ṭa·thu
lost	தொலைதல்	to·*lai*·tal
love v	அன்பு	*an*·pu
luggage	பெட்டி	*peṭ*·ṭi
lunch	மதிய உணவு	ma·*thi*·ya u·ṇa·*vu*

M

mail n	கடிதம்	ka·ṭi·*tham*
man	ஆண்	aaṇ
map	வரைபடம்	va·*rai*·pa·ṭam

market	சந்தை	san·thai
matches	தீக்குச்சி	theek·kuch·chi
meat	இறைச்சி	i·raich·chi
medicine	மருந்து	ma·run·thu
message	தகவல்	ta·ka·val
milk	பால்	paal
minute	நிமிடம்	ni·mi·ṭam
mobile phone	கைத்தொலைபேசி	kait·to·lai·pey·chi
money	பணம்	pa·ṇam
month	மாதம்	maa·tam
morning	காலை	kaa·lai
mother	அம்மா	am·maa
motorcycle	மோட்டார் சைக்கிள்	mowṭ·ṭaar saik·kiḷ
mouth	வாய்	vai

N

ame	பெயர்	pe·yar
appy	குழந்தை அணையாடைத் துணி	ku·źan·tai a·ṇai·yaa·ṭait tu·ṇi
ear	அருகே	a·ru·key
eck n	கழுத்து	ka·źut·tu
ew	புதிது	pu·ti·tu
ewspaper	பத்திரிகை	path·thi·ri·hai
ight	இரவு	i·ra·vu
o	இல்லை	il·lai
oisy	இரைச்சல்	i·raich·chal
onsmoking	புகை பிடிக்காத	pu·hai pi·ṭik·kaa·ta
orth	வடக்கு	va·ṭak·ku
ose	மூக்கு	mook·ku
ow	இப்பொழுது	ip·po·ḷu·thu
umber	எண்	eṇ

O

ld	பழையது	pa·źai·ya·thu
pen a	திறந்த	ti·ran·tha
utside	வெளியே	ve·ḷi·yey

P

assport	பாஸ்போர்ட்	paas·pawrt
ay v	பணம் கொடுத்தல்	pa·ṇam ko·duth·thal
harmacy	மருந்தகம்	ma·run·tha·ham
hoto	புகைப்படம்	pu·kaip·pa·ṭam
olice	போலீஸ்	po·lees
ostcard	அஞ்சல் அட்டை	any·chal aṭ·ṭai
ost office	தபால் நிலையம்	tha·paal ni·lai·yam
regnant	கர்ப்பம்	karp·pam
rice n	விலை	vi·lai

Q

uiet a	அமைதி	a·mai·thi

R

in n	மழை	ma·źai
zor	சவரக்கத்தி	sa·va·rak·kat·thi
ceipt n	ரசீது	ra·see·thu

registered mail	பதியப்பட்ட அஞ்சல்	pa·ti·yap·*paţ*·ţa *any*·chal
rent v	வாடகை	vaa·*ţa*·kai
repair v	பழுது பார்த்தல்	pa·*źu*·tu *paar*·thal
reservation	முன்பதிவு	*mun*·pa·ti·vu
restaurant	உணவகம்	u·ņa·va·*kam*
return v	திரும்புதல்	ti·*rum*·pu·tal
right (direction)	வலது	va·la·*thu*
road	சாலை	*saa*·lai
room n	அறை	a·*rai*

S

safe a	பாதுகாப்பு	paa·thu·*kaap*·pu
sanitary napkin	சுகாதார நாப்கின்	chu·kaa·*taa*·ra *naap*·kin
seat n	இருக்கை	i·*ruk*·kai
send	அனுப்புதல்	a·*nup*·pu·thal
sex	பாலியல் உறவு	paa·*li*·yal u·ra·*vu*
shampoo	ஷாம்பு	*shaam*·pu
she	அவள்	a·*vaļ*
sheet (bed)	விரிப்பு	vi·*rip*·pu
shirt	சட்டை	*chaţ*·ţai
shoes	காலணி	kaa·la·*ņi*
shop n	கடை	ka·*ţai*
short	கட்டை	*kaţ*·ţai
shower n	மழை பொழிதல்	ma·*źai* po·*źi*·thal
single room	தனியறை	ta·*ni*·ya·rai
skin n	தோள்	thawl
skirt n	பாவாடை	paa·vaa·*ţai*
sleep v	தூக்கம்	*thook*·kam
slowly	மெதுவாக	me·*thu*·vaa·ka
small	சிறியது	*chi*·ri·ya·tu
soap	சவர்க்காரம்	cha·*vark*·kaa·ram
some	சில	*chi*·la
soon	உடனே	u·ţa·*ney*
south	தெற்கு	*ter*·ku
stamp	அஞ்சல் தலை	*an*·chal tha·*lai*
station (train)	நிலையம்	ni·*lai*·yam
stomach	வயிறு	va·*yi*·ru
stop v	நிறுத்தும்	ni·*rut*·tum
stop (bus) n	பஸ் நிறுத்தும்	pas ni·*ruth*·tham
street	சாலை	*chaa*·lai
student	மாணவன்	maa·ņa·*van*
sun	சூரியன்	*choo*·ri·yan
swim v	நீந்துதல்	*neen*·thu·thal

T

tampons	பெண்களுக்குரிய தாம்போன்	*peņ*·ka·*ļuk*·ku·ri·ya *tam*·pon
teeth	பற்கள்	*pat*·kaļ
telephone n	தொலைபேசி	*to*·lai·pey·*chi*
temperature (weather)	வெப்ப நிலை	*vep*·pa ni·*lai*
that (one)	அது	*a*·thu
they	அவர்கள்	a·*var*·kaļ
thirsty	தாகம்	taa·*kam*
this (one)	இது	*i*·thu
throat	தொண்டை	*toņ*·ţai
ticket	டிக்கட்	ţik·*kaţ*

time	நேரம்	*ney*·ram
tired	களைப்பு	ka·*ḷaip*·pu
tissues	உறிஞ்சு தாள்	u·*rin*·chu *thaal*
today	இன்று	in·*dru*
toilet	கழிவறை	ka·*żi*·va·rai
tomorrow	நாளை	*naa*·ḷai
tonight	இன்றிரவு	in·*dri*·ra·vu
toothbrush	பல் தூரிகை	pal *too*·ri·kai
toothpaste	பற்பசை	*par*·pa·sai
torch (flashlight)	கைவிளக்கு	kai·vi·ḷa·*ku*
tour n	சுற்றுலா	*chut*·tru·laa
towel	துண்டு	*tuṇ*·ṭu
train n	இரயில்	i·ra·*yil*
translate	மொழிபெயர்த்தல்	mo·*żi*·pe·*yart*·thal
travel agency	பிரயாண அலுவலகம்	*pi*·ra·yaa·ṇa a·*lu*·va·la·kam
trousers	காற்சட்டை	kaar·*chaṭ*·ṭai
twin beds	இரட்டைப் படுக்கைகள்	i·raṭ·*ṭaip* pa·*ṭuk*·kai·kaḷ

U

underwear	உள்ளாடை	*uḷ*·ḷaa·ṭai
urgent	அவசரம்	a·va·sa·ram

V

vacant	காலி	kaa·*li*
vegetable n	காய்கறி	*kai*·ka·ri
vegetarian a	சைவம்	*sai*·vam
visa	விசா	vi·*saa*

W

walk v	நடத்தல்	na·*dath*·thal
wallet	பணப்பை	pa·*ṇap*·pai
wash (something)	கழுவுதல்	ka·*żu*·vu·thal
watch n	கடிகாரம்	ka·*ṭi*·kaa·ram
water n	தண்ணீர்	*taṇ*·ṇeyr
we	நாம்	naam
weekend	வார இறுதி *v*	aa·ra i·ru·*thi*
vest	மேற்கு	*meyr*·ku
wheelchair	சக்கர நாற்காலி	*chak*·ka·ra *naar*·kaa·li
when	எப்பொழுது	ep·po·*żu*·*thu*
where	எங்கே	*eng*·key
who	யார்	yaar
why	ஏன்	eyn
wife	மனைவி	ma·*nai*·vi
window	யன்னல்	*yan*·nal
with	உடன்	u·*ṭan*
without	இல்லாமல்	*il*·laa·mal
woman	பெண்	peṇ
write	எழுது	e·*żu*·thu

Y

yes	ஆமாம்	aa·maam
yesterday	நேற்று	*neyt*·tru
you sg inf	நீ	nee
you sg pol & pl	நீங்கள்	*neeng*·kaḷ

INDEX

H

I

J

L

M

N

O

P

Q

R

S

T

V

W